VOLUME 2   **2022**

HAYMANOT JOURNAL

SGH MAMHERS (advisory board): Tim Allison,
Vincent Bacote, Vince L. Bantu, Quonekuia Day,
Jacqueline Dyer, Carolyn Palmer, Cleotha Robertson, Nicholas Rowe

GENERAL KATABIS
VINCE L. BANTU
JACQUELINE T. DYER

urbanministries.com

Copyright © 2022 by Vince Bantu and Jacqueline Dyer, Editors
www.meachum.org

All rights reserved.
No part of this book may be reproduced or transmitted in any form or by any means, electronic or mechanical, including photocopying, recording, video, or by any information or retrieval system, without prior written permission from the publisher except for the use of brief quotations in a book review.

Published in the United States by Urban Ministries, Inc.
P. O. Box 436987
Chicago, IL 60643
www.urbanministries.com

ISBN 978-1-68353-990-2 (paperback)
ISBN 978-1-68353-991-9 (ebook)

All scripture quotations, unless otherwise indicated, are taken from the NASB, NRSV, NIV, Lexham English Bible (LEB) and Nestle-Aland Greek New Testament (Novum Testamentum Graece) 28th Edition.

Printed in the United States of America

Table of Contents

1. Introduction 1
   Vince L. Bantu & Jacqueline T. Dyer

   Dersat
   Umfundi: Quonekuia Day

2. "A Gospelist Examination of the Widow, the Orphan,
   and the Stranger in Deuteronomy" 3
   Cleotha Robertson

3. "*Ad Fontes*: An Examination of the Relationship between
   Scripture and the Negro Spirituals" 25
   Ernest D. Gray Jr.

4. "The Effects of Nationalism on the Mental and Spiritual State" . 36
   Timothy D. Allison

   Sankofa
   Umfundi: Nicholas Rowe

5. "'For You Were Slaves in Egypt': History, Memory, and
   Implications for Christian Discipleship" 46
   Nicholas Rowe

6. "Local Cultures Matter: Gospel, Identity, and
   Mission in Northern Nigeria" 58
   Yoknyam Dabale

7. "The Heresy of Prosperity 'Gospel': Trading Community
   for Commerce" 73
   Lori Banfield

8. "Nazrawis and the Zanj: Contact between Nazrawis
   of Northeastern Africa and the Swahili Coast during the
   Axumite and Early Solomonic Periods" 94
   Vince L. Bantu

   Haymanot
   Umfundi: Vincent Bacote

9. "Biblical/Social Justice as a Foundation of
   the Kingdom of God" 117
   Kenneth J. Reid

10. "Creativity, Collaboration, and Improvisation in
    Christian Systematic Theology" 135
    Preston Boone

11. "Worship, Missiological 'Blind Spots,' and Reconciliation" . 155
    Emmett G. Price

    Ujamaa
    Umfundi: Lori Banfield

12. "A Critique of the Nonviolent Ethic's Supremacy
    in the Black Church's Discourse and Teaching in
    Light of White Evangelical Theology of Violence" 165
    Tyran T. Laws

13. "Call, Chant, Cry, Shout: The Rhythms of African-Inspired
    Diaspora Preaching" 191
    Jaclyn P. Williams

14. "Dismantling the Optional Service Mentality:
    A Dire Call for Christian Preachers and Educators to
    Abandon Me-Centered Teachings that Steer Believers
    Away from Serving the Church, and Learning Practically
    How to Spark a Culture of Volunteerism" 209
    Charonda Woods

15. "*Koinonia* as Economic Development in
    the African Diaspora" 230
    Walter S. Augustine

Book Reviews

"Review of Mary K. Farag's *What Makes a Church Sacred? Legal and Ritual Perspectives from Late Antiquity*" 247
Vince L. Bantu

"Review of Jarvis J. Williams' *Redemptive Kingdom Diversity: A Biblical Theology of the People of God*" 252
Ernest Gray

"Review of Harry Singleton III's *Divine Revelation and Human Liberation*" 256
Leon Harris

"Review of Christina Barland Edmondson and Chad Brennan's *Faithful Anti-Racism: Moving Past Talk to Systemic Change*" 260
Nicholas Rowe

Introduction

Welcome to the Second Volume of the *Haymanot Journal*

The *Haymanot Journal* publishes the proceedings of the Annual Meeting of the Society of Gospel Haymanot (SGH). SGH is a consortium of Black scholars of biblical, theological, and religious studies that are dedicated to the proclamation of the Bisrat (Gospel) of Jesus Christ, the authority of the Word of Tilli (God), the liberation of the marginalized and the embracing of African-descended cultural identity. The theological landscape of academic institutions is characterized, for the most part, by a liberal-conservative binary, which is upheld by the majority of Black scholars. Meanwhile, the rich tradition of the historical Black Church—one that holds equally to the universal truth of the Bisrat and God's call upon His People for the liberation of the marginalized—is largely absent from graduate institutions of theological education. As daughters and sons of the Black Church and scholars of religious studies, the SGH exists to: 1.) bring the theological perspective of the majority Black Church—which we call Gospel Haymanot—into conversation with mainstream academia; 2.) create a scholarly community for Gospelist scholars; 3.) reclaim a Black Theology that is grounded in the authority of the Word of God and; 4.) produce Gospelist scholarship that serves the Global Church and institutions of theological education.

The *Haymanot Journal* exists to serve these goals. If one were to search for academic monographs and journal articles on Black Theology or written by Black theologians, they would overwhelmingly represent a theological perspective foreign to the majority of the Black Church. The *Haymanot Journal* exists to provide peer-reviewed scholarship from Black scholars that hold to the Bisrat and to Black liberation. This volume is organized into four disciplines framed by our African forms of knowledge and being: *Dersat* (a Ge'ez—classical Ethiopic—term meaning "biblical exegesis"); *Sankofa* (an Akan concept meaning "go back and get it" in the sense of knowing and reclaiming one's history); *Haymanot* (a Ge'ez—classical Ethiopic—term meaning "doctrine," "faith," or "theology"); and *Ujamaa* (a Swahili term meaning "collective responsibility" or "family," in the sense of practical ministry and community development). Each paper has been edited by Umfundi (Xhosa terms for "reader"), who are discipline specialists, as well as the general Katabis (Ge'ez—classical Ethiopic—term for "scribe" or "editor"). Each article was presented at the second Annual Meeting of the SGH, which was held virtually in the fall of 2021. Amidst the ongoing difficulties of viral and racialized pandemics, it was a blessing to gather virtually with a family of Gospelist scholars. We pray that the scholarship contained in this volume will enrich the academy, support the Church, and glorify the Lord Jesus Christ.

By the grace of Tilli,

Vince L. Bantu
Jacqueline T. Dyer

A Gospelist Examination of the Widow, the Orphan, and the Stranger in Deuteronomy

Cleotha Robertson

Introduction

The purpose of this paper is to examine the motif of the widow, the orphan, and the stranger in the Book of Deuteronomy. This motif occurs in Deuteronomy 14-26. In the Hebrew Bible, there is the frequent reminder that Israel was to be cognizant of and benevolent toward the widow, the orphan, and the stranger within the context of Israelite culture. These injunctions are found specifically in the following passages: 14:22-29; 16:9-12, 13-15; 24:17-18, 19-22; and 26:12-15.

This recurring motif points to the concern for the vulnerable in the Torah of Moses and reflects concerns of YHWH for the ordering and operation of a compassionate society. One even notes the pervasive concerns for this population in the literature of the larger Ancient Near East. In a survey of texts from the Ancient Near East from Mesopotamia, Ugarit, and Egypt, one notes that there was a common framework of protection for vulnerable subgroups within these cultures. In academia, these codes (Deut. 14-26) have been philosophically deconstructed with the concomitant result of dismissing the importance of supporting the marginal populations that were directly involved in these laws. In churches, insensitivity toward marginalized populations, have led to neglect and castigation.

The purpose of the paper is to examine the significance and use of the widow, orphan, and stranger motif in Deuteronomy 12-16. In this examination, the writer will note the framework issues regarding the interpretation of texts in Deuteronomy regarding the widow, orphan, and stranger. Moreover, the writer will examine the implications of this motif for a Gospelist hermeneutic with implications for the academy, the African American experience, and for a just society.

The Widow, Orphan, and Stranger in Deuteronomy

The passages that deal with the benevolence toward the widow, orphan, and the stranger are the following:

1. Deut. 14:22-29

    22. You must be certain to tithe all the produce of your seed that comes from the field year after year. 23. In the presence of the LORD your God, in the place he chooses to locate his name, you must eat from the tithe of your grain, your new wine, your olive oil, and the firstborn of your herds and flocks, so that you may learn to revere the LORD your God always. 24. When he blesses you, if the place where he chooses to locate his name is distant, 25. you may convert the tithe into money, secure the money, and travel to the place the LORD your God chooses for himself. 26. Then you may spend the money however you wish for cattle, sheep, wine, beer, or whatever you desire. You and your household may eat there in the presence of the LORD your God and enjoy it. 27. As for the Levites in your villages, you must not ignore them, for they have no allotment or inheritance along with you. 28. At the end of every three years you

must bring all the tithe of your produce, in that very year, and you must store it up in your villages. 29. Then the Levites (because they have no allotment or inheritance with you), the resident foreigners, the orphans, and the widows of your villages may come and eat their fill so that the LORD your God may bless you in all the work you do.

2. Deut. 16:9-12, 13-17

9. You must count seven weeks; you must begin to count them from the time you begin to harvest the standing grain. 10. Then you are to celebrate the Feast of Weeks before the LORD your God with the voluntary offering that you will bring, in proportion to how he has blessed you. 11. You shall rejoice before him—you, your son, your daughter, your male and female slaves, the Levites in your villages, the resident foreigners, the orphans, and the widows among you—in the place where the LORD chooses to locate his name. 12. Furthermore, remember that you were a slave in Egypt, and so be careful to observe these statutes. 13. You must celebrate the Feast of Shelters for seven days, at the time of the grain and grape harvest. 14. You are to rejoice in your festival, you, your son, your daughter, your male and female slaves, the Levites, the resident foreigners, the orphans, and the widows who are in your villages. 15. You are to celebrate the festival seven days before the LORD your God in the place he chooses, for he will bless you in all your productivity and in whatever you do; so you will indeed rejoice! 16. Three times a year all your males must appear before the LORD your God in the place he chooses for the Feast of Unleavened Bread, the Feast of Weeks, and the Feast of Shelters; and they must not appear before him empty-handed. 17. Every one of you must give as you are able, according to the blessing of the LORD your God that he has given you.

3. Deut. 24:17-18, 19-22

   17. You must not pervert justice due a resident foreigner or an orphan, or take a widow's garment as security for a loan. 18. Remember that you were slaves in Egypt and that the LORD your God redeemed you from there; therefore I am commanding you to do all this. 19. Whenever you reap your harvest in your field and leave some unraked grain there, you must not return to get it; it should go to the resident foreigner, orphan, and widow so that the LORD your God may bless all the work you do. 20. When you beat your olive tree you must not repeat the procedure; the remaining olives belong to the resident foreigner, orphan, and widow. 21. When you gather the grapes of your vineyard you must not do so a second time; they should go to the resident foreigner, orphan, and widow. 22. Remember that you were slaves in the land of Egypt; therefore, I am commanding you to do all this.

4. Deut. 26:12-15

   12. When you have finished setting aside a tenth of all your produce in the third year, the year of the tithe, you shall give it to the Levite, the foreigner, the fatherless and the widow, so that they may eat in your towns and be satisfied. 13. Then say to the LORD your God: "I have removed from my house the sacred portion and have given it to the Levite, the foreigner, the fatherless, and the widow, according to all you commanded. I have not turned aside from your commands nor have I forgotten any of them. 14. I have not eaten any of the sacred portion while I was in mourning, nor have I removed any of it while I was unclean, nor have I offered any of it to the dead. I have obeyed the LORD my God; I have done everything you commanded me. 15. Look down from heaven, your holy dwelling place, and bless your people Israel and the land you have given us as you promised on oath to our ancestors, a land flowing with milk and honey."

Definition of Terms: The Widow

The word for widow is אַלְמָנָה and it is spread all over the OT (55x). Van Leeuwen notes the following ideas connected with the widow in the Hebrew Bible. One, in the fifty-five uses in the Hebrew Bible, it is curiously missing in the outstanding widow story of Ruth and in Amos and Micah, the champions of social justice.[1] Two, the word "widow" not only evokes the notion of bereavement from having lost a husband (2 Sam. 14:5), but at the same time the loss of finances, social protection, and security. As long as the Israelites lived as semi-nomads in their tribes and clans and the family ties were still strong, the lot of the widow was not yet a problem. She returned to her parental home, where she shared in the protection and care of the clan and with the possibility of a levirate marriage (Gen. 38:11; Deut. 25:5–10; Ruth 1:8–11; cf. Mt. 22:24). Three, the widow had no right of succession of the inheritance of her late husband. Under the heirs of a dead man (sons, daughters, brothers, father's brothers, nearest relatives), the widow is not mentioned (Num. 27:8–11). In apocryphal literature, there is an exception to this. Judith inherits the rich possessions from the late husband Manasseh. This is presented as an exception to the rule (Jdt. 8:7). Four, as a result of no means of support, a widow was often obliged to live from the charity of other people (Job 31:16) or to make debts for keeping herself and her children alive. The creditor might take her only ox in pledge (Job 24:3). When she was not able to pay back the debts in due time, the creditor might come and take away her children, even her baby (Job 24:9), for using them later on as his slaves. In other cases, the widow had to suffer robbery and oppression (Isa. 10:2; Jer. 7:6; 22:3) or even death (Ps 94:6) of herself and her fatherless children. Five, a third of the widow-texts are found in legal contexts. The Lord himself is the God who "defends the cause

---

[1] Cornelis Van Leeuwen אלמ.נ.ה, *Volume 1 (New International Dictionary of Old Testament Theology and Exegesis)* (Grand Rapids, MI: Zondervan Academic, 2012), 408.

of" or "does justice to" (עֹשֶׂה מִשְׁפַּט) the fatherless and the widow (Deut. 10:18; compare Ex. 22:23 [22]). The Book of Covenant prohibits oppressing (אָנָה) them (Ex. 22:22 [21]); note that אָנָה is stronger than NIV "take advantage;" as a retaliation the Lord himself will kill the oppressors with the sword so that their own wives will become widows (Ex. 22:24 [23]). Deuteronomy forbids to take a widow's cloak as a pledge (24:17) and curses him who withholds justice (עֹשֶׂה מִשְׁפַּט) from the alien, fatherless, or widow.[2]

Deuteronomic law determines the privileges that widows along with other poor people, fatherless, alien, Levites are entitled to: the tithe of all the produce in every third year (14:28–29; 26:12–13), the gleanings of every harvest and vintage (24:19–21), participation in the sacrificial repast, and rejoicing during the Feasts of Weeks and Tabernacles (16:11, 14). Probably the widows, though not mentioned particularly, were also included among the poor who were entitled to the produce of the Sabbath year (Ex. 23:10–11) and of the edges of the field, where the owner was not allowed to reap (Lev. 19:9; 23:22). Six, in keeping with the laws of the Pentateuch, prophets accuse the leaders of Jerusalem of making many widows (Ez. 22:25), of neglecting the widow's cause (Is. 1:17, 23), of oppressing (Mal. 3:5; Zech. 7:10; Ez. 22:7) widows and the fatherless, and of making widows their prey (Is. 10:2). In Jeremiah 7:6; 22:3 not oppressing the alien, the fatherless, and the widow is one of the conditions for the survival of population and temple of Jerusalem. In Isaiah 9:17 [16] it is a sign of Israel's total depravity that the Lord will not pity the fatherless and widows any more.[3] It is part of God's judgment that He will make Israel's widows more numerous than the sand of the sea (Jer. 15:8; compare 18:21; Lam. 5:3).

Seven, in a figurative sense, "widow" is used in Lam. 1:1 for Jerusalem deserted after its destruction in Is. 47:8–9. The Prophet uses the

---

[2] Ibid.
[3] Compare God's judgment on Edom in Jer. 49:10–11.

metaphors of widowhood and the loss of children for the city of Babylon that by God's punishment will become as miserable and bereft. Similarly, in Jer. 51:5 for Israel and Judah that have not been forsaken (NIV) by God or left without his protection; in the same sense "widowhood" (אַלְמָנוּת) in Is. 54:4 for Zion. Eight, in Job and Psalms, the Lord is called the defender of the rights of the widow and the one who sustains her.[4]

Complaint is made that wicked men take the widow's ox in pledge and show no kindness to her (Job 24:3, 21), that indeed they slay the widow and the alien (Ps. 94:6). The psalmist, like Jeremiah (Jer. 18:21), prays that the wife of the wicked may become a widow and his children fatherless (Ps. 109:9), and Job (Job 27:15) is convinced that the widows of the wicked will not weep after their shameful death. Job himself testifies that he took care of the fatherless and widows (29:12–13; 31:16–17) in spite of his friends who reproached him with the opposite (22:9).

The Orphan

For the orphan, Hamilton offers the following definition. Overwhelmingly, the orphan is listed along with the widow and the alien as a compositional triad and points to the weak and helpless segments of society, the ones who are most vulnerable to injury and abuse. In almost every case a יָתוֹם is one who has lost his/her father. It is difficult, if not impossible, to isolate an instance in the OT where a יָתוֹם has lost both of his/her parents.

>   1a. There are thirty cases in which orphan יָתוֹם occurs with (אַלְמָנוּת) (H530), widow (cf. Ex. 22:21–22 [20–21], 24 [23]; Deut. 24:17, 19, 20, 21; Job 24:3; Ps. 68:5 [6]; Is. 1:17, 23; Jer. 7:6; Lam. 5:3; Ez. 22:7; Zech. 7:10; Mal. 3:5).

---

[4] Ibid.

b. In twenty-four of these cases, יָתוֹם precedes (אַלְמָנוֹת); in six, (אַלְמָנוֹת) precedes יָתוֹם. For the order *ytm:almnt* and *almnt:ytm* in Ugaritic texts.

c. In eighteen of these twenty-four, גֵּר (alien) also appears, much more often before (13x) "orphan and widow" than after (3x). Twice גֵּר breaks the pairing of יָתוֹם and (אַלְמָנוֹת).

2. Laws prohibit taking advantage of the orphan (Ex. 22:22, 24 [21, 23]; Deut. 24:17; 27:19); other laws encourage that they be provided for (Deut. 14:29; 24:19–21; 26:13). Similar injunctions are found in Near Eastern literature. Thus, Daniel is the one who "judges the cause of the widow, adjudicates the case of the fatherless." Hammurapi claims that "he governed the people of Sumer and Akkad in peace, he sheltered them in his wisdom, in order that the strong might not oppress the weak, that justice might be dealt the orphan (and) the widow."[5] Job denied any mistreatment of orphans (22:9) and testified about his befriending them (29:12; 31:17).

3. God himself is the defender of the orphan (Deut. 10:18; Ps. 10:14, 18; 68:5 [6]), even Edom's orphans (Jer. 49:11). Yet orphans, too, may become the object of his judgment (Is. 9:17 [16]).

4. In one imprecatory psalm, the writer prayed that the children of his enemies become orphans (Ps. 109:9; cf. Jer. 18:21, but with the root שָׁכַל for "childless"). The prayer is not a desire for revenge but for vengeance (i.e., an appeal to a higher authority to obtain redress and justice, cf. Deut. 32:35; נָקַם, "avenge").

---

[5] James Pritchard, *Ancient Near Eastern Texts Relating to the Old Testament with Supplement* (Princeton: Princeton University Press, 1969), 178a.

The Sojourner

The word *ger* (גֵּר) in Israel was used to denote the alien, sojourner, or the stranger. The sojourner referred to someone who did not enjoy the rights usually possessed by the resident. The clearest sense of the noun sojourner is seen when used of Israel in their time in Egypt (Ex. 23:9; Gen. 15:13). Moses named his son Gershom in memory of his stay in Midian (Ex. 18:3) for he had been exiled from both Egypt and Canaan. Abraham, Isaac, and Jacob lived as strangers in Canaan (6:4), meaning that they had no property rights there.

The sojourner in Israel was considered a proselyte. He was to be present for the solemn reading of the Law (Deut. 31:12) showing that he was exposed to its demands. The law concerning "unleavened bread" applied to him as well as the native (Ex. 12:19), and a circumcised sojourner could keep Passover (Ex. 12:48f.; Num. 9:14). He was also included in the Festival of Atonement (Lev. 16:29) and was expected to celebrate the Feast of Booths (Deut. 16:14). With the native, the sojourner was threatened with the death penalty if he offered a sacrifice to a foreign god (Lev. 17:8f.) and was forbidden to eat blood (17:10, 12, 13). Though in contrast to the native, they were allowed to eat what had died or was torn (Deut. 14:21). Like the native Israelite, they underwent special cleansing (Lev. 17:15f.). He was also included in the rites of cleansing with the ashes of the red heifer (Num. 19:10). The laws of sexual chastity applied to him as well as the native (Lev. 18:26) along with the Sabbath laws (Ex. 20:10; 23:12). The sojourner was to show the same fidelity to the Lord (Lev. 20:2).

He also enjoyed many of the same rights as the native and was not to be oppressed (Ex. 22:21 [H 20]; Lev. 19:3; Jer. 7:6; 22:3). He is mentioned in connection with the poor (Lev. 19:10; cf. 23:22) and with orphans and widows (Deut. 14:29; 16:11, 14; 24:17; 26:13; 27:19). With them he shared the sheaf left in the field (24:19) and the gleanings in the olive trees and in the vineyards (24:20–21) along with the tithe every three years (14:27; 26:12). He was to be treated righteously in judgment

(1:16; 24:17; 27:19) and the six asylum cities were also cities of refuge for him (Num. 35:15). In a word, the LORD loves the גֵר (Deut. 10:18). Israel should not oppress him because they themselves were oppressed and know his soul (Ex. 22:21; Deut. 10:19). They were to love him as themselves (Lev. 19:34). David employed them as stonecutters (1 Chr. 22:2) and they served in the army (2 Sam. 1:13). Solomon made them stonecutters and burden-bearers (2 Chr. 2:17f). In the curse formulae of Deut. 27, it is predicted that the social order would be reversed and the גֵר become the head and Israel the tail.

Textual Congruence of the Three Terms
1. Deuteronomy 14:22-29

Deut. 14:22-29 is the first of the four passages where the widow, orphan, and sojourner are listed together. Deut. 14: 22-29 deals with the tithe that was demanded of all Israelites. A tithe was demanded of all forms of income. Deut. 14:22-29 addresses five issues. One, those who maintained a farm and earned an income by crops were commanded to provide a tenth of their income to the Lord. This included the livestock and the firstborn of the flock or herd. Two, the tithe could be converted to silver for those who lived a distance from the Temple. Once at the Temple, a worshipper could use the silver for the purchase of an animal or agricultural offering that the family would use before "Yahweh your God." Three, the Israelites were commanded to remember the Levites who did not have land or an inheritance. Four, the tithe would be collected every three years. Five, the recipients of the tithe are the Levites, widows, orphans, and strangers. They received this triennial tithe because they do not have an inheritance of land.

2. Deuteronomy 16: 9-12, 13-17

This is the second passage that contains admonitions concerning the grouping of stranger, widow, and the orphan. In Deut. 16:9-12, one finds regulations regarding the Feast of Weeks. The Feast of Weeks is called the Feast of Harvest in the earlier codes (Ex. 23:16b; 34:22b).[6] In the New Testament it is called Pentecost. It marks the gathering in of all the produce that ripens during the summer months, such as grapes, dates, and olives, and is thus in an agricultural sense the end of the year (Ex. 23:16b). The precise timing is defined in Lev. 23:33–36, as beginning on the "fifteenth day of the seventh month," soon after the Day of Atonement. The Feast of Booths involved rejoicing and fellowship, and the stranger, widow, and orphan are mentioned as participants in this feast (Deut. 16:11). Only here is the Feast of Booths expressly described as a memorial of the deliverance from Egypt. The memory of servitude in Egypt and God's provision in the harvest, but was the basis for generosity towards servants, aliens, widows, and orphans.[7]

In Deuteronomy 16:13-17 one finds regulations regarding the Feast of Booths. The Feast of Booths is also called the Feast of Ingathering (Ex. 23:16; 34:22). The festival lasted seven days with a closing ceremony on the eighth day. The Feast of Booths was celebrated at the grain and the grape harvest (Deut. 16:13) and the festival included the widows, strangers, and orphans. The Feast was a commemoration of the wanderings of the Israelites after they left Egypt, in which they dwelt in temporary shelters.

3. Deuteronomy 24:17-18, 19-22

In this third passage, Moses prescribes justice and practices of liberality in the gleaning of fields. In Deuteronomy 24:17, Israelites are commanded not to pervert justice in dealing with the stranger, orphan, or the widow. The widow is singled out regarding the taking of a garment or "an item of clothing" as collateral for a loan. The term used

---

[6] J. G. McConville, *Deuteronomy: Apollos Old Testament Commentary* (Grand Rapids: IVP Academic, 2002), 275.
[7] Peter Craigie, *The Book of Deuteronomy: New International Commentary on the Old Testament* (Grand Rapids, MI: Williams B. Eerdmans, 1976), 245.

for clothing *beged* denotes the plain and unpretentious clothing of the poor.[8] Without a doubt, this law condemns creditors who demand that she pawn her clothing. It intimates that she is not to surrender in a pledge for her indebtedness, those items that were essential for comfort and for the symbols of her dignity. Additionally, Israelite farmers are enjoined not to harvest their fields so that everything is gathered. They are commanded to leave uncollected sheaves, grapes, and olives. They are to harvest only once. The produce that remains is to be left for the stranger, orphan, or the widow. The rationale for this command by Yahweh for the display of kindness is because of Israel's experience as slaves in Egypt.

4. Deuteronomy 26:12-15

The presentation of the third-year tithe is the focus of this fourth passage. This tithe of one's produce would be presented as a part of a ceremony once the children of Israel have entered into the land. About this passage, Craigie states:

> Whereas the main substance of the specific stipulations (Deut. 12–26) anticipates the continuing future life of Israel in the promised land, the legislation contained in 26:1–15 relates to two particular ceremonies which were to be held as soon as Israel had taken possession of the land and begun its new (agricultural) style of life. In this sense, 26:1–15 follows naturally from 25:17–19, which also refers to particular action to be taken once the land had been possessed; it precedes naturally the legislation of 27:1–26, in which the particular renewal of the covenant in the vicinity of Shechem is commanded, to

---

[8] Harold V. Bennett, *Injustice Made Legal: Deuteronomic Law and the Plight of Widows, Strangers, and Orphans in Ancient Israel.* (Grand Rapids, MI: Williams B. Eerdmans, 2002), 101.

be undertaken after the crossing of the Jordan and the initial stages of the conquest.[9]

Deuteronomy 26: 12-15 is the second part of ceremony. The first part is mentioned in Deuteronomy 26:1-11 and it is the offering for the first time of the first fruits of the land. This is to take place after the conquest when they are in the land of Promise. Concerning this, Craigie states:

> The first offering of the firstfruits of the ground (vv. 1–11). This ceremony was to take place in the promised land (when you enter the land), after the conquest (you take possession of it), and when the [Deut., p. 320] Israelites had begun to live in the land and be supported by its produce (you live in it: v. 1). The firstfruits of the harvest were offered at the Feast of Weeks (16:9–12; cf. 18:4)[10]

Verses 12-15 describe a ceremony that would take place two years later in the third year of full settlement. In this ceremony, the following would take place. One, the tithe of the third year took place in the Israelite towns or settlements, and that which was tithed was to be distributed among various classes of underprivileged persons (v. 12). The underprivileged included the stranger, orphan, and the widow. Two, after distributing the tithe, the worshipper made a declaration before (or "in the presence of") the Lord. Since the words were probably to be spoken in the settlements and not at the central sanctuary, these words may indicate that this worship service and declaration in the third year of settlement were performed in the home.[11]

---

[9] Craigie, *Deuteronomy*, 319.
[10] Craigie, *Deuteronomy*, 323.
[11] This declaration has three parts which are a positive statement (v.13), a negative lament statement (v. 14), and a prayer in conclusion (v. 15).

Conclusions: Rationale of Grouping of the Underprivileged and Conclusions Concerning Deuteronomy

a. Deuteronomy 14:22-29

From this passage, I conclude the following:

1. Deuteronomy 14:22-29 is forward-looking and envisioned the time when there was a central place of worship as noted in Deuteronomy 14:23: "In the presence of the LORD your God, in the place he chooses to locate his name, you must eat from the tithe of your grain, your new wine, your olive oil, and the firstborn of your herds and flocks, so that you may learn to revere the LORD your God always." The book of Deuteronomy is forward-looking, envisioning the time when Israel will inhabit the land. The care and compassion for those who do not have access to wealth (the land) is a part of the institutional framework of the covenant of Israel with Yahweh.
2. The tithe was demanded by the Lord yearly. This yearly amount could provide a national safety net for the most vulnerable of society.
3. The tithe as a social act of kindness was also reflective of their identity as a people in covenant with YHWH.
4. The mention of the Levites in the group of underprivileged is important. The Levites were the only group that did not have an ancestral inheritance of land. The calling and responsibility of the Levites were to the service of the Lord and the Cult. This is key as to why these three, the stranger, orphan, and the widow are mentioned together. They are mentioned together as a result of their direct lack of ancestral property which would

have ensured them an income or collateral that would enable them to obtain a regular income. This conclusion is supported by Deuteronomy 14:29:

> Then the Levites (because they have no allotment or inheritance with you), the resident foreigners, the orphans, and the widows of your villages may come and eat their fill so that the LORD your God may bless you in all the work you do.

5. The poor were not "otherized." The enjoyment of sharing and participation was a time of joy and sharing together. It appears that the common locale of sharing at the Temple provided a common bond between the "haves and the have nots" in terms of the possession of the land the rewards that came from the "ownership" or "stewardship of the land. The blessings of the land provided benefits to be enjoyed by all.

b. Deut. 16:9-12, 13-17

From this passage, I conclude the following:

1. The timing during the Yom Kippur points to the seriousness of the practice and how important this practice of giving is in the context of the spiritual pilgrimage of People of God.
2. The kindness of Israel to others is connected to the kindness that the YHWH has exhibited to them.
3. The institutionalization of kindness in the covenant of Yahweh with Israel towards vulnerable individuals of Israel's society reflects the character of Yahweh that is displayed elsewhere in the Bible.

c. Deut. 24:17-18, 19-22

From this passage, I conclude the following:

1. YHWH is concerned about justice. Justice is administered to the most vulnerable of society and in this case, the most vulnerable mentioned is the widow who is without support from an immediate family.
2. Justice contains both social and economic components. These components are a part of the larger framework of societal interaction. Justice contains religious, social, and economic aspects.
3. The justice of the YHWH concerns the respectability and humanity of others. Creditors are admonished not to take the garments of widows as part of collateral for loans.
4. The rationale for justice towards kindness and justice for the vulnerable of society is their experiences as slaves and God's liberation of Israel from slavery.
5. The demand for the protection of the stranger, widow, and orphan is built into the larger economy of the everyday and individual lives of farmers.

d. Deut. 26:12-15

From this fourth passage, I conclude the following:

1. This passage is forward-looking and suggests that the future welfare of the nation is connected to their faith in YHWH and compliance to the commands of the Lord. It is envisioning a time when the Israelites are in the land of promise and that the compliance with the tithe will lead to divine blessings.
2. One sees both the personal and public practice of one's faith. In Deut. 16:1-11, there is a public ceremony that is undertaken

at the central place of worship. In Deut. 16:12-15, there is the local and personal participation of the community in the lives and the needs of the vulnerable of the local community. Verse 12 indicates that the triennial tithe for the poor and disenfranchised took place in the local village.[12]

3. The inclusion of the Levites with the widows, orphans, and the sojourners. This would suggest that rationale for the vulnerability of the members of this group is that lack of access to an inheritance of land.

Bennett's Conclusions and Rationale of Grouping of the Underprivileged

Bennett notes the following:

1. The corpus of laws in Deuteronomy 14-26 deal with earlier regulations regarding the vulnerable in society, namely the stranger, orphan, and the widow. For Bennett, previous scholarship does not address why these laws were codified in Deuteronomy, which he dates to the seventh century BCE.
2. Bennett suggests that scholarship is silent concerning the grouping together of widows, strangers, and orphans in Deuteronomy. He maintains that scholarship is silent about the identity of these individuals and does not provide the common thread that connects all their lives together.
3. There is lack of clarity of scholarship regarding the lack of clarity between the problems in society and how these laws rectified the problem.
4. Bennett sees the laws of Deuteronomy 14-26 as legal remedies of problems in society. What gave rise to the promulgation of these laws and who benefits from these laws are issues that are not addressed.

---

[12] Craigie, *Deuteronomy*, 320.

5. Therefore, Bennett argues widows, strangers, and orphans were a part of a strategy to regulate their behavior and to shape the ideas of local peasant farmers regarding the distribution of goods in Ancient Israel. Specifically, Bennett argues that Deuteronomy 14-26 exacerbated the plight of widows, strangers, and orphans. This category of socially weak, but politically useful persons in the biblical communities were manipulated by intellectual elites to stave off potential uprisings by local peasant farmers in the North during the ninth century BCE. Bennett completely ignores the biblical context of Deuteronomy 14-26.

Conclusions: A Response to Dr. Harold Bennett and Gospelist Reflections

I offer the following reflections to the positions of Bennett.

1. A Question of *Sitz im Leben*: The Context of Deuteronomy

For Bennett to separate these four relevant passages addresses these marginalized groups but does so to the detriment of the group. For Bennett, biblical laws concerning widows, strangers, and orphans are drafted by a powerful elite to enhance their own material wealth and keep the vulnerable regulated.[13] Rather, the purpose of these laws, formulated in the ninth century BCE during the Omride administration, were a means to regulate behavior and shape the ideas of local farmers in Israel. For Bennett these stipulations exacerbated the plight of widows, strangers, and orphans, who were socially weak but politically useful. Intellectual elites used these biblical stipulations to stave off potential uprisings by local peasant farmers in the North during the

---

[13] Harold Bennett, *Injustice Made Legal: Deuteronomic Law and the Plight of Widow, Stranger, and Orphans in Ancient Israel* (Grand Rapids, MI: Eerdmans, 2002), 11.

ninth century BCE. In order to formulate this theory, Bennett is heavily reliant on critical law theory and social science research.

In response to Bennett, the writer views this analysis of Deuteronomy and find this faulty. Bennett can be critiqued on several points. One, Bennett totally ignores the historical context and content of Deuteronomy. The Book of Deuteronomy has traditionally been recognized as a distinctive part of the Pentateuch on the grounds of its language, style, and theology.[14] In the Pentateuchal narrative, Deuteronomy represents a long pause on the plain of Moab, where according to Numbers, Israel had arrived following its forty-year journey within the wilderness (Num. 33:49). Deuteronomy provided the farewell speeches of Moses, which comprise a majority of the book. Deuteronomy is preparing the people for a further covenant renewal to take place at Mt. Ebal near Shechem after they have entered the land of Canaan (Deut. 27: 1-8). This suggestion of a ninth-century BCE context in the Omride dynasty ignores the content of Deuteronomy and is exegetically inappropriate. Bennett postulates both a context and use of the passages of Deuteronomy that are foreign to and in tension with Deuteronomy. In his methodology of relying upon critical law theory, Bennett misconstrues both the meaning and purpose of Deuteronomy in general and specifically the stipulations dealing with the widow, orphan, and stranger.

2. Orthodoxy of Scripture

Bennett's thesis regarding the stipulations of Deuteronomy additionally reveals his perspective regarding the authorship of Deuteronomy and the orthodoxy of Scripture. Bennett posits a seventh-century BCE date for Deuteronomy. This date is at odds with the traditional date for the life of Moses which would probably have been 1526 to 1406 BCE. For Bennett, this is apparently not problematic. The Book of

---

[14] J. G. McConville, *God and Earthly Power: An Old Testament Political Theology: Genesis-Kings* (New York, NY: T&T Clark, 2008), 74.

Deuteronomy is a group of speeches given by Moses that rehearse the history of the Lord's relationship with Israel while preparing the nation for what lies ahead. The traditional view of authorship for the entire Pentateuch is that Moses is the author. The traditional view of Mosaic authorship is assumed in the Old Testament and the New Testament. The writer has a different perspective on the Scripture from Bennett. For the writer, the Holy Scripture is God's own Word.

3. Historicity and Methodology

Bennett's thesis regarding the stipulations of Deuteronomy contains additional ramifications for biblical interpretation. The Book of Deuteronomy contains these passages (14:22-29; 16:9-12, 13-15; 24:17-18, 19-22; and 26:12-15), which are part of the final speeches of Moses on the plain of Moab. Bennett's dismissal of the context in which these speeches were given, the speaker (Moses), and the original intended purpose of the Book of Deuteronomy discount the history of events narrated in the book. These relevant passages occur within the second address of Moses (4:44-26:19).[15] The Book of Deuteronomy is a series of final speeches given by Moses in preparation for the entrance of the nation of Israel into the Promised Land. Bennett's perspective on the purposes of Deuteronomy as a part of the Pentateuch are in opposition with how Deuteronomy is viewed in the remainder of the Hebrew Bible and also in the New Testament. Additionally, Bennett's perspective on Deuteronomy dismisses the historicity of the events that are assumed as historical by both the writer and the audience. Moreover, if as Bennett suggests, Deuteronomy is a seventh-century document, the historicity of Moses is also dismissed. To a large extent, this view regarding the dating of Deuteronomy and the dismissal of its historical events is reflective of the Documentary Hypothesis of the Pentateuch that was popularized by Julius Wellhausen.

---

[15] Craigie, *The Book of Deuteronomy*, 75.

Gospelist Reflections

There are some overall conclusions and contextual reflections that these four passages in Deuteronomy suggest to readers of the Hebrew Bible regarding justice for the disadvantaged of society.

1. This justice is both institutional and personal. One sees that the stipulations of Deuteronomy were mandated for individuals and also in the larger religious practices of the nations. In two of the three annual feasts, the most vulnerable of Ancient Near East society were aided by the nation of Israel and not stigmatized for being without the means proper to survival. Stephanie Coontz argues against the myth of traditional U.S. American family. For Coontz, middle-class families were never self-reliant. Through government subsidies and other support systems, families of the nineteenth and twentieth centuries were supported, with the obvious exception of African American families. Coontz contends that the solution to some of the social problems that derive from larger societal forces can begin to be externally addressed by a renewed community conscience and a "safety net" that supports the most vulnerable of society.
2. Deuteronomy stresses the importance of the lack of land for widow, orphan, stranger, and the Levite. The access to land is the access to capital and self-determination. The access to financial means for the most vulnerable of the society is not a privilege but an institutional mandate for a just society.
3. There is the obvious care and concern for the vulnerable in a just and fair society. If a society is to be just, it has to have institutional components that make justice something that is valued institutionally, corporately, and individually.
4. The institutional "safety net" for the most vulnerable is implemented on the governmental level. There should be

institutional, national, local, and individual compliance with mandates to ensure the welfare of all.

5. Justice must address the continuing attack on African Americans. The continued attack on African Americans and people of color in the United States is well documented. Almost every person of color I know has anecdotes regarding some attack either physically, psychologically, or emotionally on their personhood as a result of being a person of color. Nikole Hannah-Jones examined and reframed U.S. History through the consequences of slavery and the contributions of Black U.S. Americans. These are placed at the very center of the United States' national narrative. The lack of protection of the personhood of African Americans has been coupled with the exploitation and commoditization of persons of color and their achievements. Manning Marable argues that:

> Race is a relationship between accumulation and dispossession and that without a structural change in the economic system, disparities and discrimination would continue and perhaps worsen—correctly anticipated and analyzed current conditions. Most social indicators demonstrate that structural racism continues to flourish.[16]

For Marable, the continuing plight of African Americans is due to how people of color are victimized in the United States. Michelle Alexander traces the resumption of racial discrimination followed the Civil Rights Movement. Alexander focused on the high incarceration rate of African American men for various crimes. These Gospelist reflections suggest systemic remedies for the plight of African Americans must be multi-faceted to address the systemic nature of oppression.

---

[16] Manning Marable, *How Capitalism Underdeveloped Black America: Problems in Race, Political Economy, and Society* (Chicago, IL: Haymarket, 2015), 11.

Ad Fontes: An Examination of the Relationship between Scripture and the Negro Spirituals

Ernest Gray

Introduction

As the soil from which these expressive forms of resilience have emerged, I contend that the Spirituals developed by African American slaves in the U.S. remain an area where much reflection should be focused. The Spirituals were a complex form of artistic expression that sought to make sense of a world where Black bodies were commodified and not accepted as fully human. For this reason, the precarious institution of slavery in the Western hemisphere can adequately be compared to NT examples or as tacit witnesses to the institution. Much like the Prologue of John's Gospel, the Apostle contends that the Logos was the embodiment of divinity and humanity. However, as the introduction demonstrates, the arrival of the Logos was not one that was accepted by all. The language in John's Gospel and the predicament of African American slaves share a strange similarity, "He came to his own home, and his own people received him not."[17] This reality reminds us of Jesus' own alienation, rejection, and othering. Likewise, African Americans were subjected to dehumanizing alienation and rejection. Yet even in the midst of these realities, we find

---

[17] Jn. 1:11.

common ground in the Prologue and the Spirituals. What NT scholars purport to be an entire section of poetic prose within the Prologue can arguably be seen in certain songs which capture the same sentiment.

The institution of slavery has been the subject of numerous studies and scholarship; our interest lies in the ways and means that the antebellum and postbellum communities sought to survive. The Spirituals were a source of life. Hence, further investigations into the construction of the form and content of these artistic relics would be fruitful for purposes that relate to a greater diversity of thought within Western Christianity. These songs proved to be sources of buoyancy for the scores of men and women who were disparaged daily. A key component of resilience within people of African Descent is their ability to adapt and survive even the most challenging moments. The Spirituals served this purpose. This essay seeks to annotate the features of how the Negro Spirituals handled the disparaging circumstances associated with their existence in the Southern regions of the U.S. and seeks to corroborate how the Christian Scriptures were embedded in a program of resistance and survival. They proved buoyant and aided those who relied upon them. Related to this theme of resilience is John 1:10-11 and the reality of rejection that both Jesus and many African Americans have faced. Therefore, with the Incarnation of Christ, there is a great sense of illumination that has been inaugurated within the earth. At the same time, most rejected this light and chose unbelief and ignorance instead. A reminder of this reality tethers the experiences of the Messiah to the plight of people of African Descent. Our focus will attend to the prologue of John in general—and 1:11 in particular—to examine the rejection of Jesus and the sustained rejection of the men and women who lacked voices, agency, and freedom.

This paper seeks to proffer the following idea: Hymns sung within communities of faith have been a source of resilience in the face of persecution. Their existence among people of African descent is redolent within the various Negro Spirituals that emerged prior to and during the era of slavery. However, due to the paucity of research upon Negro Spirituals and biblical texts, this study aims to ascertain the manner that these texts are deployed as sources of resilience during and after the era of slavery. Building upon the work of NT hymnody research, this essay will investigate a few African American Spirituals and the corresponding texts that demonstrate their literary allusion. It will be determined that the biblical texts served as liberating language that promoted resilience and resistance for the possessor. Considered together, Scripture and Negro Spirituals provided a powerful counter to the horrors of the American institution of slavery.

While a survey of instances of hymnody throughout the NT would be profitable, that is a much larger project and beyond the scope of this essay. To annotate an instance of correlation, the ideational meaning of John 1:1-18 and the Spirituals that discuss the Incarnation, rejection, and alienation shall serve as correlates. This correlation will demonstrate the manner that a biblical text can inform the creation of songs and hymns, which engender acceptance and divine closeness. These two aspects were pursued within the theological outworking of various Negro Spirituals.

To compare the difference between a sample NT hymn and early African American Spirituals, a comparative model which analyzes that the narrative navigates between the two sources will be employed. The theory that I employ in this essay is derived from the realm of intertextual allusions. It would appear that, like most literary borrowing, the shorter reading represents the original or the narrative borrowing from donor text to ultimate text. However, given the history of creation that surrounds the existence of Negro Spirituals, the direction does not always reflect the direction one would inspect. In other words, artisans and hymn creators who engaged in the process of hymn fashioning generally drew from their own experience and found resonance within the Bible to support their predicament.

Scriptural Hymnody

The text of Scripture remains a primary source for Christian Hymnody. The Old and New Testaments provide the content for use in artistic form as the primary means to remind the oppressed of the places, events, and outcomes that have been recalled in connection to God: "Christian hymnody has drawn deeply from the biblical well for both content and form."[18] This takes the form of "orally transmitted Bible stories."[19]

Methodology

To restate my claim, this study seeks to establish that to detect the existence of hymns in extra biblical accounts or within the Scriptures, several criterial can be used.[20]

1. Quotations: distinctive biblical words or phrases that are found in numerous hymns and from a variety of versions of the Scriptures.
2. Mosaics: biblical quotes, which may be found in the hymns of writers who have a special command of Scripture.
3. Metrical versions: a casting of the biblical text into meter but following closely the biblical use of words, word order, and sequence of thought.
4. Paraphrase: a freer instance of metrical version in its use of biblical word, word order, and sequence of thought.
5. Allusion: an indirect use of scriptural reference which often allude to specific people, places, items, and events of Scripture.

---

[18] Scotty Gray, *Hermeneutics of Hymnody: A Comprehensive and Integrated Approach to Understanding Hymns* (Macon, GA: Smyth & Helwys Publishing, 2015), 39.

[19] Brian K. Blount, *Cultural Interpretations: Reorienting New Testament Criticism* (Minneapolis, MN: Fortress Press, 1995), 57. Blount adds: "The fact that the spiritual is an oral phenomenon opens it all the more to contextual influence; the literary control that exist in written works are absent."

[20] Gray, *Hermeneutics of Hymnody*, 45-50.

It is within the realm of allusion that correlates exist between Negro Spirituals and scriptural hymns, which will be elaborated upon in the balance of this study. Due to the oral realty of each song that was constructed, the initial methods of constructing hymns would not represent an accurate depiction of literary borrowing or intertextuality. At best, to allude to a story shared or truth exposited from the Scripture is likely all one can summon to recreate any literary interaction. As shall be demonstrated, this type of literary existence does make it challenging to establish any dependence between biblical text and song. Blount opines,

> As one might expect, however, there could be no textual control. Slave laws mandated black illiteracy; the slave therefore had little ability to consider the English versions of the stories much less Greek…This does not mean, however, that a "spiritual" interpretation of a biblical story must necessarily be inaccurate. There is never one single, inviolate lexical-literal textual meaning…therefore the mere fact that the slaves could not have employed textual control in their interpretative moves does not automatically invalidate the interpretative conclusions reached in their music.[21]

Let us consider how Old Testament hymns present and the manner they resonate within the African American community during the antebellum and postbellum periods.

Old Testament Hymns

The Old Testament is a key source of liberation for oppressed groups including African Americans in the antebellum south:

---

[21] Blount, *Cultural Interpretations*, 58.

It is not possible to estimate the sustaining influence that the story of the trials and tribulations of the Jews as related in the Old Testament exerted upon the Negro.

This story at once caught and fired the imaginations of the Negro bards, and they sang, sang their hungry listeners into a firm faith that as God saved Daniel in the lion's den, so would He save them; as God preserved the Hebrew children in the fiery furnace, so would He preserve them; as God delivered Israel out of bondage in Egypt, so would He deliver them. How much this firm faith had to do with the Negro's physical and spiritual survival of two and a half centuries of slavery cannot be known.[22]

As the alignment of both the Hebrew Scriptures and deep resonance to the era of American slavery are well established, we see that vindication of the Jews from captivity and the abolishment of slavery in America are generally read together.[23] Something all the more evident as these songs serve as tools for liberation in both a spiritual and physical sense.

New Testament Hymns

Within the New Testament, we encounter a different textual witness. Many of the so-called hymns in the NT are shorter, apocopated prose with poetic features. Instances of NT hymns and their approximate numbers do not have a consensus due to the creep between language

---

[22] James Weldon Johnson & J. Rosamond Johnson, *The Books of the American Negro Spirituals* (New York, NY: The Viking Press, 1925), 20-21. Cf. Thurman, "the experiences of frustration and divine deliverance, as set forth in the stories of the Hebrews in bondage, spoke at once to the deep need in the life of the slaves. They were literalists in their interpretations, not only because such was the dominant pattern of the religious thinking of the environment but also because their needs demanded it," Howard Thurman, *Deep River and the Negro Spiritual Speaks of Life and Death* (Richmond, IN: Friends United Press, 1975), 14.

[23] See Willie James Jennings, *After Whiteness: An Education in Belonging* (Grand Rapids, MI: Wm. B. Eerdmans, 2020).

and definitions regarding their function.²⁴ Among the agreed upon, many have come from the Pauline corpus, though those outside of the Pauline text tend to be much more didactic and lengthy.

John's Prologue (1:10-18) as Exemplar

> *This* was the true Light that, coming into the world, enlightens every person. ¹⁰ He was in the world, and the world came into being through Him, and *yet* the world did not know Him. ¹¹ He came to His own, and His own people did not accept Him.¹² But as many as received Him, to them He gave the right to become children of God, to those who believe in His name, ¹³ who were born, not of blood, nor of the will of the flesh, nor of the will of a man, but of God. ¹⁴ And the Word became flesh, and dwelt among us; and we saw His glory, glory as of the only *Son* from the Father, full of grace and truth. ¹⁵ John testified about Him and called out, saying, "This was He of whom I said, 'He who is coming after me has proved to be my superior, because He existed before me.'" ¹⁶ For of His fullness we have all received, and grace upon grace. ¹⁷ For the Law was given through Moses; grace and truth were realized through Jesus Christ. ¹⁸ No one has seen God at any time; God the only *Son*, who is in the arms of the Father, He has explained Him.

Although establishment of the Prologue remains tenuous among scholars as to its actual existence as a hymn, many agree that it is one

---

[24] For instance, terminology shifts, between encomium, hymn, prose hymn, and poem. The following have been suggested by Robert J. Karris, *A Symphony of New Testament Hymns: Commentary on Phil. 2:5-11, Col. 1:15-20, Eph. 2:14-16, 1 Tim. 3:16, Tit. 3:4-7, 1 Pet. 3:18-22, 2 Tim. 2:11-13* (Collegeville, MN: Liturgical Press, 1996). A brief glance at this list suggests that Pauline hymnic texts are more numerous than other NT collections. This does not, however, exhaust the list of examples one might find scattered throughout the NT.

of the "most profound poems in the NT."[25] Interpretative approaches abound, including comparative studies: Mandean redeemer myths, Gnostic comparisons, and creation accounts. Studies of the Prologue of John are not in short supply. However, given the relationship it bears to items of Creation, humanity, and the Incarnation, this text is apt to address the similar circumstances to which African Americans were experiencing, especially in the section of interest 1:10-11. This was the rejection of the Word in the World. Regarding the manner that rejection is expressed in the discourse, Gordley notes:

> Our understanding of the ways in which hymns at times functioned as part of a strategy of resistance for Jewish and Greco-Roman communities during this era allows us to consider how a hymn with this kind of language might have functioned similarly for the Johannine Community…like other kinds of resistance literature, the prologue exhibits a concern for remembering key events of the past in a way that challenges the prevailing narrative of the dominant group.[26]

With vv. 10-11 under consideration, some translations capture the poignancy of John's description of rejection. The construction ἐν τῷ κόσμῳ ἦν, καὶ ὁ κόσμος δι' αὐτοῦ ἐγένετο, καὶ ὁ κόσμος αὐτὸν οὐκ ἔγνω, demonstrates a narrative irony that is sometimes lost in translation: "he was in the world, and the world was made by him, but the world didn't know him." The term ἔγνω here suggests that

---

[25] Philip Wesley Comfort, *The Poems and Hymns of the New Testament* (Eugene, OR: Wipf & Stock, 2010), 39. Cf. Matthew E. Gordley, who notes, "although I view the prologue as a Christian hymnic composition, my claim in presenting this arrangement is not that it represents an original, preexisting hymn that predated the Gospel of John…but it seems most likely to me that the prologue was written in a hymnic register for the purpose of introducing the Gospel and is itself the result of deep and extended reflection on the contents of this Gospel." *New Testament Christological Hymns: Exploring Texts, Contexts, and Significance* (Downers Grove, IL: InterVarsity Press Academic, 2018), 148.

[26] Gordley, *New Testament Christological Hymns,* 146.

the world's ignorance forestalled its knowledge of His creative act in tandem with God the Father. Furthermore, vv. 11, deepens this notion: εἰς τὰ ἴδια ἦλθεν, καὶ οἱ ἴδιοι αὐτὸν οὐ παρέλαβον as the referent to "one's own" normally remains ambiguous. What exactly is "one's own"? The relative ambiguity has rendered many translations in dire need of clarity, others have simply chosen not to specify. Note the following versions:

> RSV. "He came to his own home, and his own people received him not."
>
> NASB. "He came to his own, and those who were his own did not receive him."
>
> NIV. "He came to that which was his own, but his own did not receive him."

As the options in rendering these verses demonstrates, the sense conveyed here is replete of the same irony of vv. 10: "The Lord Jesus arrived on earth, and was rejected by those he came to save." This common experience suggests that Jesus has always been relatable to the suffering than to those who carry out the othering, alienation, and rejection.

Rejection at times does pervade several Spirituals wherein, focusing upon Jesus, African Americans identified greatly with the suffering of Jesus. Notice the similarities between Jesus' silence during the Passion and the silence of slaves during their own life sufferings:

> Oh, dey whupped him up de hill, up de hill
>
> Oh, dey whupped hi, up de hill, an' he never said a mumbalin word,
>
> Oh, dey whupped hi, up de hill, an' he never said a mumbalin' word,
>
> He jus, hung down his head an' he cried.

As the mistreatment, lynching, and beating of Jesus could be comprehended vicariously amongst other groups of humans, for the slaves in America, such would not be the case. Their experiences were his experiences, and He is acquainted with their grief. Such tools for survival took shape in their perspectives, which did not allow them to rest in sorrow. In another example of such fortitude, the idea of Jesus suffering is captured in his atonement. This Spiritual speaks to this idea of universal suffering that touches all:

> But He ain't comin here t' die no mo',
>
> Ain't comin' here t' die no mo',
>
> Hallelujah t' de Lamb
>
> Jesus died for every man.
>
> But He ain't comin' here t' die no mo'
>
> Ain't comin here t' die no mo'

Comparatively, it can be said that though the African American slave had no access to educational pursuits, reading aids, nor interpretive skills, her/his ability to reorient the story to explain their lives remains paramount throughout the Spirituals.

Observations

So what can be said regarding this proposal of literary kinship? First, it must be noted that contrary to the proposition of this essay, very little evidence suggests that the Scriptures served as the borrowed source for the construction of Negro Spirituals. This reality in no way undermines the theologizing we witness throughout most spirituals; it simply means that the most evident way to show dependence is through oral recitation, not orthography. Second, the experiences of African American slaves serve as the interpretive lens for which the Bible aligns and affirms their dignity. In other words, they experienced the cruelty of slavery and wrote a song about it with the Bible as a means of validation. Third, as Howard Thurman has suggested, the Pauline texts are not as engaged within the bevy of songs that were created during the era of slavery: "Some blacks rejected Paul because of the way whites preached and interpreted his texts."[27] This tenuous relationship deserves a deeper dive to consider how African American slaves renegotiated their relationship with these texts; texts which were maligned and used to perpetuate the sin of slavery. Finally, if Jewish literature and hymns served to embed resistance for the community, how much more redolent does this resistance and resilience lie within the texts of Negro Spirituals? This query will likely need to be taken up at a later time.

Conclusion

This study sought to evaluate the relationship between the biblical text and Negro Spirituals. Though literary borrowing appears to be a non-factor in the creation of Negro Spirituals, the use of the biblical text shows the existence of allusion throughout to ensure that the slaves who wielded them were aware of the liberative power that they possessed.

---

[27] Lisa M. Bowens, *African-American Readings of Paul: Reception, Resistance, and Transformation* (Grand Rapids, MI: Wm. B. Eerdmans, 2020), 2.

The Effects of Nationalism on the Mental and Spiritual State

Timothy D. Allison

Introduction

The Book of Jonah gives a riveting account of the Prophet Jonah as he attempted to flee to Tarshish after God commanded him to prophesy to Nineveh. Throughout the text, Jonah's erratic behavior reveals his lack of compassion for Nineveh and his anger toward God for wanting to save the people of Nineveh. This paper will examine the Book of Jonah with a focus on Jonah's mental and spiritual state to demonstrate that Jonah's actions were fueled by depression. Further, evidence exists to argue that Jonah's depressive state resulted from his internal battle of loyalty to his nation or his God, opposition to Nineveh, and his conflict with God for wanting to save a group of people that Jonah saw as unredeemable. The conflict of allegiance between God and country caused problems for Jonah and the Church today, as we will examine later in this paper.

Historical Context

There is not much history given to us in the Book of Jonah concerning his background. We know that he was a Hebrew, a prophet, and the son of Amittai. We find a prophet named Jonah in the book of 2 Kings during the reign of Jeroboam II, a king who did evil in the sight of

Yahweh.[28] The text tells us that the prophet Jonah gave the prophecy of the restoration of Israel's borders. With this information, the date of the events in the Book of Jonah would have been during the eighth century BCE.

Nineveh was a city of violence, known for its brutal treatment of those they conquered. Reliefs from the Assyrian King Sennacherib's palace depict naked Judaeans impaled on poles and sieged ramps built by Judaean slaves. These reliefs depict the cruelty with which Assyrian forces treated defeated people groups. The Assyrians would amputate their enemies' hands and feet, pluck their eyes out, and skin their captives.[29] Jonah's pride in Israel, coupled with the treacherous nature of Assyria toward Israel, could have easily caused him to have internal conflict when given the command to go and preach repentance to Nineveh.

Range of Meaning רָדַם (ra-dam)

In exploring this internal conflict, let us examine the state of Jonah in Jonah 1:5 (CSB): "The sailors were afraid, and each cried out to his god. They threw the ship's cargo into the sea to lighten the load. Meanwhile, Jonah had gone down to the lowest part of the vessel and had stretched out and fallen into a deep sleep." Yahweh spoke to Prophet Jonah and directed him to go to Nineveh and preach repentance. Instead, Jonah went the opposite way down to Joppa and boarded a ship heading to Tarshish, attempting to flee from the presence of Yahweh. While at sea, Yahweh sent a great storm. The storm is so massive that the sailors begin to throw the cargo overboard to save themselves. They even began to pray to their gods. Through all of this commotion, Jonah was in the lower part of the ship in *ra-dam*, a "deep sleep."

---

[28] Billy K. Smith and Franklin S. Page, *The New American Commentary: Amos, Obadiah, Jonah*, vol. 19B (Nashville, TN: Broadman & Holman Publishers, 1995), 206.

[29] Anna Sieges, "Nineveh," in *The Lexham Bible Dictionary*, John D. Barry (Bellingham, WA: Lexham Press, 2016).

An examination of the Hebrew language will further give us insight into possible reasons for Jonah's ability to sleep deeply through so much chaos. It is quite apparent that Jonah was experiencing heavy exhaustion. But this exhaustion was more than physical. Jonah's exhaustion was yet another attempt to escape, brought on by the strain on his mental and spiritual state.

The author of Jonah chose the word וַיֵּרָדַם (va-ye-ra-dam) to describe the state of Jonah's sleep. Exploring how this word is used throughout the biblical text will give us more insight into its meaning and the possible reason for the author's use of this word in Jonah 1:5. Deep sleep וַיֵּרָדַם (va-ye-ra-dam) in Jonah 1:5 is a Niphal verb, which indicates the action of the verb as a completed action. The previous verb וַיִּשְׁכַּב (vay-yis-kab) "laid down" is also a Niphal verb.[30] In context, this does not give us a reason for Jonah's deep sleep. Furthermore, we must not rush to fill in the blanks by saying the cause of his deep sleep was physical exhaustion alone. All that we can say is that Jonah was at the bottom of the ship, and he was in a state of deep sleep.

The root for וַיֵּרָדַם (va-ye-ra-dam) is רָדַם (ra-dam).[31] We encounter this root in its noun form in Genesis 2:21, when Yahweh causes Adam to fall into a deep sleep. The sleep state that Adam experienced is described as sedation by Yahweh in preparation for the formation of the woman by the removal of Adam's rib. The sedation could have been caused by a loss of consciousness or simply the inability to move or feel the environment around him. In the case of Jonah, he was at the bottom of the ship, completely unaware of the effects of the storm. The sailors were trained for this environment and were yet afraid. They were throwing cargo overboard while the ship itself was "threatening" to break, but Jonah was oblivious to it all.

---

[30] W. Dennis Tucker Jr., *Jonah: A Handbook on the Hebrew Text* (Waco, TX: Baylor University Press, 2018), 20-23.
[31] Francis Brown et al., *The Enhanced Brown-Driver-Briggs Hebrew and English Lexicon: With an Appendix Containing the Biblical Aramaic* (Oak Harbor, WA: Logos Research Systems, 2000).

Other uses of רָדַם (*ra-dam*) can be found in 1 Samuel where the same form, תַּרְדֵּמָה (*tar-de-mah*), that is found in Genesis 2 is used. In this context, David spared the life of Saul by taking a spear and a water jug that was sitting by his head.[32] They were unaware of his presence because Yahweh had caused them to be in a deep sleep, as in Genesis. In Judges, we encounter the gruesome murder of Sisera by Jael where she took a tent peg and hammered it into the temple of Sisera.[33] This was done while Sisera was in רָדַם (*ra-dam*), a "deep sleep." The context suggests that Sisera's reason for being in such a deep sleep was because of exhaustion. This type of sleep causes a person to be unaware and unreactive to the events around them. This can be initiated by Yahweh for His purpose or even by exhaustion, such as in the case with Sisera. It is also plausible that neither of these were contributing factors to Jonah's רָדַם (*ra-dam*).

Clinical Criteria for Depression

It is plausible that Jonah's state of רָדַם (*ra-dam*) could be diagnosed as Major Depressive Disorder. To examine this idea, we must look at the criteria for Major Depressive Disorder and the condition of Jonah as revealed in the biblical text. Major Depressive Disorder is diagnosed by utilizing the American Psychiatric Association's Diagnostic and Statistical Manual (DSM).[34]

The criteria are as listed.

A minimum of five symptoms from the following list have been occurring nearly every day during the same two-week period and represent a change from previous functioning. At least one of the symptoms must be (1) or (2) as listed below:

---

[32] 1 Sam. 26:12
[33] Judg. 4:21
[34] *Diagnostic and Statistical Manual of Mental Disorders: DSM-IV.* (Washington, DC: American Psychiatric Association, 1994).

1. Depressed mood most of the day, nearly every day, as indicated either by subjective report (e.g., feels sad or empty) or observation made by others (e.g., appears tearful), or
2. Markedly diminished interest or pleasure in all, or almost all, activities most of the day, nearly every day, as indicated either by subjective account or observation made by others (does not include symptoms that are clearly due to general medical condition or mood-incongruent delusions or hallucinations)

    Jonah's Condition: We encounter very odd behavior with Jonah. After the captain finds Jonah at the bottom of the ship, pagan men prompt him to pray, yet he does not (Jonah 1:6). It is odd behavior for a prophet not to pray; only when Jonah is sinking in the ocean after being thrown overboard does he decide to pray.

3. Significant weight loss when not dieting or weight gain (e.g., a change of more than 5% of body weight in a month) or decrease or increase in appetite

    Jonah's Condition: N/A

4. Insomnia or hypersomnia

    Jonah's Condition: Jonah was in such a deep sleep that neither the storm nor the commotion of the sailors throwing cargo overboard could wake him. (Jonah 1:4-5).

5. Psychomotor agitation or retardation (observable by others, not merely subjective feelings of restlessness or being slowed down)

    Jonah's Condition: N/A

6. Fatigue or loss of energy

    Jonah's Condition: Jonah went to the bottom of the boat to sleep.

7. Feelings of worthlessness or excessive or inappropriate guilt (which may be delusional, not merely self-reproach or guilt about being sick)

Jonah's Condition: N/A

8. Diminished ability to think or concentrate, or indecisiveness (either by subjective account or as observed by others)

   Jonah's Condition: N/A

9. Recurrent thoughts of death (not just fear of dying), recurrent suicidal ideation without a plan, or a suicide attempt or specific plan for committing suicide

   Jonah's Condition: Jonah persuades the sailors to throw him overboard (Jonah 1:12). This was an attempt at suicide. Jonah prays for Yahweh to take his life (Jonah 4:3). Jonah states that it is better for him to die than live (Jonah 4:8). The last words that are recorded of Jonah are these "I am angry enough to die" (Jonah 4:9).

Through this comparison, we can conclude that Jonah meets the requirements for Major Depressive Disorder, according to the DSM.

God and Country

"However you are feeling at this moment—happy or sad, calm or anxious—is most likely related to what is happening in the immediate world around you. The daily ebb and flow of human emotions represent adaptive responses to life's ongoing demands, accomplishments, and disasters and are especially sensitive to changes in one's social environment."[35] Yahweh's command for Jonah to preach repentance to the Ninevites and Jonah's allegiance to Israel in light of Assyria's treacherous past with Israel could have spun Jonah into a stressful whirlwind that would have impacted him both spiritually and mentally.

The Book of Jonah stands out from any of the other major or minor prophets. This is because the emphasis of other prophetic books is on the words of the prophet. However, the Book of Jonah focuses more

---

[35] Scott M. Monroe and Mark W. Reid, "Life Stress and Major Depression," *Current Directions in Psychological Science* 18.2, (2009): 68-72

on the actions of the prophet such as his failed attempt to flee from Yahweh, his time spent in the belly of a whale, and his anger with Yahweh for his mercy given to Nineveh.

Chapter one reveals to us that the command of Yahweh to Jonah began with a double imperative קוּם (*qum*) לֵךְ (*la-k*). In this construction, the principal idea is introduced in the second verb לֵךְ ("go"). This is known as hortatory discourse. Hortatory discourse is meant to persuade the audience or change the audience's behavior.[36] Therefore, Jonah was to "hurry up," "get up," and "go" to Nineveh. We must ask, was the immediacy of Yahweh's command for Ninevites? Or was it to challenge the negative attitude that Jonah harbored? Whatever the case, perhaps the immediacy of the command caused Jonah to act in an abnormal way. He immediately "got up" and headed in the opposite direction of Nineveh.

It is not until chapter four that Jonah explains the reason for his actions. He clarifies that his original flight was because he knew that God was gracious, compassionate, slow to anger, abounding in love, and one who relents from sending disaster. He knew God could possibly forgive Nineveh, and that was problematic for him. Some suggest that he was angry because the destruction of Nineveh would ultimately mean preservation for Israel, as their great enemy would be no more. The stigma of being a part of the preservation of Israel's greatest threat would be too much for him to bear.[37] His reputation may have been at stake because he proclaimed destruction to Nineveh, and Yahweh granted them mercy. Another option is that Jonah's nationalistic disposition gripped him and caused him to shun Yahweh's mercy on his nation's enemies.[38] I believe this to be the most significant answer to Jonah's anger. Worries about the preservation of Israel or the stigma of

---

[36] W. Dennis Tucker Jr., *Jonah: A Handbook on the Hebrew Text* (Waco, TX: Baylor University Press, 2018), 20-23.
[37] Smith and Page, *Amos, Obadiah, Jonah*, 272.
[38] Smith and Page, *Amos, Obadiah, Jonah*, 272.

being a part of the preservation of Israel's greatest enemy can easily fit under the umbrella of Jonah's nationalism.

To better understand Jonah's nationalistic allegiance, I would like to offer this definition given by sociologist Anthony D. Smith who describes nationalism as "substituting the nation for the deity, the citizen body for the church and the political kingdom for the kingdom of God, but in every other respect replicated the forms and qualities of traditional religions."[39] The term "nationalism" is generally used to describe two phenomena:[40]

- the attitude that the members of a nation have when they care about their national identity, and
- the actions that the members of a nation take when seeking to achieve (or sustain) self-determination.

These definitions confirm Jonah's national identity yet expose his allegiance to Israel as greater than his allegiance to Yahweh. Jonah's nationalism robs him of the vastness of Yahweh's mercy. In the story of Jonah, the treacherous undeserving pagans seem to be the more remarkable examples than the Prophet himself. They willfully respond to Yahweh while His Prophet was frustrated by His divine nature. The Prophet's spiritual state is frustrated because he knows Yahweh. He knows that Yahweh is merciful because Yahweh spoke through him to an evil king of Israel, and He displayed His mercy to them. Perhaps Jonah could accept this mercy because Yahweh was Israel's God, and their God should destroy their enemies, not save them. I believe that nationalism can be a scheme used by Satan to blur the lines and distort the view of believers.

---

[39] Stephen Backhouse, "Nations and Nationalism," in *Kierkegaard's Critique of Christian Nationalism*, vol. 3 (Oxford: Oxford University Press, 2011).

[40] Miscevic, Nenad, "Nationalism," *The Stanford Encyclopedia of Philosophy* (Fall 2020 Edition), Edward N. Zalta, ed.: https://plato.stanford.edu/archives/fall2020/entries/nationalism/.

Awake, O Sleeper, and Rise

Christian nationalism is "a cultural framework—a collection of myths, traditions, symbols, narratives, and value systems—that idealizes and advocates a fusion of Christianity with American civic life."[41] Blurring the lines between Christian nationalism and Gospelist Christianity can cause its proponent to falsely equate the country's values with the values of the Church. A consequence of this is determining what is inclusive or exclusive based on their constitution instead of the Holy Scriptures. It is possible for one not to affirm the tenants of Gospelist Christianity and still subscribe to Christian nationalism. Gospelist Christianity is a belief system that is founded on faith in Jesus Christ as Lord of one's life. Christian nationalism can be adopted and passed on through generations as a normative way of life. An example of this is giving the U.S. flag the same reverence as the cross that Jesus hung on while boldly stating, "I kneel for the cross and I stand for the flag."

On January 6, 2021, a group of rioters stormed the Capitol building intending to take the country back. This action is in line with the phenomenon of nationalism. It was alarming to see signs with the word "Jesus Saves" and "In God, We Trust," crosses, and other Christian imagery. It is a stark reminder that Christian nationalism is alive and well in the U.S. However, unlike Jonah and Israel, the U.S. is not the oppressed but has been found guilty of being the oppressor.

For those who claim to be followers of Yeshua, Christian nationalism must be rejected at all costs. It is nothing but another false gospel. Far too many professing followers of Yeshua have fallen into *ra-dam* (deep sleep). They have allowed their allegiance to their country to supersede their allegiance to the one and only true God.

Mental health encompasses one's emotional, psychological, and social well-being. As Gospelists, we must allow each of these sectors

---

[41] Andrew L. Whitehead and Samuel L. Perry, "Understanding Christian Nationalism and Its Consequences," in *Taking America Back for God: Christian Nationalism in the United States* (New York, NY: Oxford University Press, 2020).

of life to be shaped from a biblical perspective.[42] Our minds are to be renewed by the truth of the Gospel while rejecting the patterns of this world. We must awake from any slumber that has diverted our attention and let the light of Yeshua shine on us.[43] There are varying degrees of mental illness. We should never be ashamed to seek professional help. We can trust Jesus and have a counselor.

---

[42] Rom. 12:2
[43] Eph. 5:14

"For You Were Slaves in Egypt": History, Memory, and Implications for Christian Discipleship

Nicholas Rowe

In May 2021, *The Washington Post* reported numerous political efforts prohibiting so-called Critical Race Theory (CRT) teaching in public schools. While the reasons were varied, a common concern was how its content is "hostile to white people," is "teaching kids to hate their country and to hate each other," and challenged a supposed understanding of the past.[44] This went forward, despite little or no understanding of the nature of CRT.[45] These efforts resulted from intentional ideological misrepresentation of the theory for political power. It further marginalized discussions about systemic racism in U.S. society by labeling it as an extension of illegitimate

---

[44] Marisa Iati, "What is critical race theory, and why do Republicans want to ban it in schools?" *The Washington Post*, May 29, 2021, https://www.washingtonpost.com/education/2021/05/29/critical-race-theory-bans-schools.

[45] This is a problem not just in popular understanding but also among academics. Nathan Cartagena cites Kimberlé Crenshaw, one of the founders and a proponent of this theory, as saying "the name Critical Race theory…[is] now used interchangeably for race scholarship as Kleenex is used for tissue." See Nathan Cartagena, "What Christians Get Wrong About Critical Race Theory," *FaithfullyMagazine.com*, February 27, 2020, https://faithfullymagazine.com/critical-race-theory-christians/.

Marxist thought.[46] While many continue to discuss CRT and its misappropriation, this will not be the focus of this essay.[47] I am more concerned about other things. First, the effect of the banning legislation was to proscribe any teaching that highlighted the history of racism and its continuing impact on the present. It dictates an official state narrative of the past that prioritizes a particular cultural understanding of race that downplays how white European racial thought has oppressed people of color, especially persons of African descent. The appropriation of the past is a significant part of group identity and how this shapes interactions between different social groups. This has significant ramifications for identity-based conflict and its resolution. Rather than heal the open wound of racial division within U.S. society, this attempt to impose a silencing of racism's roots will have the opposite effect. We must discuss how groups construct their defining narratives, particularly in ways that marginalize other groups to the detriment of all. Second, we must examine the fear-based motivations for this process and compare this directly with how the Body of Christ, the global community of Christ-followers, receives its identity and formation. Critical to this is how the Body of Christ appropriates the past. This has ramifications for Christian spiritual formation and the practical theology of peacemaking and healing from historical conflict trauma (including, very specifically, race-based trauma). The hope is that this will raise discussions about how to prepare Christ-followers for ministry in a context where identity conflict resolution is necessary.

Not all means of appropriating the past are the same. Academic history insists on producing narratives adhering to rigorous standards

---

[46] Christopher Rufo, a political activist, is considered the originator of anti-CRT activism. See Laura Meckler and Josh Dawsey, "Republicans, spurred by an unlikely figure, see political promise in targeting critical race theory," *The Washington Post*, June 21, 2021, https://www.washingtonpost.com/education/2021/06/19/critical-race-theory-rufo-republicans/.

[47] Cartagena, "What Christians Get Wrong About Critical Race Theory," is an excellent assessment of this matter.

of evidence. According to John Tosh, it also should not settle for reinforcing our presuppositions, "but should pay special attention to what is different and remote from our experience."[48] The informal appropriation of the past practiced in everyday life, especially on a collective level, is called memory—specifically, *collective memory*. It is far more subjective and selective of past events, serving the purpose of creating a shared understanding of the past that reinforces shared values, group cultural priorities, and norms. It deliberately eschews the complexities of the past, which historians are cautious to preserve and articulate. In the words of Peter Novick, collective memory "simplifies; sees events from a single, committed perspective; is impatient with ambiguities of any kind; reduces events to mythic archetypes."[49] In short, collective memory is a phenomenon that arises in a group context, in which the group chooses what parts of the past it will remember and what parts it will forget. Moreover, as Maurice Halbwachs has argued, this function is shaped by concerns the group is facing in the present.[50] It promotes a social cohesion and group response that protects the group's interests, what the group is, and how it sees itself. Historian David Blight claims that "collective memory should be seen as a set of practices and ideas embedded in a culture, which people learn to decode and convert into their identities."[51] Furthermore, Halbwachs stresses that individual recollections of the past are shaped by the collective they belong to, from families up to the nation-state citizenship

---

[48] John Tosh, *The Pursuit of History*, 5th ed. (London: Longman, 2010), 304.

[49] Peter Novick, "The Holocaust in American Life," in Jeremy K. Yamashiro and Henry L. Roediger III, "The collective memory bias that flatters our homelands," *Psyche,* February 14, 2022, https://psyche.co/ideas/the-collective-memory-bias-that-flatters-our-homelands.

[50] See Lewis A. Coser, "The Revival of the Sociology of Culture: The Case of Collective Memory," *Sociological Forum* 7.2 (1992): 365-373. Coser mentions Maurice Halbwachs, *La topographie légendaire des évangiles en Terre sainte* (Paris: Presses Universitaires de France, 1941) as the text where he develops this argument.

[51] David Blight, "Historians and 'Memory,'" *Common-place,* 2.3 (April 2002). http://commonplace.online/article/historians-and-memory/ (accessed October 2021).

level.[52] In this sense, this collective ordering of the past is an essential part of *group identity*.

This reframing of the past has its distortive and reductionistic effects, especially regarding a group's self-perception and perception of others. A group's picking and choosing historical events for its collective memory reveals its investment in creating a self-defining narrative that builds its self-esteem. Henri Tajfel and John Turner confirm Halbwachs's argument in their work on intergroup conflict. Where this occurs, an individual can move from social identification (adopting the hallmarks of the group you have determined yourself to be a part of) to social comparison (comparison of "our" group with "other" groups). To maintain its self-esteem, a group must look better than other groups. This is critical to understanding prejudice. When two groups identify each other as rivals, each feels they must compete successfully against the other group for their members to maintain their self-esteem.[53] And because self-esteem is on the line, it becomes critical to avoid any aspect of a group's past that brings shame or denigrates the group in question. In response to this, the shame-producing memory must be intentionally forgotten, and its evidence must be silenced. In addition, narratives of competing groups that re-emphasize the shame-producing events must also be muted.[54]

This is the dynamic at play in these attempts to dictate the public-school curriculum. As the contested debate about the U.S. past continues, some white U.S. Americans feel threatened by the competing

---

[52] Maurice Halbwachs, *The Collective Memory*, Eng. trans. Francis J. Ditter, Vida Yazdi Ditter (New York: Harper & Row, 1980), 50-51.
[53] Henri Tajfel and John C. Turner, "The Social Identity Theory of Intergroup Behavior," in J. T. Jost and J. Sidanius, *Political psychology: Key readings* (New York, NY: Psychology Press, 2004), 276-293.
[54] Pierre Nora, "The Era of Commemorations" in *Realms of Memory: the Construction of the French Past*, Volume III, Lawrence Kritzman ed., trans. by Arthur Goldhammer (New York: Columbia University Press, 1996), 609-637. Also see Dee K. Britton, "What is Collective Memory?" *Memorial Worlds: Thinking about the who, what, and why we remember…and those that we forget,* https://memorialworlds.com/what-is-collective-memory/.

narratives dictated in the space of public education and are willing to use state power to shut down the threats to their identity. It seeks to re-center their view of the past to affirm their need to maintain cultural and social control. At best, this is an irrational response to the clear historical evidence of U.S. racism and its personal and systemic effects. At worst, it is an idolatrous response borne out of shame and the fear of some white U.S. Americans that they are losing control of the narrative—which has always centered their view of the past. Therefore, it is disturbing when these cultural agendas and habits find their way into the Christian community.

Unlike other types of human-defined social collectives, the Body of Christ, the global community of Christ-followers past, present, and future, is defined by Divine initiative. It includes Christ and humanity, receives its identity from God through Christ, and is animated through the Holy Spirit.[55] By contrast, human-based communities define their boundaries (their members) from within and prioritize the control of their destinies to survive. This creates the climate for aggressive competition and conflict if the group perceives its survival (or at the very least, its pre-eminence) is at stake.[56] God's priority is to His Kingdom (the restoration of the created order) through the work of Christ; in submission to Him, the Body of Christ extends the Kingdom throughout the world. The Kingdom of God and its citizens (the Body of Christ) strive toward *shalom,* a proper ordering of relationships and vocation that promotes total human flourishing for *all* persons, not just its members. It does not engage in the type of competition that necessarily seeks dominion over other groups, nor does it seek power at the expense of others. It is not necessary since, by the death and resurrection of Christ, "God has put everything under His feet."[57] Instead,

---

[55] See 1 Cor. 12.
[56] Henri Tajfel, "Social Psychology of Intergroup Relations," *Annual Review of Psychology*, 33, 1-39 (1982): 14.
[57] Eph. 1:22; 1 Cor. 15:27.

through the transforming power of the Holy Spirit in its members, it sees the *Imago Dei* in others and invites them to experience the *shalom* of God through a relationship to Him, first, and then through relationships with its members.[58]

Conversely, human-defined groups, with no connection to their Creator, cannot see the image of God in other groups. Humanity's relational brokenness from its Creator means that people cannot see Him as the reference for identity or being. The search for identity becomes self-referential. Human-based collectives evaluate others according to how much of themselves they see in the other. If one cannot see that, one either dismisses the humanity of the other, or one forces the other to conform to one's image, always in ways that undermine the dignity of the other. Imperialism, racism, and sexism are all examples of this dynamic. Rather than looking for the *Imago Dei,* a group seeks its *imago sui* (the image of itself).[59] With this orientation, human-based collectives can quickly weaponize the past by reinforcing their collective memory in public spaces. It is an attempt to control whose version of the past gets remembered while others are silenced and elevates the group at the expense of others.

The Body of Christ, however, should engage the past differently. Ideally, it can hold all of the past, including the parts that do not conform neatly to an idolatrous self-centered group memory. The *imago sui* functions with a deformed practice of memory that hides the shameful things of the past because it does not make the collective look good. However, the Body of Christ is a collective shaped by the Word of God, the sacrifice and resurrection of Christ, and the regenerative power of the Holy Spirit, through which the *Imago Dei* is fully revealed. And the defining sacramental ritual of this Body is the

---

[58] Mt. 22:34-40.
[59] Nicholas Rowe, "Worshipping While Black," in *Gospel Haymanot: A Constructive Theology and Critical Reflection on African and Diasporic Christianity,* ed. Vince Bantu, 145-168 (Calumet City, IL: UMI, 2020), 148.

command *to remember*, not selectively *but completely.* It preserves the *Imago Dei* in the community.

In the fifth of the Ten Commandments (Deut. 5:6-21), God instructs the Israelites of the keeping of the Sabbath. The community works for six days, but the seventh is a sabbath rest, during which *nobody* works, not even those who do not have control over their labor. They were to rest like everyone else. The community has to

> Remember that you were slaves in Egypt and that the Lord your God brought you out of there with a mighty hand and an outstretched arm. Therefore, the Lord your God has commanded you to observe the Sabbath day.

God makes it plain *why* this commandment is crucial: they were to remember that they were enslaved people in Egypt and that the only reason they were able to function as a community was that their identity rested on the work of God. God did for them what they could not do. This phrase, "remember you were slaves in Egypt," appears five more times in the Book of Deuteronomy. The imperative to remember is formational for the community defined by God's redemptive action. It is a memory in the way I have explained the term. Similar to other group contexts, it is a critical part of group identity. There is no way in this short essay that I can plumb the full richness of this, but allow me to suggest a partial list.[60]

First, Israelite memory in Deuteronomy insists on *vulnerability*. It demands that members of this chosen community never forget that, though they came from a common ancestor and were made so by God's promise, they were also marginalized, instrumentalized, and dehumanized persons. They were subject to the whims of an overlord and oppressor. Many other narratives of memory rarely mention the

---

[60] See A. J. Culp, *Memoir of Moses: The Literary Creation of Covenantal Memory in Deuteronomy* (Lanham, MD: Lexington Books/Fortress Academic, 2020) for a detailed investigation into this process.

hard times of the past unless to demonstrate a group's ability to overcome them by their strength. Otherwise, the recovered story forgets or deletes these parts. In the Deuteronomy account, Israel does not deliver itself. It is hopelessly in bondage until God saves it. The God of Israel is the central actor. Deliverance by God is the action defining Israel's identity.

Conversely, this also implies that the Israelites are not *allowed* to forget. They are not to edit past events in the retelling; they are not to remember selectively to foster their comfort. Any collective events or realities of the past that might elicit collective shame or guilt must *remain* in the memory. Removing them removes God's action from memory. It removes both human vulnerability and God's agency. This type of memory centers on the Israelites and not God; it implies self-sufficiency, that their state of autonomy is self-generated. The memory generated by the *imago sui*, not the *Imago Dei*, refuses to declare that only God can save and restore. Moreover, the work of removing shame is not left to the Israelites to figure out. God does that work so that the past no longer is a place of psychic burden, but a place of recalling God's total work of deliverance from oppression *and* shame.[61]

Second, memory here carries *ethical freight*. The command to remember is the foundation of ethical action. For example, in chapter 15, the imperative to remember that they were enslaved people in Egypt is why persons must free those who have bonded their labor because of poverty or deprivation. Every seventh year, they became free to re-establish themselves as fully thriving persons in their own right. It reminded them that every Israelite descended from those who could not save themselves. In chapter 16, the command to remember forms part of the Festival of Weeks, the celebration of the harvest. The festival is a ritual noting God's provision. But they must also

---

[61] See Josh. 5:9; Rom. 5:3-4. The Joshua passage discussed the monument at The Gilgal (The Circle), where God "rolled away the reproach (shame) of Egypt" from the Israelites.

not forget that at one time, they were enslaved, and the fruits of their labor belonged to their oppressors. Therefore, all members were part of this celebration, not only those who possessed land and controlled labor but also the bondservants and others whose labor was part of the harvest production.[62]

Chapter 24 twice issues the command to remember. First, it clarifies the imperative not to take advantage of the marginalized and powerless by denying them justice. One must also not take advantage by asserting one's rights if, by doing so, you put the life of the vulnerable in jeopardy. For example, by taking a widow's cloak as collateral, you were leaving her exposed to the elements.[63] Later it lays out the law of gleaning. Landowners must not pick their fields clean; they must leave some for "the foreigner, the fatherless, and the widow,"[64] the most vulnerable community members. These classes of people are mentioned three times in this chapter to emphasize the point. Why? Because at one time, every Israelite was like "the foreigner, the fatherless, and the widow." They had no one acting on their behalf until God intervened.[65] In all these actions, the community ritualizes and encodes the act of redemption modeled by the God who redeemed them. The ethic of the Israelite community is always bent toward the most vulnerable because, at one point, *all* Israelites were helpless.

May I suggest something else? They *remain* vulnerable. An African reading suggests that any reference to a collective never refers only to the living but also includes their *ancestors*. It implies that their *ancestors* were enslaved in Egypt until God delivered them, and this salvific action continues in their descendants. The salvation of God is what marks the community—past, present, and future.

---

[62] Dt. 16:9-12.
[63] Dt. 24:17-18.
[64] Dt. 24:19
[65] Dt. 24:19-22

The framework of memory laid out in Deuteronomy for the Israelites finds its full expression in the Body of Christ in the New Testament. It has implications for discipleship and praxis for the Church today. The central part of the sacrament of Eucharist is the command to remember: "Do this in remembrance of Me."[66] We engage in the sacrament precisely to remember, not to forget, the Body and work of Christ, which was both an expression of *vulnerability* and an expression of salvation. Christ on the cross represents broken, vulnerable humanity. This was not a demonstration of self-sufficient strength but total surrender. This is unlike those enslaved to their sin in metaphorical Egypt, like the Israelites. It was God who raised Him from the dead. Only He could do that. He alone saved and delivered Israel from bondage just as He delivers humanity from enslavement.

Thus, like the Israelites, the Church must never edit the past to promote human self-sufficiency in its identity narrative. This must not happen, individually or corporately. We do not clean up our timelines to obscure faults or places of vulnerability or weakness. Conversely, as Paul so clearly emphasizes, our weaknesses are the heart of the story because they invite the action of the saving God. This is the same God of the Old Testament, now present through the work of Christ. In our weakness, we find His strength. It is entirely the opposite of the *imago sui* that promotes an identity based on the self-contained and all-sufficient self. This image is a walking fallacy by definition. We make a bolder claim for the Body of Christ, walking in vulnerability, honesty, and truth about its past, present, and future. There is no distinction between history and memory. For the believing community, memory *is* history, and history *is* memory.

This does not mean the total rejection of former group collectives. When Paul refers to the hallmarks of his former identity—his circumcision, his Israelite ancestry, his tribal identity, his membership

---

[66] Lk. 22:19. See also 1 Cor. 11:24, 25.

as a Pharisee[67]—as "excrement," it does not mean that he has forgotten any of those aspects. What he rejects is their deployment for an identity based on the *imago sui*: self-sufficiency, self-made power, clout, and the currency of privilege in a context where vulnerability and weakness bring on the heights of contempt. However, when they get redeployed into the collective narrative of the Body of Christ, the community of the Christ-followers, those elements are insufficient to set him free from his slavery to his tendency to "blasphemy, persecution, and violence,"[68] slavery to brokenness and delusion against which all his credentials were utterly useless. These aspects of his identity become powerful only when the person and action of God become the center, and he joins the Body of Christ rather than fights against it. His experiences matter as a means of demonstrating how God expresses His salvation in multiple and diverse ways.

As a concluding example, we can consider how the Black Church in the U.S. is a gift to the Body of Christ and U.S. society. Healthy Christian communities in marginalized groups are essentially prophetic communities to the rest of their society. Marginalized communities exist in a state of vulnerability, which varies depending upon the security of the dominant group. Dominant groups often have triumphalist origin narratives emphasizing their self-sufficiency, ability to control their destiny, and perceived superior capacity against rivals. However, Christian marginalized communities readily find identification with the Deuteronomy narrative, which invites the action of God. The Black Church found meaning in their experience in the Scriptures and identified with the Israelites's slavery in Egypt. The vulnerability of the Israelites gave sense to their deep vulnerability. It became logical for them to center their collective identity, not on their self-sufficiency but the hope for spiritual and physical deliverance. The power of that Gospelist narrative was such that the dominant white

---

[67] Phil. 3:5
[68] 1 Tim. 1:13

order tried to prevent access to those parts of the Scriptures, but to no avail.[69] The revelation of a salvific God oriented their identity as bearers of His image, and it retains that power to this day. Any healing between groups that reside within the Body of Christ must look at the conflict's history to face its needs for healing. In this process, it is more than *Sankofa* (literally, "to go back and get"),[70] because good practice *never* leaves things behind. They are kept in the light. It remains a prophetic practice in a context of self-sufficiency that can never know full justice and shalom.

---

[69] Esau McCaulley, *Reading While Black: African American Biblical Interpretation as an Exercise in Hope* (Downers Grove, IL: InterVarsity Press, 2020), 170. McCaulley's volume is an excellent discussion about Black Church biblical interpretation and a refutation of the incorrect thesis that African American Christianity is derivative of white slave-owner religious practice.

[70] The term *Sankofa,* from the Twi language in Ghana, means "to retrieve," but also names a cultural practice of the African Diaspora. It comes from the proverb, *Se wo were fin a wo Sankofa a yenkyi* ("It is not a taboo to return and fetch it when you forget"). See Christel N. Temple, "The Emergence of Sankofa Practice in the United States: A Modern History," *Journal of Black Studies,* 41.1 (2010): 127-150.

Local Cultures Matter: Gospel, Identity, and Mission in Northern Nigeria

Yoknyam Dabale

Introduction

A subset of Europeans weaponized Christianity in the non-Western world, and the result was devastating—genocide, slavery, colonialism, and white supremacy.[71] This historical context has made many people hesitate to align themselves with Christianity. Additionally, debates about the nature of mission and its function remained a fierce debate for decades. In this paper, I take up R. Daniel Shaw's concept of hybridity to show how mission can prosper in the Global South if the knowledge, theological insights, and work of local devotees are supported and centered.[72] I first highlight diverse meanings of missions and specific ideas about mission that complement my research

---

[71] Michael W. Stroope, *Transcending Mission: The Eclipse of a Modern Tradition* (Downers Grove, IL: IVP Academic, 2017), 166-175.

[72] Shaw argues that every society has the ability to understand and make use of Christianity through its culture. Thus, foreign missionaries do not have to force their interpretation of scriptures on the people they minister to in the mission field; rather, they should allow the Holy Spirit to work within the specific culture. See Daniel R. Shaw, "Beyond Syncretism: A Dynamic Approach to Hybridity," *International Bulletin of Mission Research* 42(1):6-19: https://doi.org/10.1177/2396939317708954 (accessed October 31, 2018).

on Christian women in northern Nigeria. I then examine the relationship between culture and the Gospel in the Global South. I conclude by encouraging a view of mission that is African-women-focused.

The Meaning and Practice of Missions

For many years now, the term "mission" has been debated and contested. Scholars and practitioners have offered a broad range of perspectives on the topic. Michael Stroope interrogates how Christians have used what they term mission in their denominations. He observed that churches claim that their mission (outreach) work locally and internationally is their response to God's command as inscribed in the Bible. Stroope, however, rejects the widely held belief that mission is biblical. He bases his perspective on a close reading of Scripture and concludes that there is no evidence supporting a Bible-based mission for Christians.[73] Additionally, according to Stroope, Christians have engaged the term "mission" in conflicting ways. For these reasons, he concludes that the term and concept should be abandoned altogether.[74]

As an African woman and a daughter of European colonialism, I empathize with Stroope's position.[75] Foreign missionaries, as agents of Western imperialism, exploited Africa. The outcome was catastrophic. On the other hand, words and institutions can carry different meanings and interpretations based on context and culture. This is a matter of what I call the *hermeneutics of the oppressed*. Take, for example, the status of women in the Church and the home. Ephesians 5:22-24 demands that, "wives, submit yourselves to your own husbands as you do to the Lord. For the husband is the head of the wife as Christ is the head of the church, his body, of which he is the Savior. Now as the church submits to Christ, so also wives should submit

---

[73] Stroope, *Transcending Mission*, 139.
[74] Stroope, *Transcending Mission*, 279-281.
[75] Walter Rodney, *How Europe Underdeveloped Africa* (Washington, DC: Howard University Press, 1981), 308-309.

to their husbands in everything."[76] Conservative Christians often use this passage to justify women's subordination in the Church and their households. But some liberal thinkers argue that the Bible is a "living text"[77] written in a particular historical context. Therefore, in our time, it must be read with a lens that is empowering to contemporary women.[78]

Likewise, some Europeans used missions to cause significant harm in Africa. Some Africans have, in turn, reproduced that harm. But there are also many examples of Africans refashioning mission and other harmful things brought by Europeans to do incredibly productive work in Africa. In the remainder of this section, I will discuss four denominations' approach to mission work.

Four approaches to mission

The Evangelical approach to mission foregrounds a concern with human suffering in the world, which they attribute to sin. They maintain that with the help of the Holy Spirit, the Church's mission is to go into the world and preach the Gospel to save it from its sinful ways. This, in turn, will eliminate suffering. Furthermore, as it relates to religious pluralism and dialogue, Evangelicals are willing to participate, but ultimately see it as an opportunity to convert non-Christians. This goes back to what they consider their role in the world.[79] By comparison, as John Paul II puts it in *Redemptoris Missio*, the Roman Catholic Church preaches the Gospel to all nations to save them. Their concern

---

[76] Unless otherwise noted, all biblical citations are taken from the New International Version (NIV).

[77] A.B. Caneday, "Is Theological Truth Functional or Propositional? Postconservatism's Use of Language Games and Speech-Act Theory," in *Reclaiming the Center: Confronting Evangelical Accommodation in Postmodern Times*, eds. Millard J. Erickson, eds. Millard J. Erickson, Paul Helseth, and Justin Taylor, 365 (Wheaton, IL: Crossway Books, 2004), 152.

[78] Elisabeth Schüssler Fiorenza. *In Memory of Her: A Feminist Theological Reconstruction of Christian Origins* (New York, NY: Crossroad, 1983).

[79] John Stott, "Lausanne Covenant," 1974. Lausanne Movement. https://www.lausanne.org/content/covenant/lausanne-covenant (accessed October 31, 2018).

is not merely about sin as the Evangelicals see it. Instead, the primary vision of the Catholic Church's mission is to reach those who have not yet heard the Gospel. This is not suggesting that sin should be ignored. It is just not central to the approach of Catholics. John Paul II pointed out that there are still communities in the world that have not heard the Word of God, and the Church should commit itself to spread the Gospel to all corners of the earth before the Second Coming of Jesus Christ. He states that *akin Allah a dukanuniya* ("God's work in all nations") can only be done with the help of the Holy Spirit (John Paul II 1990, 1-4). Unlike Evangelicals, the Catholic Church sees religious pluralism and interreligious dialogue as an opportunity to learn from others, not necessarily a platform to convert others (John Paul II 1990, 38-40).[80] This approach is likely an attempt to avoid reproducing the oppressive colonial method that the Catholic Church historically utilized to gain converts.[81]

The United Methodist Church (UMC) and the Eastern Orthodox Church[82] inform my understanding of missiology. Together, these two ideas give me a holistic understanding of the mission project. The UMC defines mission as the effort "to make disciples of Jesus Christ for the transformation of the world."[83] This means that the Church prioritizes converting non-Christians hoping that once they internalize their faith in Jesus Christ, they will go into the world and create

---

[80] See "Christian Witness in a Multi-Religious World," *Pontifical Council for Interreligious Dialogue*, January 28, 2011, http://www.vatican.va/roman_curia/pontifical_councils/interelg/documents/rc_pc_interelg_doc_20111110_testimonianza-cristiana_en.html (accessed October 31, 2018).

[81] Michael W. Stroope, *Transcending Mission: The Eclipse of a Modern Tradition* (Downers Grove, IL: IVP Academic, 2017), 166.

[82] Unless otherwise noted, throughout this text, I am referring to all of the patriarchs that fall under the category of "Orthodox church." See definition by Petros Vassiliadis, *Orthodox Perspectives on Mission* (Oxford: Regnum Book International, 2013), 1-2.

[83] United Methodist Church. *The Book of Discipline for the United Methodist Church.* (Nashville, TN: The United Methodist Publishing House, 2016).

positive change. As a member of the United Methodist Church,[84] I am inspired by my denomination's commitment to living out its faith. One could also interpret their vision as adhering to James 2:14-26, which encourages Christians to act upon their belief and not simply profess it. A limitation of this approach to mission is the emphasis on winning souls for the transformation of the world and not so much on the Body of Christ being constantly inspired by the Word of God.

The Eastern Orthodox Church highlights the limitation of the UMC by framing the local church as missional. It sees its mission as the local congregation's commitment to the liturgy. This belief is embodied by constantly participating in the Eucharist as a Christian family unit. Secondly, Eastern Orthodox devotees are expected to express compassion to the suffering of the vulnerable in the world.[85] The Eucharist is central to the Orthodox Church's missionary work. The understanding is that the local congregation is a mission field. It is not simply where individuals meet once a week on Sunday to worship. Instead, it is a family of believers collectively sharing life together. The Eucharist energizes and unites believers. This, in turn, enables the devotees to reach out to the suffering world and offer their compassion. The emphasis on communal life also has some potential pitfalls. Namely, it can encourage individuals to be overly dependent on the collective. In this way, the development of the individual can be compromised.

The Eastern Orthodox Church's expression of mission encourages Christians to share the love of Christ in their local church by sharing communion before reaching out to others outside the Church. However, the emphasis on physically being together is not realistic in a global world wherein individuals are frequently pushed or pulled away from their local communities. Communities can be stretched

---

[84] I have been a member of the United Methodist Church since 1992; however, I am currently discerning where I belong as the denomination is disputing over the issue of homosexuality.
[85] Vassiliadis, *Orthodox Perspectives*, 190, 237.

across different continents but linked in real-time on social media. What happens when members of the congregation are no longer living in proximity to their home church?[86] One possible resolution of the missional limitations of the United Methodist Church and the Eastern Orthodox Church comes from Yotti/Bali culture. The indigenous moral philosophical idea of *tuku bini* conveys the need to unite to tackle problems and the belief that working alone on an important task is inconceivable. The Yotti/Bali people are mostly family-oriented farmers. They rely on the social collective for their survival. Family includes the living and the dead (ancestors) who are in continual relationships with each other. The relationship between the living and the dead is managed by the *mypa* or spirit medium.[87] The family goes beyond the nuclear and extends to uncles, aunties, cousins, and grandparents. It also includes non-biological people who have a close relationship with the family. Work is divided based on one's skills and ability. Suppose a family has farm work that it is unable to get done. In that case, the community rallies to relieve the burden by dividing the workload among each community member that can work based on their skills and ability. This dynamic approach to family structure reinforces the idea of the local church as a mission field. It strengthens the familial bonds of the Eucharist when individual members of the church are not physically present. Additionally, it can reduce the tendency to be dependent on the patronage of Westerners.

Mission, Hybridity, and Anti-Racism

What I have found to be especially compelling are mainstream missiologists who have affirmed my view that racism is deeply entrenched within the Western theological tradition. For centuries, the Western

---

[86] Vassiliadis, *Orthodox Perspectives*, 34-45.
[87] Richard Fardon, *Between God, The Dead and the Wild: Chamba Interpretations of Ritual and Religion* (George Square: Edinburgh University Press, 1990), 23-123.

world has controlled the dominant Christian narrative.[88] This is despite the sharp decline of Christian devotees in the West and the rapid growth of Christianity in the Global South. Kwesi Dickson argues that the Christian mission sees itself as a Western project among indigenous communities. According to Dickson, Western missionaries believed that indigenous people who were missionized lacked the capacity to rationalize their Christian faith.[89] Africans could only be objects of missionary programs as opposed to mutual participants with equal standing who were the authorities on their own lives and experiences. This colonial-era holdover lingers even today, especially in Africa. In turn, many Africans have internalized the view that they are inferior to think and provide for their congregation.[90] Over the past decades, African church membership has proliferated. Homegrown theology, however, has not kept pace with numerical growth. Furthermore, traditional mainline churches in Nigeria, such as Anglicans, Catholics, and United Methodists, are dependent on Western funding to thrive even when they are founded by local leadership.

I am not suggesting there have not been any African initiatives to do missions on their terms. In fact, there are examples of Africans from African Independent Churches (AICs) who left missionary churches because they wanted an African-centered Christian experience. And some African Christians within the mainline churches (post-colonial) have indeed ushered in the creation of African Theology. For example, the revolutionary women's organization Ruwadzano in Zimbabwe was created in the 1920s by women in the Methodist Episcopal Church who wanted to express themselves

---

[88] Andrew F. Walls, *Crossing Cultural Frontiers: Studies in the History of World Christianity* (Maryknoll, NY: Orbis Books, 2017).

[89] Kwesi Dickson, *Uncompleted Mission: Christianity and Exclusivism.* (Maryknoll, NY: Orbis Books, 1991), 3-4.

[90] E. Julu Swen. "Nigerian Church faces fine, possible demolition." UM News, June 12, 2019, https://www.umnews.org/en/news/nigerian-church-facing-fine-demolition (accessed March 25, 2020).

freely within the colonized mission church. As Tumani M. Nyajeka puts it: "The mission church was teaching [African women] that they needed God to save them from the "darkness" of their skin, flesh, culture, and environment."[91] These racist messages created an atmosphere of timidity among the women. In response to this crisis, Ruwadzano combined Shona and Christian worldviews in a way that resonated with local women. It provided a platform for women to pray and be possessed by the spirits. It was also a place where the women felt free from the gaze of colonialists. In the Shona indigenous spirituality, mid-morning is when spirits are free to express themselves. They held their meetings in the deep forest at 4:00 am, believing human beings could transcend into the spirit realm. Their prayer sessions would go for several hours, where they bared their hearts to each other and the spirit world. From the outside looking in, one might assume Ruwadzano is just a prayer group. However, it is actually a platform for protest and revolutionary Christian expression to reclaim African souls and land in a hostile environment. The women of Ruwadzano wanted Christianity that did not police their souls. They found ways to protest their religiosity and reconnect with the land taken away from them as colonized people. Their meeting in the forest reunited them with the land, their ancestors, and the entire African cosmology.[92] But most mainline churches in Africa have not entirely abandoned their deference to Western views.

While applauding the growth of Global Christianity, Willie J. Jennings[93] observes that it is not developing on a solid foundation due to the legacy of Western colonialism. Jennings believes that white Christians have taken the position of biblical Israel as forebearers of the Gospel. By doing so, they have disrupted God's plan and used

---

[91] Tumani Mutasa Nyajeka, *The Unwritten Text: The Indigenous African Christian Women's Movement in Zimbabwe* (Mutare, Zimbabwe: Africa University Press, 2006), 147.

[92] Nyajeka, *The Unwritten Text,* 147-148.

[93] Willie James Jennings, *The Christian Imagination: Theology and the Origins of Race* (New Haven, CT: Yale University Press, 2010), 1-64.

their power to serve their greed and pride. For Christianity to be truly global, it must return Israel to its rightful position so that God's vision of including all human beings under his roof can be realized. Bryant L. Myers observes that human beings tend to pursue their own glory as opposed to the glory of God.[94] He suggests that removing human ego and replacing it with God's purpose for humankind would solve issues affecting the decline of Christianity in the West and churches in the Global South can find their voice.

Oscar Garcia-Johnson maintains that to address the colonial legacy of Western hegemony in Christianity, we must confront the white-controlled production of knowledge.[95] Garcia-Johnson believes that Christianity is profoundly flawed because it is Eurocentric. He suggests that to deconstruct this model of knowledge, Indigenous ways of knowledge ought to be celebrated by foregrounding them in academic settings. Garcia-Johnson's critique reminds us of the major role that racism plays in knowledge production in seminaries and divinity schools in the West. I wonder how mainline seminaries in formerly colonized spaces like Nigeria can break away from Eurocentric theology when they depend on Western benevolence?

Guiding missionaries on respecting local cultures, Douglas McConnell[96] suggests that instead of preemptively imposing their ways on local communities, they should see themselves as learners of the Gospel, not teachers. McConnell observes that this will create a platform for the Indigenous leadership to thrive and offer ideas to benefit their mission. Adding to the critique of the Western approach to missionaries' work overseas, Dan Shaw's *Traditional Ritual as*

---

[94] Jennings, *The Christian Imagination*, 23-30. See also, Bryant L. Myers, *Engaging Globalization: The Poor, Christian Mission, and Our Hyperconnected World* (Grand Rapids, MI: Baker Academic, 2017), 176-185.

[95] Oscar Garcia-Johnson, *Spirit Outside the Gate: Decolonial Pneumatologies of the American Global South* (Downers Grove, IL: IVP Academic, 2019), 38, 58, 150, 200.

[96] Douglas McConnell, *Cultural Insights for Christian Leaders: New Directions for Organizations Serving God's Mission* (Grand Rapids, MI: Baker Academic, 2018), 155-180.

Christian Worship: Dangerous Syncretism or Necessary Hybridity? looks at mission activities in the past through an anthropological lens.[97] According to Shaw, missionaries had blind spots, which prevented them from seeing God's presence and activities in the lives and cultures of Indigenous people. Because of that, they force-fed their theology on them. He then introduced what he calls hybridity: that the role of the missionary should be to deliver the Gospel and then allow the Gospel to be understood through the cultural experiences and lens of the Indigenous people it encounters. Rt. Rev. Dr. Done Peter Dabale and his wife, Mrs. Christiana Kerike Peter Dabale, co-founders of the United Methodist Church of Nigeria (UMCN), are examples of Indigenous leaders who contributed to localizing the Gospel. They also happen to be my parents. *Mama da Babah* (Hausa, "mother and father") committed themselves to the Methodist mission of making disciples for Christ and transforming lives. My parents (hereafter the Dabales) did mission work in their own communities because they knew the cultural landscape. The Dabales were able to help members understand the Gospel using their Indigenous traditions.[98] They also incorporated the Yotti/Bali philosophy of *tuku bini* (unity for progress) by recruiting community members to help them spread the Gospel. They regarded members of their congregation as family. For example, because the Dabales received guests at their home frequently, whenever Mrs. Dabale cooked, she would save a portion of it for potential overnight guests. In addition to that, they planted churches, opened schools and hospitals, and established women's outreach programs that helped women learn a trade.[99] Historically, mainstream missionaries,

---

[97] R. Daniel Shaw and William R. Burrows, *Traditional Ritual as Christian Worship: Dangerous Syncretism or Necessary Hybridity?* (Maryknoll, NY: Orbis Books, 2018), 18-26.

[98] Marubitoba Peter Dong, *The History of the United Methodist Church in Nigeria* (Nashville, TN: Abingdon Press, 2000), 75-76,92-98.

[99] The Reverend Athanasius T. Nah, Jr, *Know Your Bishop* (Jalingo, Nigeria: Amune House, 1993), 9. Also see Esther L. Megill, *Return to Africa: A Journal* (Bloomington, IN: AuthorHouse, 2008), 103, 457-458.

by contrast, have tended not to respect local cultures. Thus, their behaviors sometimes created a hostile environment and prevented them from genuinely fulfilling their *akin Allah* (Hausa, "mission of God").[100] Their lack of knowledge of local cultures and appreciation of Indigenous ideas prevented them from gaining converts.[101]

God is working in Indigenous communities. Missionaries do not have the power to control where God's Spirit works. Their roles should be delivering the Gospel and allowing people the opportunity to understand it through their local rituals. Instead of demonizing Indigenous practices and cultures, they can be vehicles that carry Indigenous people to the throne of Jesus Christ.

What these scholars share is a call for hybridity. Mission, and the theology behind it, have been Eurocentric, and local cultural ideas should inform the texture of Christianity in non-Western locales. The recommendations to democratize mission by indigenization is a sign that mainstream scholars are wrestling with the issue of the lack of diversity of mission. Since the future of Christianity is no longer in the hands of Europeans and U.S. Americans, it creates an urgent need for self-reflection about the place of the West in Global Christianity. Doing further research on this topic encourages me to reflect on my context in Northern Nigeria, where mission is still Western-driven. But it also reminds me of how colonialism did not discriminate based on gender. Both men and women were affected, even though the degree and detail of their dehumanization varied. This discovery cautions me about generalizing that Northern Nigerian men are oppressors of women without offering nuances to the issue of women's marginalization in the region and the Church.

---

[100] Marijke Steegstra, *Dipo and the Politics of Culture in Ghana* (Accra: Woeli Publishing Services, 2005), 7, 238. Also read A.E. Afigbo, *The Warrant Chiefs: Indirect Rule in Southeastern Nigeria, 1891-1929* (London: Longman Group Ltd, 1972), 237-241.

[101] Helen Callaway, *Gender, Culture and Empire: European Women in Colonial Nigeria* (Oxford, London: Macmillan Press, 1987), 3-205.

Nigerian Example of Mission

Some of the victims of colonial missionary enterprise have challenged the devastation of Western Christian imposition. The Dabales actualized the Church's mission by highlighting that Gospel bearers have an obligation to redeem the body and the soul.[102] This propelled their zeal to utilize the Methodist social Gospel principles in their ministry.[103] They often cited John 10:10 as a foundational text: "The thief comes only to steal and kill and destroy; I have come that they may have life, and have it to the full." Nigeria is rich in natural resources, but most Nigerians are poor.[104]

This problem is compounded in Northern Nigeria, a region that has always been underdeveloped compared to the rest of the country. Comparatively, higher levels of violence are another challenge. In fact, my village was attacked and burned down in December 2021 and a number of villagers were killed.[105] These challenges meant that any efforts at development to the region would be complicated. However, the Dabales did not abandon their community. Instead, they did whatever they could to make the community thrive. They exemplified the Yotti/Bali philosophy of *wehnam* ("family looking after itself") and extended their hands to the community.[106]

---

[102] For more information on the UMC as a denomination see Richard P. Heitzenrater, *Wesley and the People Called Methodists*. (Nashville, TN: Abingdon Press, 1995).

[103] General Board of Global Ministries, Bishop Dabale of Nigeria Speaks on "Hope for the Children of Africa." General Board of Global Ministries, December 2000, https://archive.is/20140920011357/http://gbgm-umc.org/news/2001/jan/hopedabale.stm (accessed March 21, 2019).

[104] Kazeem Yomi, "Nigeria is set to stay the world's poverty capital for at least a generation." *Quartz Africa*, October 12, 2018, https://qz.com/africa/1421543/nigerias-poverty-crisis-is-worsening-oxfam-world-bank-data/ (accessed March 21, 2019).

[105] Rafiu Ajakaye, "16 Killed in fresh attacks in Nigeria's Taraba State." Anadolu Agency, December 7, 2018, https://www.aa.com.tr/en/africa/16-killed-in-fresh-attacks-in-nigerias-taraba-state/1202442 (accessed March 21, 2019).

[106] Esther L. Megill, *Return to Africa: A Journal* (Bloomington, IN: AuthorHouse, 2008), 458.

For example, whenever Mrs. Dabale cooked, she saved a portion of it for the unannounced visitors. Additionally, they planted churches and, in partnership with the United Methodist Church in the U.S., built hospitals, schools, and crisis centers. Within ten years of their ministry, they mobilized close to half a million believers when other denominations attempted to do the same and failed.[107]

Centering African Women

In future versions of missiology as a discipline, I envision a stronger focus on women of color. The dominant theme in missiology is how the former Christendom (the West) can relate to the Church in the Global South, where Christianity is thriving. We cannot speak of Global Christianity without engaging women in a sustained manner. As the proverbial wisdom of the Yotti/Bali people of Northern Nigeria teaches us, *pe nya tip bile ke kabok bora* ("when you are hit, you will feel it"). Women know what they want; we must give them the floor to speak it. If Christian leaders and scholars are interested in uplifting the entire Body of Christ, women must not be just included but prominently featured. Women comprise the majority of Global Christianity, yet their voices have remained muted in the Church and in academia.[108] African women are, in fact, writing about their experiences and that of their church communities. For example, The Circle of Concerned African Women Theologians (also known as "The Circle"), an organization I recently became a member of, has existed for three decades. This Pan-African organization provides a platform for

---

[107] The Reverend Athanasius T. Nah, Jr, *Know Your Bishop* (Jalingo: Amune House,1993), 9. Also see Stephen Drachler, "First United Methodist Bishop of Nigeria, Done Peter Dabale, Dies in US Hospital." UM News, August 27, 2006, https://www.umnews.org/en/news/first-united-methodist-bishop-in-nigeria-done-peter-dabale-dies-in-us-hospi (accessed August 28, 2006).

[108] Robert J. Priest and Robert DeGeorge, "Doctoral Dissertations on Mission: Ten-Year Update, 2002-2011 (Revised)," in *International Bulletin of Missionary Research* 37.4 (2013): 195–200.

African women theologians from all religious traditions represented on the continent (Islam, Christianity, African Traditional Religions, and others) to speak on various topics impacting their lives.[109] Over the years, members of The Circle produced an impressive collection of articles and books that told the stories of African women in the Church.

There has also been a long tradition of African women spearheading the hybridizing or Africanizing of the Gospel. Kimpa Vita, also known by her Christian name, Dona Beatriz, from the seventh century Kongo Kingdom, protested against colonialists and the Catholic Church in her home country. She claimed to be possessed by the spirit of St. Anthony to protest colonial powers and the Catholic Church's exclusion of and discrimination against African members. This motivated her to replace Eurocentric images in the Church with local Kongolese icons and to speak against colonial authorities. Vita's actions threatened and angered the missionaries in Kongo. Subsequently, she was charged with blasphemy and burned at the stake.[110] This "Africanizing'" of the Church and revolt against colonial authority tells us how she committed herself to reclaim Kongolese identity and protect Kongolese land. Her work and death, just like Christ's death and resurrection, brought forth a new life in her country. Musa W. Dube credits Vita's protest for establishing what is now known as African Initiated Churches (AICs) and inspiring the biblical hermeneutics of The Circle of Concerned African Women Theologians.[111] Vita's story tells us that African women have not been passive bystanders in the Christian encounter in Africa. Indeed,

---

[109] Mercy Amba Oduyoye, *Introducing African Women's Theology* (Sheffield: Sheffield Academic Press, 2001), 9-120.

[110] John K. Thornton. *The Kongolese Saint Anthony: Dona Beatriz Kimpa Vita and the Antonian Movement, 1684-1706* (Cambridge: Cambridge University Press, 1998), 177-195.

[111] Musa W. Dube, "Talitha Cum! Some African Women's Ways of Reading the Bible," in *Semeia Studies: Twenty-Five Years of Liberation Theology*, eds. Botha (Atlanta, GA: SBL, 2009), 133-146.

they have frequently led the charge. Thus, the Church needs to make room for women's participation. Lastly, I argue that for Christianity to be truly global and penetrate the hearts of people it encounters, it must speak and listen to Indigenous people.

The Heresy of Prosperity "Gospel": Trading Community for Commerce

Lori Banfield

Introduction

You have heard it said that humanity is endowed with an inalienable right to pursue happiness.[112] But the Scripture has said, "let us pursue what makes for peace and mutual upbuilding."[113] Now don't misunderstand, I take no qualm with the declaration of our nation's forefather Thomas Jefferson; especially considering the desperate posture towards liberation for which he wrote this manifesto. However, I cannot ignore how such a sentiment has been interpreted to ignite individualist and meritocratic ideals that center this nation's capitalist and conquistador ethos. Philosophically speaking, the method of pursuant interaction has historically proved hedonistic—led by pleasure principles expressed in the values of money and prestige. It would appear we have become "lovers of self, lovers of money, proud, arrogant, abusive...reckless, swollen with conceit, lovers of pleasure rather

---

[112] "The Declaration of Independence: The Unanimous Declaration of the Thirteen United States of America in Congress," in *From Many, One: Readings in American Political and Social Thought*, ed. Richard C. Sinopoli (Washington, DC: Georgetown University Press, 1996), 27-30.

[113] Rom. 14:19. Unless otherwise noted, all biblical citations are from the English Standard Version (ESV).

than lovers of God, having the appearance of godliness, but denying its power."[114] In our pursuit of the "right" to more, we have missed the Everything. It is the Everything—Creator God and King who has established us in the community to be conduits of His abundance.

As such, what I find most disheartening is that the very space and people trusted and anointed to display the splendor of God's shalom—the Church—has too, been tainted by the hedonistic value systems of this civilization. The tainted doctrine I call into account is the Prosperity "Gospel." In exploring the roots of Prosperity Theology, I will draw foundational connections to the indoctrination of this nation's individualist and capitalist ethos. The maleficent impact the Prosperity Gospel has had, particularly in urban contexts on community engagement, scriptural reliability, and an authentic Christian identity has revealed it as antithetical to the Jesus-centered Bisrat ("Gospel").

Origins of Prosperity "Gospel"?

Prosperity "Gospel," or the Word of Faith Movement, is defined as a "Gospel according to which the full blessings of God available to those who approach Him in faith and obedience include wealth, health, and power."[115] Also known as the "Health and Wealth Gospel," this theological framework conveys that the preeminent will of God is wrapped within the glorification of humanity: to heal people physically, increase people's earthly wealth, and secure people's happiness through positive thinking and confession.[116] The witness of Prosperity "Gospel" uses biblical scriptures that, uncontextualized, focus the reader on self-centered, human advancement and materialistic

---

[114] 2 Tim. 3:2-5.

[115] "Prosperity Gospel Definition & Meaning," Dictionary.com (accessed January 28, 2021). https://www.dictionary.com/browse/prosperity-gospel.

[116] Joe Carter, "What You Should Know About the Prosperity Gospel," The Gospel Coalition, May 3, 2017. Retrieved from https://www.thegospelcoalition.org/article/what-you-should-know-about-the-prosperity-gospel/; Brandon Kimber, *American Gospel: Christ Alone*, Netflix. United States: Transition Studios, 2018.

expression assessed by one's amount of faith that compels God to act.[117]

The Prosperity "Gospel" finds its origins in an Anglo-American revivalist by the name of Kenneth Hagin. This "Father of Prosperity Gospel" was influenced by a charismatic Baptist preacher named E. W. Kenyon who preached a blessing-centered message in the late American 1800s.[118] Rev. Hagin's charismatic approach to financial freedom and material prosperity would spread across the "Bible belt" southern evangelical circles from the 1950s into the early '80s. The Age of Reaganomics (1981–1989) could be identified as a social affirmation of prosperity principles as U.S. Americans, wearied by wars and unrest, sought to re-stabilize American dream ideals and economic vigor. Evangelist Oral Roberts would be the next to assert this theology with his faith-healing revival ministry. This ministry exploded in prestige and revenue, grossing over $110 million annually. Evangelist Roberts and his team "encouraged" congregants to "sow a seed" as a tangible expression of faith that God would reward them with their desires. Claiming to be inspired by 3 John 1:2, followers of Roberts began to proclaim: "God wants you to be rich."[119] One Oral Roberts University student, Kenneth Copeland, took this theological framework and expanded its global reach. Following the proliferation of television, televangelists like Jimmy Swaggart, Tammy Faye Bakker, and Benny Hinn would streamline these principles into the Black evangelical and charismatic spaces. A trend in debt-relief literature, financial literacy, and stewardship seminars began to engage church

---

[117] M.O. Maura, C. Mbewe, K. Mbugua, J. Piper, W. Grudem, *Prosperity? Seeking the True Gospel*. (Plateau State, Nigeria: Africa Christian Textbooks, 2016).

[118] Brandon Kimber, *American Gospel: Christ Alone*. Netflix. United States: Transition Studios, 2018.

[119] "Prosperity Gospel," *Christianity Today*, July 22, 2020. Retrieved from https://www.christianitytoday.com/ct/topics/p/prosperity-gospel/; Paul Pilzer. *God Wants You to Be Rich: How and Why Everyone Can Enjoy Material and Spiritual Wealth in Our Abundant World* (Chicago, IL: Touchstone Faith, 2007).

communities and garner the attention of Black clergy throughout the Northern and Western regions. The principles would then be carried on by a string of infamous Black preachers throughout the 1970s and into the 1990s like Rev. Ike (Frederick J. Eikerenkoetter II) in New York. Rev. Ike spoke of a "Blessing Plan" and "green power" mind science philosophy. Then there was the aptly named Creflo Dollar, a catalyst within the celebrity preacher, mega-church movement.[120] In this collection of preachers, America revealed that it had created for itself a false theology and exported it globally.

I am particularly vexed by the way it has infiltrated my beloved tradition of the Black Church experience. The origins of the Black Church emphasized carrying the cross of Jesus. It never included materialistic ends but were instead founded in liberation and reconciliation through Christ-centered fellowship, and biblical teaching that shaped livelihood. In the words of Bishop William Barber, "How did we go from I have a dream to bling-bling?"[121] It is not within our origins and is yet another extension of the indoctrination and pathological projection of this nation. With that being said, the Black Church must still be held accountable and repent for its role in perpetuating these values. We can do so while remaining diligent in our effort to decolonize our origin stories.

Historically, the Black Church in the U.S., regardless of denominational affiliation, has been committed to the holistic progression of people and community. This notion of progress was not so heavily inundated with talks of riches. During the late 1970s-early 2000s, in stride with the "moving-on-up phenomenon," Prosperity Gospel began to seep into the Black Church experience and capitalized off Black social misery (i.e., war trauma, AIDS, and drug epidemics) and

---

[120] Henry Louis Gates Jr., *The Black Church: This Is Our Story, This Is Our Song* (New York: Penguin Publishing Group, 2021).
[121] Henry Louis Gates Jr., *The Black Church: This Is Our Story, This Is Our Song* (New York: Penguin Publishing Group, 2021).

the American apartheid (i.e., exploitation of poverty, mass criminalization, and incarceration through the war of drugs).[122] As I reflect on growing up (circa the 1990s) in a Holiness Church tradition, I consider how my great-grandmother, Bishop Lena Thomas (Grandma Bishop, as I affectionately called her) was unimpressed with the propagation of Prosperity doctrine making its way through the airwaves. Though the values were spreading and being exalted all around us in the Philadelphia, PA region, I felt protected from its framework. I conversed with my pastor, Bishop Keith Thomas, who also raised under the tutelage of Bishop Lena Thomas but having a more proximate context to Prosperity Gospel's proliferation in the '70s and '80s. He affirmed that our trailblazing founder didn't even give it much energy. Instead, she maintained a profession of faith and a discipleship mandate that stipulated that authentic "progress comes through a fervent prayer life (intimate and communal), a meditation on the Word, and diligence in basic spiritual disciplines." The results of this model were closer fellowship to the person and power of Jesus, which ultimately was expressed in the care of neighbors.

I find it is important to reclaim the authenticity and reliability of the sacred text, that is, to detox from sandy interpretation as it pertains to the claim of prosperity as a supreme feature of salvation. What do the Scriptures declare to humanity concerning prosperity? How does God define and impart a prosperous life to His beloved? What does that look like throughout the scriptural narrative and in our day for the glory of God being revealed? In the next section, we will examine the key term "prosperity" and seek to uncover the authentic doctrinal

---

[122] Michelle Alexander and Harold Dean Trulear, *Fighting the U.S. Caste Culture* in *Prism Magazine*, Winter 2014. Retrieved from https://issuu.com/prismmagazine/docs/prism-winter-2014/19?e=2263645/6029402; S .E. Moore, A. C. Adedoyin, M. A. Robinson, and D. A. Boamah, "The Black Church: responding to the drug-related mass incarceration of young Black males: 'If you had been here my brother would not have died!'" in *Social Work and Christianity* 42.3 (2015): 313-331.

application of three of the core scriptural passages used within the Prosperity Gospel movement.

Biblical Interpretation: Prosperity

Between the Old and New Testaments of the biblical canon there are sixty-eight verses that reference or use the term prosper or prosperity.[123] We will examine three passages that are a recurring reference for proponents of Prosperity Theology: Jeremiah 29:11, Malachi 3:10, and 3 John 1:2. First, let us keep in mind that whenever we approach God's Word for contextual revelation, it is important to remember the overall scope of the biblical narrative. The Bible is a communicative act by God and about the character and heart of God to His beloved.[124] No matter how much its message has been manipulated and abused, God's Word is truth and the principles and promises of His kingdom lie in every crevice of His Word. In this case, the Kingdom principle of stewardship is in question as it has been the victim of exploitation for perverse gain. My mission in this exercise is to reclaim the pure heart of stewardship principles and thereby liberate this generation to the life abundantly their soul so longs.

In our U.S. English vernacular, the term "prosper" means to "succeed in an enterprise or activity; to succeed in especially material terms, be financially successful."[125] Unfortunately, this is the association and lens this era of Western people have brought to their readings of the biblical text. Contextually, the U.S. English lens of prospering along with many other words is a reductive interpretation of what a term authentically means in the biblical society's origin—a collectivist society in Northern Africa. The languages of Hebrew and Greek

---

[123] F. Brown, S.R. Driver, and C. Briggs., *Hebrew Lexicon* entry for "Tsalach" (Peabody, MA: Hendrickson Academic, 1994).

[124] Jeannine K. Brown, *Scripture As Communication: Introducing Biblical Hermeneutics* (Grand Rapids, MI: Baker, 2007).

[125] "Prosper." Merriam-Webster.com. 2011. https://www.merriam-webster.com/dictionary/prosper (accessed May 8, 2020).

will provide an authentic understanding of the term and its usage in context. The Hebrew word for prosper is *tsalach* (pronounced "tsaw-lakh"), which means "to thrive and to push forward in various senses; to break out, come (mightily), go over, be good, be profitable." Similarly, in the New Testament Greek, εύοδόω (*euodóō,* pronounced yoo-od-o-o) means "to thrive, do well, speed; to help on the road" or "succeed in reaching." These two languages would have been most prominently used within any scriptural account that pens the expression. Scripture, and the languages from which the word "prosperity" is derived, would have meant "more than money and the accumulation of wealth, but rather an ongoing state of success [and guidance] that touches every area of our lives."[126] It is pertinent that we keep this understanding of the term "prosper" at the forefront of our scriptural exposition: "For I know the plans I have for you," declares the LORD, "plans to prosper you and not to harm you, plans to give you hope and a future."[127] This message of the Prophet Jeremiah is often purported as a message of permission to flee one's perceived space of suffering and leap for the greener grass God has *planned* for us. Like the Israelites of Jeremiah's day fearful of exilic punishment and discomforts, we mistakenly assume that God perceives place and space as distinct states or denotes preferences and evaluations of worth as we do. Jeremiah exposes in the greater context of these prophetic letters and specifically that God's intention is to have His beloved be atmosphere-changers in the very place of their consequential misery. He has assigned them to permeate the space as well as to dwell in, invest in, and steward it and its people into its thriving. They are not called to abandon it as a space of perpetual doom.[128]

---

[126] M. D. Jordan, "Spiritual Life: Choose to Have a Healthy Soul and Prosper" in *Tri-City Herald*, January 28, 2021. Retrieved from https://www.tri-cityherald.com/living/religion/spiritual-life/article139572563.html.

[127] Jer. 29:11, taken from the New International Version (NIV).

[128] Jonathan Brooks, *Church Forsaken: Practicing Presence in Neglected Neighborhoods* (Downers Grove, IL: InterVarsity Press, 2018), 6-28.

I find it interesting that in this same series of letters, Jeremiah warns Kings Jehoiakim and Jehoiachin against other prophets and diviners that had arisen with messages of quick-fix escape, beguiled pacts of allegiances, and false hopes of ambitious ascension dripping with no accountability. Jeremiah staunchly calls these people out as false witnesses! He warns King Jehoiakim not to trust Israel's victory over Egypt and that captivity by Babylon was inevitable because of their continuous transgression.[129] Moreover, he warned them to "stop their transgressions," just as Ezekiel did from Babylon.

Contextualizing the passage reveals to the reader (then and now) that God intends to flourish his people in the very place of their affliction. We can truly learn from the Israelites that God is intentional even when we step out of his intention. God uses discomforts as an accountability measure to display his transformative power in the practice of presence; "a very present help in the time of trouble."[130] As opposed to fleeing or remaining focused on their perception of where God was, the gift to dwell with God where He is requires renewed dedication and a posture of trust in the sovereignty of the Lord. The restoration promised in verse 11 isn't just concerning our place in body but is more fully tied to our heart posture of repentance. Jeremiah continues this sentiment in Lamentations 3:40 as he appeals, "Let us examine our ways and test them, and let us return to the Lord."

> Malachi 3:10 "Bring the full tithe into the storehouse, that there may be food in my house. And thereby put me to the test," says the Lord of hosts, "if I will not open the windows of heaven for you and pour down for you a blessing until there is no more need."

---

[129] P. L. Maier, *Josephus*. (Grand Rapids, MI: Kregel Publications, 1995), 179.
[130] Ps. 46:1.

Considered a minor prophet book, Malachi conveys the major message in stride with that of Jeremiah: God is calling his people to a repented heart, postured with intentional trust towards Him as key to holistic thriving. Before we can hold the direction of verse 10, let us step back a little and review verse seven to gain a greater understanding of the thesis of Malachi's matter. It reads, "return to me and I will return to you." The Lord is making a plea to His people from the top-down; the priest and worship shepherds have abandoned the service of the Lord and become callous and cynical in their witness. God used Malachi to declare a season of repentance and return to the origins of their worship. The instruction in verse 10 is an honorable action when one recognizes that everything belongs to God alone. It is only God's good and merciful pleasure to gift us with stewardship rights. However, these stewardship rights are voided if we do not present ourselves fully. They are subject to our honor of God.

This passage often reminds me of the encounter Jesus has with a group of Pharisees and Herodians over the topic of taxation to Caesar.[131] It demonstrates that they approached Jesus (with intentions to trap him) regarding the legitimacy of Israelites participating in the practice of paying taxes to Caesar. Upon asking one of them for a denarius, Jesus responded: "Render to Caesar the things that are Caesar's and unto God the things that are God's." Now consider, for a moment, the face or image engraved upon every human person. God is the image we humans bear. Since we are fashioned in the image of God, it is our reasonable service to render ourselves back unto God. People will invest their substance where they perceive an attachment. In Malachi 3:10b, God used their practice of stewardship and generosity as an example in beseeching his leaders to trust His character and His covenant. He says: "put me to the test." God behooves His image-bearers to trust in their source that provides, produces, and protects (see v. 12). Malachi 3:10 is not a promise of earthly wealth. God is

---

[131] Mt. 22:15-22; Mk. 12:13-17; Lk. 20:19-26.

not a slot machine. The promise of blessing is more substantive than carnal accumulation. It is the eternal enjoyment and security in the goodness of God Himself.

"Beloved, I wish above all things that thou mayest prosper and be in health, even as thy soul prospereth."[132] One of the shortest books of the sacred canon, 3 John is the final letter of John to a dear friend Gaius. Little is known of the details concerning Gaius, but it is presumed that he served in an eldership role. Gaius received a great commendation from John for his faithfulness in leadership. This passage was written in the context of a commonplace greeting. We might modernly express the pleasantry "peace." It was not written with any prophetic intent but simply a pleasant salutation and expression of genuine good wishes for a close friend. I am fascinated by how such a simple colloquial salutation could evolve into the origin of an entire theological framework. 3 John 1:2 is not written to foster a doctrine of material prosperity. Rather, this interpretation is a prime example of the slippery slope of eisegesis. With that being said, I affirm that God desires His beloved to prosper and be in good health. But the key to such thriving is expressed in the latter portion of John's greeting to Gaius: "even as your soul prospers." Wellness and thriving in the fullness of life flows from and centers on the perpetual surrender to the fullness of our soul to God. If our soul is made to reflect the likeness of God, then it can only experience fullness in community. Carnal accumulation will never provide the substance for which our soul craves.

Keep in mind that the early apostles developed the foundational elements of our Christ-centered witness amidst the growing capitalist influence of their day (Rome). Paul made a point to warn his mentee, Timothy, and the larger community of believers: "For the love of money is a root of all kinds of evils. It is through this craving that some have wandered away from the faith and pierced themselves with

---

[132] 3 Jn. 2. King James' Version (KJV).

many pangs."[133] This message reaffirmed the sentiments of our Lord Jesus as he taught the Disciples proper pursuits of their hearts: "No one can serve two masters, for either he will hate the one and love the other, or he will be devoted to the one and despise the other. You cannot serve God and money."[134]

At the same time, it would be irresponsible to superimpose the opposite sentiment that God desires His creation to be impoverished and destitute. Certainly, that too is not a sound biblical interpretation. Scripture declares in Genesis 1:28 that "God blessed them." God said to them: "Be fruitful and multiply and fill the earth and subdue it, and have dominion over the fish of the sea and over the birds of the heavens and over every living thing that moves on the earth." Moreover, in our redemption, we have been justified as joint heirs with Christ Jesus. This same Christ has promised us life and that more abundantly with a given assignment to display the splendor of *shalom* and reconciliation as His kingdom comes: "His divine power has granted to us all things that pertain to life and godliness, through the knowledge of him who called us to his own glory and excellence."[135] This is not a matter of God's concern with the status of poor or rich but rather with the eternal state of the dead and the living.

What I hope has been accomplished from the brief analysis of these three core texts is that human prosperity is wrapped up in the Lordship of God, not the piety of humanity. God imparts a prosperous life to His beloved through the person of Jesus who promised life abundantly in John 10:10b. God's prosperity in Scripture is the life abundantly for which Christ speaks. Life abundantly is the embodied fullness of God, the filling of His spirit resulting in the thriving of human existence whose vessel overflows to provide community (e.g., kingdoms and nations). This is aligned with Jesus' prayer for

---

[133] 1 Tim. 6:10.
[134] Mt. 6:24.
[135] 2 Pet. 1:3.

"Kingdom come;" that God's glory will be revealed through the igniting of a people to the ultimate pursuit of shalom. There will be nothing missing, nothing broken, nothing lacking. *Shalom* includes revelation and the manifestation of all being replenished, restored, renewed, and reckoned through the *Ramah* ("Word").[136]

The kingdoms of this world seek to perpetuate this Kingdom quality. But because the world's values are perverse, its counterfeit structure can only provide an illusion of fortitude. We must ask ourselves: "what does a particular kingdom or nation value?" The answer reveals how that nation indoctrinates the culture of prosperity. In the United States of America, the purported values are monetary currency and prestige or fame with the end being happiness. The citizens are conditioned to join a quest in the all-consuming pursuit of happiness. Pursuits of happiness are fleeting, emotion-driven states of consciousness tied to insatiable races to trophies of achievement. Hedonistic pursuits of happiness as sovereign inconspicuously "steal, kill, and destroy"[137] the very fabric of a beloved people. Greed creates division, not unity; it belittles and does not edify; it poaches instead of develops. It trains us to be consumers of temporal emptiness instead of carriers of eternal light empowered to shift an atmosphere. It trains us to be apathetic towards meritocracy and corrupt injustice, instead of lamenting partners and restorative justice activists. 1 John 5:21 (NLT) warns us: "Dear children, keep away from anything that might take God's place in your hearts."

Happiness pursuits are a perversion of the authentic promised kingdom intention for flourishing and joy. Joy is a perpetual fountain, developed in one's soul. It can be stirred, it can be capped, it can be bursting but it is always accessible: "Our capacity for joy is likely hardwired and is not solely dictated by our experiences and

---

[136] Rom. 10:13-15.
[137] Jn. 10:10a.

circumstances."[138] When we bask in it or live out of it, the atmospheres we venture into will shift and even grant us warning wisdom. Consider the posture of Jesus as conveyed in Hebrews 12:2: "for the joy set before him [Jesus] he endured cross despising the shame." The Apostle Paul asserts this posture as he prays "that God, the source of hope, will fill you with joy and peace because you trust in him. Then you will overflow with confident hope through the power of the Holy Spirit."[139] It is time that we call the Prosperity Gospel out for what it is, a heresy—belief at odds with orthodox doctrine. A poor interpretation of the Scripture intertwined with toxic, self-centered doctrine. Long enough has this framework ripped at the seams of our integrity, edification, and effectiveness as the body of Christ.

The Consumer Identity

Prosperity doctrine has exposed itself as an antithetical sect of Christianity in its placation, individualism, and meritocracy that have proliferated systemic oppression and social and economic inequity. At this time in our nation's history, urban communities were being attacked on all social and political fronts. Too many within our one ally and catalyst for change—the Black church—chose to accept the rhetoric of meritocracy. Many in the Black Church ignored the issues and instead focused on individual facades of self-improvement and escapist mentalities. This approach only furthered the oppression of our people. This oppression was no longer limited to social and economic status but was now extended to our spiritual development, which is so heavily tied to our communal attachment:[140] The spiritual and

---

[138] Markham Heid, "Are we Hardwired for Happiness?" in *Time Special Edition: The Power of Joy*. (New York: TIME, 2020), page 16.
[139] Rom. 15:13.
[140] Nancy Boyd-Franklin, *Black Families in Therapy: Understanding the African American Experience* (New York: Guilford Press, 2006), 125-131.

psychological impact of individualism has previously been articulated by Mwalimu Julius Nyerere and Joseph Brandt respectively:

> The indoctrination of individualism has enslaved us with apathy concerning our communal responsibility.[141] According to researchers, Sensoy and DiAngelo (2017), individualism is the belief that we are all unique and outside the forces of socialization…any differences between social groups are seen as a result of individual strengths or weaknesses. Individualism is considered a "problematic cultural belief." An ideology steeped in American civility; "it permeates almost every aspect of our lives, [with an] emphasis on the needs and desires of the individual, and over-reliance on the self. Individualism expresses such self-righteous concepts as "I don't need anyone, I only need to rely on myself; My relationship with God is strictly private and an individual matter."[142]

Such a belief lies at the core of the theological discourse of the Prosperity Gospel. Brandon Kimber's *American Gospel: Christ Alone* documentary, beautifully summed up the founding antithetical agenda of Prosperity Gospel: "Create a God that only wants to give you the desires of your heart…That is idolatry, the elevation of the gift above the giver." In a nation inundated with accumulation pursuits, this challenges believers to ask, "Is Jesus all satisfying to you?"

America is a colonized territory founded on capitalist, revisionist ideals whose settlers were emboldened by Pope Alexander VI's 1493 "Doctrine of Discovery."[143] However unintentional, the words in the Doctrine of Discovery ignited a conquistador siege that included

---

[141] Julius K. Nyerere, *Ujamaa: Essays on Socialism* (Oxford: Oxford University Press, 1974).
[142] Joseph Brandt as told by A. Tappin, "Keynote Address: White Supremacy and Christianity in the United States" in *Eastern University Faculty Workshop* (March 2021).
[143] Mark Charles and Soong-Chan Rah, *Unsettling Truths: The Ongoing, Dehumanizing Legacy of the Doctrine of Discovery* (Downers Grove, IL: IVP Books, 2019).

the co-opting of land, genocidal desecration of the indigenous, and dehumanization of persons within the system of chattel slavery. This overlooked ideal birthed the indoctrination of the "consumer" identity. U.S. Americans have been taught that we were consumers and thus only valuable as producers or consumers. When most production moved overseas, ending the American Industrial age, consumerist ideals became more prevalent as a major means of status evaluation.

As a nation, we have engaged in gluttonous consumption resulting in some of the worst eating, spending, and toxic habits.[144] We have consumed products, adoration, attention, fantasy, media platforms, and sensuality. And when that left us empty and bewildered, we debased ourselves further to the consumption of substances. What an expansive yet shallow appetite we have discovered: "it would seem that our Lord finds our desires not too strong, but too weak. We are halfhearted creatures, fooling about with drink, and sex, and ambition when infinite joy is offered us...we are too easily pleased."[145] Such shallow consumerist identities have resulted in idle states and idolatrous behavior—heavy, but empty and powerless.[146] And just like Dagon, we cannot stand in the most holy presence of God in this state. When we do, we will fall on our faces broken in reverence to the fullness of the Holy God.

The proliferation of Prosperity doctrine has spread to the point that we built a theology around its tenets and goals. We have four generations of people approaching the Church and worshiping with a capitalist-revisionist consumer mentality. The Church edifice has been reduced to just another store where people approach asking, "what can God do for me, what does he have to offer me for my loyalty and faith?" Some Black churches have historically lacked endowments

---

[144] David G. Myers and C. N. DeWall, *Psychology in Modules,* 12th ed. (New York, NY: Worth, 2018).
[145] C. S. Lewis, *The Weight of Glory: And Other Addresses* (San Francisco, CA: HarperOne, 2001), 26.
[146] 1 Sam. 5:1-5.

and equitable mortgage terms and are dependent solely on tithing to stay afloat. Because of this, many have bought into this consumer profile and shifted their service (product) to motivational social clubs and entertainment centers, focused on attendance numbers (traction) and offering collections (sales).

But isn't that the way the enemy works: he eases us into hypocrisy? He entices us by displaying the present "effectiveness" of his evil in the mainstream culture. The enemy seduces us to turn a blind eye to injustice and thereby lulling us to sleep as our minds focus on our present lack instead of the *kairos* ("appointed time") and *koinonia* ("community"). The strategy to leverage our perceived lack is easily amplified in a society engrossed in the consumption Olympics, a rat race of gluttonous pillaging.

At a minimum, two generations of Prosperity theologies have led the infrastructure of our faith, ethnic identity, and hearts to be exposed as faulty. The dysfunctionality is like the infrastructures in many major American cities such as Flint's water crisis, Philadelphia's school building COVID-19 crisis, and Houston's electrical crisis. Founded in capitalist "profit over people" ideologies, it lacks the very fiber and capacity to hold up under pressure. A theology built on Prosperity principles leave a people mystified and ill-equipped to stand and fight. Furthermore, it cannot sustain us in the more founded promised season of trial, discomfort, and devastation.[147] Today, there is an entire generation that has experienced continuous devastation, tragedy, and unrest from birth. This began with the 9/11 terrorist attack. This is a people born in a wilderness of warfare, famine, and disease. This generation needs a resilient faith in a sovereign Emmanuel God, a Gospel witness of redemption and glorious hope at work in them: "A wounded culture finds its best answers in a wounded Savior."[148] That Savior is Jesus.

---

[147] Jn. 16:33.

[148] Ravi Zacharias and A. Murray, *Seeing Jesus from the East: A Fresh Look at History's Most Influential Figure* (Grand Rapids, MI: Zondervan, 2020), 57.

The theological framework of Prosperity "Gospel" does not meet the soul's cry. They have the appearance of sound fortification but lack the power thereof. Because of this, they are responsible for the collateral damage of devastated hope, stolen purpose, and even lost lives. What did the children of Israel do in the wilderness with their riches? They made an idol out of them. That idol was only responsible for debasing them into idle, disgraced people.

Reconciliatory Action: Repent, Revive, Reestablish

Thanks be to God who does not abandon us to our self-righteous endeavors. It is in those very moments that God reveals Himself so that His beloved will repent. They witness to their LORD and are empowered to walk in integrity. A powerful witness can only take our faith so far. We need to reclaim a knowing witness of God. These mountainous, hard-pressed structures of greed, racism, and individualist ideologies must be eroded from their roots with the waters from on high. Rivers in the desert. Rivers in the wilderness. A voice crying out full of the Spirit has poured out, declaring "prepare ye the way of the Lord," "your kingdom come!"[149] This anointing has a promise to reach and propel the cleansing, refreshing, and purifying process of the hidden spaces of faulty, toxic, and heretical indoctrination: "Pure and genuine religion in the sight of God the Father means caring for orphans and widows in their distress and refusing to let the world corrupt you."[150]

We now seek to reestablish the gift of the Church: the authentic Word-formed lives, the testimony of Jesus that liberates, the evangelism that reconciles, the posture of praise that stirs joy in and out of due season, and an incarnate faith that lives out acts of justice to

---

[149] Is. 43:19, 40:3; Mk. 1:3.
[150] Jas. 1:27.

display the splendor and majesty of the King of kings and Lord of lords. We can no longer afford to be led astray by the double-minded syncretistic doctrine of Prosperity. This doctrine speaks not to the needs of the community but to the fanciful pursuits of "happiness" that this nation has sold here and abroad: "You are not here for wealth accumulation but to be a vehicle of wealth distribution."[151] Repent! Be no longer conformed or consumed by this world, but be transformed by the renewal, the refreshing, the restoring, and the release of your individual and social mind in the *shalom* of God. "You have made us for yourself, O Lord, and our hearts are restless until they rest in you."[152]

We are not consumers. Though it may be a social activity we perform, it is not the identity of humanity. We are the beloved image-bearers of the Most High God, redeemed by Christ Jesus to mature into the fullness of His likeness. We are called to be His hands and feet in the service of Kingdom come. You cannot buy and sell this salvation and sanctification. Didn't Martin Luther expose this very perversion in the Catholic Church and spark the Reformation?[153] Better yet, didn't our Lord Jesus expose this same corruption in the temple of Jerusalem and proceed to disrupt the system so heavily influenced by the dominant capitalist political authority of that day—Caesar and the Roman Empire?[154]

Salvation and abundant life are gifts of God alone so that no man can boast! This gift does not give us permission to negate human suffering nor abandon those to it. Rather, salvation liberates us to

---

[151] Goode, Wilson. 2019. *"Eastern University Graduation Speech."* Transcript of speech delivered at Eastern University, May 11, 2019.

[152] Augustine of Hippo, *Confessions,* ed. Albert Cook Outler (Oxford: Oxford University Press, 1998).

[153] Eddie L. Hyatt, *2000 Years of Charismatic Christianity* (Lake Mary, FL: Charisma House, 2002), 73-77.

[154] See. Matt. 21:12-13; Mark 11:15-18.

reconcile community with God and with fellow people.[155] We must repent for accepting and perpetuating a theology that had nothing to do with the God of the Bible, nothing to do with Christ, nothing to do with salvation, and everything to do with the god of this nation—money. Jemar Tisby's historical survey of the role of racism within U.S. American Church history leads us to conclude that in the U.S., the color of compromise is ultimately green.[156]

In our repentance, let us engage in lamentation and reclaim it as a unique anointing in this current great awakening. Historically, great awakenings have emerged out of struggle or tension in the greater culture and more prominently in the face of derision within the Church, be it of doctrine, worship expression, or witness.[157] Our modern tension has been amplified by the unprecedented coronavirus pandemic, political warfare, economic misery, and violent desecration of image-bearers. This has ultimately been represented in a common mistrust of faith organizations and the person of Jesus Christ. We cannot afford to sit idly by, avoid, demonize, or devalue the suffering grief and angst of this generation. Our role is not that of condemner, for no condemnation should be found in us. We have experienced its liberation and justification firsthand.[158] Rather our role has been revealed by Christ: we have the ministry of reconciliation and reconciliation requires presence.[159] Thus, we must emphasize the Emmanuel anointing—God with us.[160]

Let us come down from our pious escapist towers and be present to God's wounded heart in the valley of dry bones. The revival of

---

[155] 2 Cor. 5:11-21.
[156] Jemar Tisby, *The Color of Compromise: The Truth about the American Church's Complicity in Racism* (Grand Rapids, MI: Zondervan, 2020).
[157] Vernon M. Whaley, *Exalt His Name Understanding Music and Worship, Book 2* (Calumet City, IL: Evangelical Training Association, 2019), 41-60.
[158] Rom. 8:1.
[159] 2 Cor. 5:18.
[160] Mt. 1:23.

this generation of dry bones has already been stirred by God. Listen. Can you hear the "rattling noise," and feel them reverberate off the walls of your soul.[161] Submit to God as He finds us bare, washes and resuscitates us by His spirit, and restores our weight. Every sinew, muscle, epidermis layer returns—may the Word of God return flesh to our ravished carcasses. The state of dry bones is the consequence of a consuming appetite for the illusions of substance. We ate empty and thus wasted away. This revival does not look like what you have imagined. A peculiar revival will reestablish the peculiar Kingdom of God on the earth. We are a nation of Word-formed image-bearers armed with an authentic knowing witness. This revival will be experienced in the streets and on the margins of borders, prisons, hospitals, schools, and voting booths. These contexts are where feet and hands protest injustice and call into account the corrupt kingdoms of this world. It will be led by all ages, genders, and creeds as God will pour out His spirit on all flesh postured at His wounded heart.[162] Revival is present and ordained as God's spirit is released from the confines of church buildings. It is present where rituals and traditions are abated, and we sit in our homes with those He has anointed us to steward. Will we respond, rising as an army in formation asking our Lord and commander: "How do you want to be worshiped? How do I serve you, now? What are you revealing to us, God?" The Spirit is freshly pouring out and stirring a groan, a moan, a labor-intense lamentation. This call to repentance includes exposure and boldness to tear down idols in sacred spaces and detox sandy scriptural interpretations. It helps us to discern spirits of seduction and perversion that have long enough wreaked havoc on the sacred covenant of worship. A concern for human dignity and, most of all, a resurrection of the powerful person of Jesus as a banner over us is rising!

---

[161] Ez. 35.
[162] Acts 2:17.

This is where our prosperity lies—the Bisrat is the person of Jesus. The ultimate end and gift of the gospel is God Himself—both the giver and the gift. The good news for me and my neighbor is that "He who has God and everything else has no more than he who has God only."[163] He will liberate and prosper our souls. He will perform His promises. He will make individuals and creation whole again. The good news is not what I have, but who has me! The good news is not expressed in how much I can accumulate. The good news is expressed in my posture of service unto God and His beloved creation. God's word is true regardless of how poorly it has been misused. The sacred passages of Jeremiah, Malachi, and 3 John are truth and speak to us in this season. Now that we have received them afresh, let us apply them as instructed. They each will mature us into a witness of God himself and ignite us in reconciliatory action: "Let the message about Christ [alone], in all its richness, fill your lives. Teach and counsel each other with all the wisdom he gives."[164]

---

[163] C. S. Lewis, *The Weight of Glory: And Other Addresses* (San Francisco, CA: HarperOne, 2001), 34.
[164] Col. 3:16.

Nazrawis and the Zanj: Contact between Nazrawis of Northeastern Africa and the Swahili Coast during the Axumite and Early Solomonic Periods

Vince L. Bantu

During the Axumite Period, the Bisrat spread across all of the major civilizations in the continent now known as Africa for which textual documentation is extant. These regions included: the North African provinces of the Western Roman Empire—Byzacena, Africa Proconsularis, Numidia, and Mauretania; Egypt; the Nubian Kingdoms of Nobatia, Makouria, and Alodia/Alwa; and the Ag'azi (Ethiopian) kingdom centered in Axum. Africans were included among the earliest Nazrawis mentioned in the New Testament and became missionaries throughout the continent. The Roman colonies in North Africa were predominately Christian in the earliest centuries despite intense persecution at the hands of the Roman Empire. The independent African nations in the Nubian and Ag'azi regions chose to adopt the Urpeh as their national religion in the sixth and fourth centuries respectively. By the end of the Axumite Period, the Urpeh was the dominant religion in all of these regions of the African continent. The North African regions under Western Roman colonization maintained a Chalcedonian form of the Urpeh that was in agreement with the dominant Roman Church centered in Rome and Constantinople. By contrast, the Urpeh of Egypt, the Nubian kingdoms, and Agʻazi followed the Miaphysite confession which held to a haymanot of one *helawie* (*physis*; "nature") in Yeshua. These independent and colonized Nazrawi regions of Africa engaged in extensive trade with one another, the European mainland of the Roman Empire, the Near East, the Persian Empire, and the Indian Subcontinent. African Nazrawis travelled throughout these regions of the world, traded goods, and exchanged cultural and religious influences. Extant data attests to a great deal of interaction between North and East African civilizations and the European and Asian continents. However, there is also evidence of interaction between Northeastern African Nazrawis with their African neighbors along the Sahel. Northeastern African Nazrawis had long established trade routes across the Sahara that connected them to neighboring people groups. Amidst the trade and military conflict between African Nazrawis and their neighbors, African missionaries and travelers made contact with surrounding communities. As the Bisrat was spreading across the African continent, another world religion emerged across the Red Sea and began to spread in Africa through militaristic means.

After the Arab Muslim armies conquered Egypt and destroyed Carthage, they unsuccessfully attempted to dominate the Nubian Nazrawi kingdoms. There was no attempted conquest of Agʻazi, with whom the Arab Muslims had amicable relations prior to the Conquest. Soon after the Arab Muslim Conquest of the Northwest African coast, the presence of the Urpeh disappeared from this region and Islam continued to spread south into Central and West Africa. The spread of Islam facilitated the expansion of Central and West African civilizations such as Mali, Songhai, and Ghana, upon whom Islam was forced through North African Islamic conquests during the tenth and eleventh centuries. An extensive trade connected the continent of Africa with European and Asian continents known to the modern world as the Trans-Saharan Trade. Northeastern African Islamic and Nazrawi communities traded slaves, metals, and crops with emerging communities in Central and West Africa as well as European and Asian empires. Many Central and West African kingdoms embraced Islam as the dominant religion, as trade routes to North Africa and the Near East were controlled by Islamic societies. Indigenous African religions persisted in Central and West Africa and often clashed with emerging Islamic African societies. Nazrawis in Egypt remained populous and would have likely interacted with North and West Africans travelling through Egypt to the Near East. The Nubian kingdoms entered a golden era during the early Solomonic period while the Nazrawi Ag'azi kingdom centered in Axum declined and the Ag'azi Urpeh was largely diminished for some time. The Ag'azi region was again dominated by Nazrawis following the emergence of the Zagwe and Solomonic Dynasties. The Nazrawis of the Nile Valley continued to spread the Bisrat throughout the Northern half of the African continent, as attested in multiple medieval sources.[165] In sum, the Bisrat spread across the entire Northern half of the African continent prior to the advent of Western colonialism. The spread of the Bisrat across North, East, Central, and West Africa occurred through Indigenous Africans. However, does evidence exist for the spread of the Bisrat in the Southern portion of the African continent? What was the extent and nature of trade and contact between southern African civilizations and the rest of the continent? The following study will explore these questions and survey the relevant sources narrating the formation of South and Southeastern African civilizations.

The Indian Ocean Trade led to increased development of urbanized civilizations across the continent as well as detailed reports of these communities. Archaeological evidence demonstrates connections

---

[165] I am currently developing a project that explores this Westward Nazrawi expansion.

between the Southeastern African coast and the Near East stretching back to the first millennium BCE.[166] In the southern portion of the African continent, one of the earliest-documented urbanized civilizations was the Swahili coast. Late antique Romans referred to the East African coast as "Azania" (lit. "dry area"). The first-century Roman historian Pliny, in his *Natural History*, refers to an "Azanian Sea" (*Azanium*) across from the Arabian Peninsula.[167] Pliny describes Azania as the region of the Troglodytae along the Red Sea: "From this place is the Azanian Sea (*Azanium mare*), a peninsula which some writers called Hispalus, Lake Mandalum, and the island of Colocasitis, with many others lying out along the horizon, in which are many turtles. The town of Suche, the island of Daphnidis, and the town of the Adulitae—which was founded by Egyptian slaves who had escaped their captors."[168] The locations provided by Pliny correspond to the Red Sea coast of modern Egypt, Sudan, and Eritrea. However, the account of Azania in the first-century *Periplus of the Erythraean Sea* describes the beginning of the Azanian region as the Western tip of the Horn of Africa in modern Somalia: "From Opone the cape goes back to the south, and first are what are called the Lesser and Greater Bluffs of Azania (Ἀζανίας), having harbors, roadsteads and anchors for six courses towards the south-west. Then the Lesser and Greater Beaches, of another six courses, and after them in order, the courses of Azania (τῆς Ἀςανίας δρόμοι)."[169] The *Periplus* further indicates that the region of Azania extended further along the East African coast south of the Horn region:

---

[166] Felix A. Chami, Madame Françoise Le Guennec-Coppens, and Sophie Mery, "East Africa and the Middle East Relationship from the First Millennium BC to about 1500 AD," in *Journal des Africanistes*, 72.2, 21-37 (2002): 23.

[167] Pliny the Elder, *Natural History*, Books 3-7, ed. H. Rackham (Cambridge, MA: Harvard University Press, 1942), 420. For a survey of the earliest Greco-Roman sources on Azania, see G.W.B. Huntingford, "Azania," in *Anthropos* 35/36 (1940/1941): 208-220.

[168] Pliny, *Natural History*, 466.

[169] *The Periplus of the Erythraean Sea*, ed. B. Fabricius (Leipzig: Verlag von Veit, 1883), 52.

From here after two courses from the land lies the last marketplace of Azania, called Rhapta (Ἀζανίας ἐμπόριον κεῖται, τὰ Ραπτὰ), which has its name from the aforementioned stitched (ῥαπτῶν) boats, in which there is an abundance of ivory and tortoiseshell. The people of this land have huge bodies and they act like pirates. And each location likewise has its own leader. The Mopharitic ruler (ὁ Μαφαρείτης τύραννος) governs it according to the old treaty by which it lies in the kingdom which has become first in Arabia. Under the king, those from Mouza (Μούζης) control it by payment of tribute, and send ships with captains and servants who are majority of the Arab skin (Ἄπαψι χρώμενοι) and have experience with the place and their language by intermingling and intermarriage.[170]

Mouza likely is the ancient antecedent of the modern Mawza District of Yemen. This would likely indicate that Azania was in close contact with the Himyarite Kingdom of Southern Arabia. The picture of a multiethnic blend of Arabian and Sub-Saharan African trade during the Axumite period indicate that the multiethnic foundation of Swahili identity started in ancient times. The *Periplus* claims that Azania is near Barbaria, a region also mentioned by the second-century historian Claudius Ptolemy:

That which is near the Arabian (Sea) and the Avalites gulf, along the sea is called Troglodytica (Τρωγλοδθτικὴ) as far as Elephantas mountains, where the Adulitae (Ἀδουλῖται) are. And the Avalitae near a bay with a similar name. And the Mosyli (Μόσυλοι) are near the promontory with a market

---

[170] *Periplus*, 54-56. Azania also participated in the slave trade which was centered around Nubia, Stanley M. Burstein, *Graeco-Afrciana: Studies in the History of Greek Relations with Egypt and Nubia* (New Rochelle, NY: Aristide D. Caratzas, 1995), 197. This would have increased the likelihood of Christian contact during Nubia's Christian period.

place with a similar name. All of the shore of the Rhaptum promontory—the interior of Barbaria (Βαρβαρὶα)—is called Azania (Ἀζανία), in which there are many elephants.[171]

Barbaria is also mentioned in the sixth-century travelogue of Cosmas Indicopleustes. Cosmas was an Egyptian monk who was a member of the Church of the East centered in the Persian Empire. Cosmas made a journey throughout the Red Sea and Indian Ocean and wrote about his travels in *Christian Topography*. Cosmas not only mentions the Somali coast, or "Barbaria," but he also describes a vibrant trade between this region, the Nazrawi Agʻazi empire centered in Axum and African regions further to the interior:

> The land (χώρα) bearing frankincense is situated in the cape region of Ethiopia (Αἰθιοπίας), being in the interior and is contained by the ocean further. Hence, the residents of Barbaria (Βαρβαρίαν), being near, go up into the interior and, exchange and supply them an abundance spices, frankincense, cassia, calamus and many other things. Afterwards, they send supplies by sea to Adulis and to the Homerites (Ἀδούλῃ καὶ ἐν τῷ Ὁμηρίτῃ) and to Inner India and to Persia. And you will find this written in Kings, that the Queen of Sheba—that is, of the Homerites, who later our Lord in the Gospels calls "the Queen of the South"—brought spices to Solomon the same Barbaria which is the neighbor on the border, along with rods of ebony, apes and gold from Ethiopia, as all of Ethiopia is a neighbor according to the border of the Arabian Gulf. Again, it is knowable from the Word of the Lord that He calls these places the ends of the earth, as it says: "The Queen of the South will rise up in judgement against this generation and condemn it,

---

[171] Claudius Ptolemy, *Geography*, ed. Carolus Fridericus Augustus Nobbe (Lepizig: Caroli Tauchnitii, 1843), 279-280.

for she came from the ends of the earth to hear the wisdom of Solomon." For the Homerites are not far away from Barbaria, as the sea-journey across the sea that is between them is two days. And then what remains beyond the Ocean is called Zingion (Ζίγγιον). The province that is called Sasu (Σάσου) is near the ocean, as the land bordering the Ocean is the frankincense-producing region and it has many goldmines. The King of the Axumites (Ἀξωμιτῶν), through the ruler of Agaw (Ἀγαῦ), sends their own men there in order to trade for gold. And there are many other traders that accompany them, above five-hundred people. They bring with them there oxen, salt and iron. And when they are near the land, they make a camp at that place. Then they make a fence bearing a great abundance of thorns, and they stay within it. And when they sacrifice the oxen and dismember them and place them on top of the thorns with the salt and the iron. Then the indigenous people (ἐγχώριοι) come there bearing gold (χρυσίον) like lupine, which is called "gold" (ταγχάραν), and they place one or two lupines usually above that which they desire—on the flesh, salt or iron—and they continue on a ways. Then the manager of the cattle comes up and, if he is satisfied, he takes the gold and if not, then he leaves it and takes his gold and departs. This is the exchange in that place, since they speak a different language and interpreters are indeed greatly lacking. And they are at the place in that country (χώραν) for five days more or less and based on access, they come and trade until they finish trading. And during the return, again they agree to bear arms, since those who must be passed through in the interior of that country (χώρας) threaten them from a desire to take the gold. It takes six months to do this trade, both the departure and the return. They proceed slowly in the departure, mainly because of the cattle. But on the return, they speed up so that the winter and rain do not create problems for them on the way. For the source of the Nile River is there and during winter, because of its abundant rain, many rivers come from it into the road. Their winter is equivalent to our summer. The beginning is the Egyptian month of Epiph until Toth, the showers are exceedingly vehement for three months, to the point that multiple rivers form, all of which flow into the Nile. This has been received from my own observation and also from hearing from those who have written of trading in these areas.[172]

It seems likely, based on Cosmas' description of the gold trade between Ag'azi and the enigmatic "Sasu," that "Barbaria" refers to a location south of the Ag'azi kingdom centered at Axum, beyond which lay the ocean.[173] Furthermore, Cosmas' mention of "Zingion" indicates that the Ag'azi Empire had direct connections with the Swahili coast. There has been speculation that this "Zingion" refers to a region in the Ag'azi Red Sea.[174] However, Cosmas' mention that "Zingion" lay "beyond Barbaria," a region referring to the Somali Coast, indicates that this region Cosmas heard about during his time in Adulis referred to regions beyond the Horn of Africa. In his travel journal, Cosmas provides information not only about the world of the Indian Ocean during the sixth century, but also regarding the presence of Christians in India, Ag'azi, and Arabia:

---

[172] Cosmas Indicopleustes, *Christian Topography*, ed. Wanda Wolska-Conus (Paris: Les éditions du cerf, 1968), 357-363. Cf. 1 Ki. 10:1-13; Mt. 12:42; Lk. 11:31.

[173] Wanda Wolska-Conus, "Cosmas Indikopleustes (Cosmas the "Indian Sea Traveler") (fl. 540 C.E.)," in *Trade, Travel and Exploration in the Middle Ages: An Encyclopedia*, ed. John Block Friedman and Kristen Mossler Figg, 129-131 (New York, NY: Routledge, 2016), 130. Another interpretation of Cosmas' description of the Ethiopian gold trade was previously offered by L.P. Kirwan, "The Christian Topography and the Kingdom of Axum," in *The Geographical Journal*, 138.2, 166-177 (1972).

[174] George Hatke, "South Arabia, the Arabs, and the East African Trade in Pre-Islamic Times," in *South Arabian Long-Distance Trade in Antiquity "Out of Arabia,"* ed.George Hatke and Ronald Ruzicka, 1-62 (Cambridge: Cambridge Scholars Publishing, 2021), 23, n. 132.

In Taprobane (Ταπροβάνη), an island in Inner India, where the Indian Sea is, there is a Church of Christians there, with clergy and believers. I do not know if there are beyond it. Likewise, in the place called Male (Μαλέ),[175] where the pepper grows, and in the place called Calliana (Καλλιάνα), there is a bishop who is ordained from Persia (Περσίδος). Likewise, in the island that is called Dioskoridous (Διοσκορίδους),[176] which is located in the same Indian Sea and in which the inhabitants speak Greek, having been initially inhabited the Ptolemies following Alexander the Macedonian, there are clergy that are ordained from Persia and are sent there and there are many Christians. I sailed around the island but I did not go on it. But I met with some Greek-speaking people there who came into Ethiopia (Αἰθιοπία).[177]

While the Christian communities that Cosmas visited in South Asia were clearly a part of Cosmas' own Church of the East centered in Persia, it seems likely that the Christians of Socotra may have been part of the Miaphyhsite Christian communities of Egypt, Nubia, and Ethiopia.

Following the rise of Islam, commerce and trade across the Indian Ocean and Red Sea intensified and developed in new areas. The tenth-century Muslim historian Al-Masudi witnessed the gold trade in Sofala in modern Mozambique. In describing the extent of the Indian Ocean, al-Masudi provides a description of the East African coast using categories reflective of his time period:

> It has a bay stretching from the land of Habesha (الحبشة) passing to the region of Barbaria (بربرا ناحية), a land between the Zanj (الزنج) and Habesha. This bay is called "The Barbarian" and its length was five-hundred and the width, from the edge,

---

[175] The Malabar Coast of Southwestern India.
[176] Sokotra.
[177] Cosmas, *Christian Topography*, 503-5.

is one hundred miles. These are not the Barbarians that hail from the land of Barbaria that is west of the land of Africa (ارض افريقية), for this region is referred to differently than this name. And all of the captains from Oman (العمانيين) travel on this sea to Kanbalu Island (جزيرة قنبلو) in the Zanj Sea (بحر الزنج). And in this city are Muslims among Zanj non-Muslims (الكفار من الزنج).[178]

While the location of Kanbalu has been extensively debated, it is clear that this island was located along the Southeastern African coast.[179] This island was part of the region Al-Masudi refers to as "Zanj," which also lay along the Southeastern African coast. It is likely that the Arabic name Zanj was influenced by the Greek "Zangion" and "Azania" used by Roman historians centuries earlier. The ninth-century theologian Al-Jahiz commented on the Trans-Saharan slave trade and made interesting distinctions of the "Zanj" that were being trafficked to his native Basra:

> You (the whites) have yet to see the true Zanj, since you only know the enslaved kind brought from the shores of Qanbalu… But the people of Qanbalu are devoid of brains, Qanbalu being the one place at which your vessels dock. And that is because the Zanj are of two main lines of descent, Qanbalu and Langawiya, just as are the Arabs of two main lines of descent, Qahtan and 'Adnan. You have yet to see a member of the Langawiya kind, either from the coast (al-Sawahil), or from the interior (al-Jouf). If you could meet these, you would forget the issue of fair looks

---

[178] Al-Masudi, *Les Prairies d'Or*, vol. I, ed. C. Barbier de Meynard and Pavet de Courteille (Paris: Imprimerie Impériale, 1840), 231-2.

[179] Adria LaViolette, "Swahili Archaeology and History of Pemba, Tanzania: A Critique and Case Study of the Use of Written and Oral Sources in Archaeology," in *African Historical Archaeologies*, ed. Andrew M. Reid and Paul J. Lane, 125-162 (New York, NY: Kluwer/Plenum Publishers, 2004), 135.

and perfection. Now, if you refuse to believe this, saying that you have yet to meet a Zanji with the brains even of a boy or a woman, we would reply to you, have you ever met among the enslaved of India and Sindh individuals with brains, education, culture and manners so as to expect these same qualities in what has fallen to you from among the Zanj.[180]

Al-Jahiz provides a fascinating account of Blackness from the perspective of a person of African descent from the Abbasid homeland. Al-Jahiz's statements were remarkable given the immensely racist climate of the Abbasid world. The eleventh-century Christian physician Ibn Butlan distinguishes between four categories of Black people: the Zanj from the Swahili Coast, the Habash from the Horn of Africa, the Zaghawa from the Lake Chad region, and the Nuba from the Nile Valley.[181] The presence in the Near East of African slaves from Nazrawi kingdoms along with those from other parts of the continent further attests to the exposure of Southern Africans to the Bisrat during the early Solomonic period. Arabian ports such as Aden were a significant crossroads where slaves and merchants from the Nazrawi African regions of Egypt, Nubia, and Ag'azi would have met with those from the Swahili coast. The medieval Cairo Geniza manuscripts claim that, at Aden, there were "ships from India and its environs, ships from the land of Zanj and environs, ships from Berbera and Habash and environs, ships from al-Ashhar and al-Qamr and environs."[182] The Trans-Saharan slave trade resulted in the Arabian Peninsula serving as a point of triangulation between Nazrawi communities

---

[180] Ghada Hashem Talhami, "The Zanj Rebellion Reconsidered," in *The International Journal of African Historical Studies* 10.3, 443-461 (1977): 450-451.
[181] John O. Hunwick, "A Region of the Mind: Medieval Arab Views of African Geography and Ethnography and Their Legacy," in *Sudanic Africa* 16, 103-136 (2005): 122.
[182] Roxani Eleni Margariti, *Aden and the Indian Ocean Trade: 150 Years in the Life of a Medieval Arabian Port* (Chapel Hill, NC: The University of North Carolina Press, 2007), 154.

in Northeast Africa and the Swahili Coast. However, there was also direct connections between Zanj and Nazrawi Abyssinia.

Al-Masudi goes on to identify the coast of modern Mozambique as the extremity of the Zanj region: "The furthest end in the Zanj Sea is Kanbalu Island and the country of Sofalah of the Wakwak (سفالة والواق واق), which is in the most remote parts of the Zanj country and Sofalah is cut off from this sea."[183] Sofalah referred generally to the coast of modern Mozambique.[184] Mombasa was another significant port city in the "Zanj" region of the Southeastern African coast. It appears that its inhabitants practiced Islam by the time of Ibn-Battuta's fourteenth-century visit:

> We arrived at the island of Mambasa (منبسى)…a large island that, between it and the coastal land (ارض السواحل) is two days by the sea. It does not have a mainland. Its trees are the banana, the lemon and the citron. They had a fruit called jammun, and it resembles and olive tree, and its fruit pit are like it. It is very sweet. The people of that island do not sow (grain) there, and it is brought to them from the coast (السواحل). The majority of their food is bananas and fish. They are of the Shaf'i denomination. They are devout, virtuous and upright. Their mosques are of wood, expertly administered.[185]

Two centuries earlier, Al-Idrisi visited Mombasa and made no mention of mosques or the presence of Muslims, though he did notice

---

[183] Al-Masudi, *Les Prairies d'Or*, 233.

[184] John Iliffe, *Africans: The History of a Continent* (Cambridge: Cambridge University Press, 1995), 54.

[185] Ibn Battuta, *Voyages d'Ibn Batoutah*, vol. 2, ed. C. Defrémery and B.R. Sanguinetti (Paris: L'Imprimeri Nationale, 1877), 191. See also, Rosemary McConkey and Thomas McErlean, "Mombasa Island: A Maritime Perspective," in *International Journal of Historical Archaeology* 11.2, 99-121 (2007): 105; Mombasa was founded no later than the ninth century, Kai Kresse, *Philosophising in Mombasa: Knowledge, Islam and Intellectual Practice on the Swahili Coast* (Edinburgh: Edinburgh University Press, 2007), 36.

Muslims at Zanzibar. Al-Idirisi only mentioned that the island had no "proper buildings" and that the Zanj inhabitants engaged in iron mining.[186] The lack of Islamic presence strongly indicates that the inhabitants were still largely practitioners of Indigenous religions during Al-Idrisi's visit. Al-Idrisi describes the trade between the Swahili coast and the Arabian Peninsula thusly:

> In the whole of Zendj country the main products are iron and the hides of tigers from Zanzibar...Since they have not pack animals, they themselves carry their loads. They carry their goods on their heads to two towns, Mombassa and Malindi. There they sell and buy. They Zanj have no ships in which they can voyage, but boats land in their country from Oman, as do others that are going to Zabaj (or Djawaga) (Endonezya). These foreigners sell their goods there, and buy the produce of the country. The inhabitants of Zabaj (or Djawaga) call at Zanj in both large and small ships and trade their merchandise with them, as they understand each other's language. The Zendj have at the bottom of their hearts a great respect for the Arabs. For this reason, when they see an Arab, whether a traveler or merchants they prostrate themselves before him. They say in their language: "Welcome son of Yemen." The visitors to this country steal their children, enticing them away by means of giving them fruit. They carry the children from place to place and finally take possession of them and carry them off to their own country.[187]

Al-Masudi goes on to describe the military tensions between the Zanj and the Abyssinians: "The arm of the Nile, of which we have mentioned that is drawn into the Zanj Sea (بحر الزنج), is a canal which

---

[186] McConkey and McErlean, "Mombasa Island," 105.
[187] Al-Idrisi, *Géographie d'Édrisi*, vol. I, ed. P. Amédée Jaubert (Paris: L'imprimerie royale, 1836), 58.

proceeds from the upper mouth of the Zanj and it separates the Zanj land from the frontier land of the Abyssinian races (بلاد اجناس الاحابيش). If they did not have this channel and sandy deserts, the numerous and fierce Zanj would have forced the Abyssinians from their homeland."[188] Al-Masudi describes an interconnected Indian Ocean Trade that included Christian Ag'azi and the Southeastern African coast, which he describes as a religious mixture of Muslim and non-Muslim. This report indicates that Christian Ag'azi encountered the Swahili communities along the Southeastern African coast. Furthermore, the coastal communities in Southern Africa traded and communicated with South-Central African civilizations from the beginning of their development. According to Ibn Battuta's fourteenth-century report of Southeastern Africa, much of the coastal cities were under Islamic dominance while the interior regions practiced traditional religion. As noted above, Ibn Battuta visited a Mombasa that was under Islamic dominance. He gives a similar report regarding the capital of the Kilwa Sultanate:

> We stayed for the night at this island and journeyed by sea to the city of Kilwa (الكلوا), and its name is determined by the proximity of all of it and the homes are assembled and open by the owners. It is a great city of the coast (ساحلية). The majority of its people are Zanj, blackity-black (السوداد المسستحموا اللزنوج). They have cuts on their faces like those on the faces of the Limiyyin of Janada (جناادة من الليميين). One of the merchants mentioned to me that the city of Sofala (سفالة) is half a month's journey from the city of Kilwa, and there is a month's journey between Sofala and Yufi of the country of the Limiyyin (يوفى من بلاد الليميين). They bring gold nuggets from Yufi to Sofala. Kilwa is one of the most beautiful cities and is perfectly built. All of it is wood and its houses are of reeds.

---

[188] Al-Masudi, *Les Prairies d'Or*, 211.

The rains in it are heavy. They are a people who do not lose vigor for Holy War (جهاد), since they have one common mainland with the unbelieving Zanj (كفار الزنوج). Their highest virtue is religion and prayer, for they are Shaf'i in faith (المذهب شافعية وهم والصلاح الدين).[189]

Given Ibn Battuta's observations, it would appear that that the East African coast was predominately Islamic. In the fourteenth century, Ibn Battuta indicated that the Islamic Sultanate of Kilwa participated in trade that connected them to the Asian continent on one hand and the Swahili coast on the other:

> At the time of my entrance, its (Kilwa) sultan was Abu al-Muzaffar Hazan, who is also "Father of Gifts," due to an abundance of gifts and noble deeds. He carried out many raids on the country of the Zanj (ارض الزنوج) and he took its property. And he reserved one fifth of the booty that he took and he seized it as is specified in the Book of Allah the Exalted. And he placed a portion for the relatives in a designated account. And when the nobles came to him, he lavished it to them. And the nobles came to him from Iraq (العراق) and Hijaz (الحجاز) and the like. I saw in his place some nobles from Hijaz, from Muhammad bin Jammaz, Mansur bin Lebidah bin Abu Nemy and Muhammad bin Shemilah bin Abu Nemy. And I met in Mogadishu Tabl bin Kabish bin Jammaz. And he was preparing to come to him. This sultan is exceedingly humble. He eats with the poor and he honors religious people and the nobles.[190]

Though his report does not mention Christians, Ibn Battuta further demonstrates the interconnected world of Southeast Africa and

---

[189] Ibn Battuta, *Voyages*, 192-193.
[190] Ibn Battuta, *Voyages*, 193-194.

the world of the Indian Ocean. Kilwa is said to have been founded by a Persian traveler whose mother was an "Ethiopian" slave.[191] The fourteenth-century traveler Ibn al-Mujawir witnessed the maritime connections between Kilwa along the coast of modern Kenya, Tanzania and Mozambique and Madagascar, the Horn of Africa, the Arabian Peninsula, and the Persian Gulf:

> From Aden to Mogadishu is one monsoon (sailing season), from Mogadishu to Kilwa another monsoon, and from Kilwa to al-Qumr the third. But those people combined the three sailing seasons in one. In the year 626 (1228-9 AD – M.T.) there arrived at Aden a ship from al-Qumr that followed that route: it departed from al-Qumr, steered for Kilwa and anchored at Aden. Their vessels have outriggers because sailing in their seas is difficult due to frequent sea storms and many shallows. When these people's authority weakened, the Barbara (al-Barabir) took over and forced them out. They took control of the country and settled the valley. This area is now built up with palm-leaf cabins, and they were the first to build them in Aden. After them this place became destroyed and remained desolate until the people of Siraf moved there from Sifar, as mentioned previously.[192]

In the midst of the international context of the Horn of Africa, Nazrawis were not only present but at times exerted political hegemony. During the twelfth century, the Horn of Africa was described as being under the leadership of Ag'azi: "Habesha borders on the sea side with the land of Barbria, which comes under the Habesha

---

[191] P.M. Holt, Ann K. S. Lambton, and Bernard Lewis, *The Cambridge History of Islam, Volume 2A: The Indian Sub-Continent, South-East Asia, Africa and the Muslim West* (Cambridge: Cambridge University Press, 1970), 382.
[192] Akshay Sarathi, *Early Maritime Cultures in East Africa and the Western Indian Ocean* (Oxford: Archaeopress Publishing, 2018), 220.

(ثحت طلعة الحبشة ويتصل ايمنا بارض الحبشة على البحر بلاد بربرة وهم), and there are endless villages."[193] According to Al-Idrisi, not only did the "Berbera" region of modern Somalia have contact with Ag'azi but that Ag'azi exercised political authority over Somalia. As Islamic empires continued to emerge throughout the early Solomonic period, they indeed clashed at different times with the Nazrawi Empire of Ag'azi. During the fourteenth century, the Ag'azi King Amda Seyon conquered the Islamic Sulanate of Ifat, which had previously dominated the area of modern Somalia. Of the several people groups reported to have been dominated by Amda Seyon, some included people groups that were situated south of the Ethiopian Empire:

> He sent other battalions who were known as Damot, Säqalt, Gʷändär, and Ḥädya, men on horses and foot, powerful and expertly trained in combat, champions who have no equal in killing, with their commander Bägey-Medr Ṣäga Krestos—he sent them to attack the land of the rebels who resemble the crucifying Jews which are Sämeyn, Wägära, Ṣälämt, and Ṣägädey. Long ago, they were Christians (*krestiyan*), but now they have denied Christ-like the crucifying Jews (*'ähud säqalyan*).[194]

The modern Hadiya people reside in the Southern Nations of Ethiopia which is a region that borders modern Kenya. Solomonic Ag'azi sources indicate that the Hadiya, among many other groups, were incorporated into the Christian army of Amda Seyon. The Nazrawi empire of Ag'azi also traded slaves from another African people group to the south known as the Washlu. The Washlu appealed to the Ag'azi as partners in slave trading because of their willingness to perform castration on slaves in order to create eunuchs, a practice

---

[193] Al-Idrisi, *Kitab al-nuzhat al-mushtaq*, ed. R. Dozy and M.J. De Goeje (Leiden: Brill, 1866), 27.
[194] *The Glorious Victories of 'Amdä Ṣeyon*, ed. Manfred Kropp (Leuven: Secrétariat du SCO, 1994), 11.

that would have been disagreeable to the Ag'azi.¹⁹⁵ Washlu lay further south from the Hadiya people, perhaps even within the borders of modern Kenya.¹⁹⁶ The contact between the Hadiya and the Washlu with the Nazrawi Ag'azi further demonstrate contact with the Urpeh in Southeastern Africa.

Visitors from regions with heavy Christian populations visited the Swahili coast regularly; the possibility of Christians being among these travelers is high. Al-Idrisi also indicated that there was another Nazrawi community that existed at the crossroads of the Indian Ocean Trade—the Socotra archipelago just off the Somalian Cape Guardafui:

> The island of Socotra (سقطري) is an island of vast land and it is renown for the extent of land in it and the multitude of trees…As we have said, along the north and west sides, it falls to the land of Yemen (بلاد اليمن), for it is connected to it and a similar area to it which neighbors it, facing the Zanj region, the city of Malindi and Mombasa (بلاد الزنج مدينة ملندرومنبسه). The majority of the people in the city of Socotra are Christians (اكثر اهل مدينة سوقطره نصاري).¹⁹⁷

Socotra played a long role in commerce and travel between Egypt, Arabia, the Horn of Africa, and the Indian Subcontinent. Cosmas Indicopleustes had already witnessed a Nazrawi community there centuries before Al-Idrisi. It is surprising to hear Al-Idiri's comment that the population was predominately Nazrawi during the twelfth century. However, there were Nazrawis said to have been from Socotra from early Axumite times. The Arian historian Philostorgius reported

---

¹⁹⁵ Fauvelle, *The Golden Rhinoceros*, 213.
¹⁹⁶ Taddesse Tamrat, *Church and State in Ethiopia 1270-1527* (Oxford: Oxford University Press, 1972), 87.
¹⁹⁷ Al-Idrisi, *Kitab al-Nuzhat al-Mushtaq*, ed. Kenelm Digby (Rome: Medici Printing Press, 1591), 26-27.

a missionary named Theophilus the Indian who went from Socotra to the Arabian Peninsula and to Axum and "corrected" some of the practices of the Christians there.[198] Al-Idrisi further described Socotra as a place where surrounding African and Arabian communities seek refuge, including the Ag'azi. If the Ag'azi frequented Socotra during the twelfth century, it is possible that Christianity was introduced through these refugees. Like other Islamic cartographers, Al-Idirisi describes an interconnected Indian Ocean Trade which involved the Southeastern African coast:

> This section consists of the description of a part of the Indian sea and all the islands that are in it, in which people of different races live. In the south of the countries in this section is the rest of the countries of the black kaffirs, and several countries close to the sea. Our intention is to describe all those things with clarity. So we say that the sea is the Indian Sea and on its shore is situated the town of Bedouna, at the extremity of the country of the kaffirs, unbelievers who have no revealed religion, but take standing stones which they anoint with fish oil and to which they prostrate themselves in worship. That high is the stupidity in which these people live and the absurdity of their beliefs. Part of this country obeys the Berber king and the rest the Ethiopian one.[199]

Al-Idirisi goes on to describe other sections of the Somali coast which are the "Zanj" government, such as the port city of Malindi, that he claims is inhabited by practitioners of Indigenous religion.[200] The Bisrat made contact with the Southeastern African coast throughout the Axumite and early Solomonic periods. It is likely that the Bisrat

---

[198] Nathanael J. Andrade, *The Journey of Christianity to India in Late Antiquity: Networks and the Movement of Culture* (Cambridge: Cambridge University Press, 2018), 76.
[199] Al-Idrisi, *Géographie d'Édrisi*, 55.
[200] Al-Idrisi, *Géographie d'Édrisi*, 56.

may have reached the interior kingdoms that later developed through trade with the Swahili coast.

One of the earliest urbanized civilizations in the interior of Southern Africa was the Zhizo community centered at Schroda which was developed during the tenth century. The capital of Schroda developed through the Indian Ocean Trade, as evidenced by the presence of glass beads at Schroda and rhino horns on the Sofala coast of modern Mozambique.[201] Furthermore, the community at Schroda had developed sophisticated gold work which was traded with the Swahili coast and across the Indian Ocean. In the eleventh century, the original inhabitants of Schroda migrated further west into modern Botswana and the Limpopo Valley was dominated by a civilization referred to by archaeologists as K2. Further evidence of Indian Ocean glass beads were not only discovered at K2, but also much further west in modern Botswana and Northern Cape.[202] A third civilization developed in the Limpopo Valley during the early-thirteenth century called Mapungubwe. Also during the mid-thirteenth century, a neighboring civilization of Mapungubwe developed in the Limpopo valley called Thulamela. Like other late Iron Age civilizations in Southern Africa, Thulamela participated in the Indian Ocean Trade, as is evidenced by the presence of Chinese pottery.[203] However, evidence for international trade is much higher in Mapungubwe. Tens of thousands of Indian beads as well as Chinese celadon were discovered at Mapungubwe, along with clay spindles from the Swahili coast.[204] Indian, Chinese, and Arab merchants served as an important connecting point between the emerging city-states of Southern Africa, and the more

---

[201] Thomas N. Huffman, *Mapungubwe: Ancient African Civilisation on the Limpopo* (Johannesburg: Wits University Press, 2005), 14.

[202] Huffman, *Mapungubwe*, 21.

[203] Maryna Steyn, Sidney Miller, Willem C. Nienaber, and Marius Loots, "Late Iron Age Gold Burials from Thulamela (Pafuri Region, Kruger National Park)," in *The South African Archaeological Bulletin*, 53.168, 73-85 (1998): 76.

[204] Huffman, *Mapungubwe*, 52-4.

ancient civilizations in Northeastern Africa in which Christianity had a long history. For example, the first documented arrival of a Chinese person in Africa was an eighth-century traveler named Du Huan who came to Nubia and Axum and noted the Christian presence in these regions.[205]

Further north from the Limpopo Valley, another civilization developed beginning in the eleventh century that has been known as Great Zimbabwe. Likely due to the decrease of Mapungubwe in the fourteenth century, this century represented the zenith of Great Zimbabwe, most vividly depicted in the construction of an enormous city lined with massive stone-walled buildings.[206] The ascendance of Great Zimbabwe during the fourteenth century as the dominant entity of South-Central Africa corresponded to the increase of gold production and trade in the Zimbabwean plateau. South-Central African kingdoms developed through trade and contact with the Swahili communities.[207] The Kilwa Sultanate along the Swahili coast maintained strong control of the interior gold trade with Mapungubwe and Great Zimbabwe that also connected to the Asian continent.[208] There is a strong probability that among the inter-religious travelers that the merchants of Mapungubwe and Great Zimbabwe interacted with at Mombasa, Kilwa, and Sofala, that Nazrawis would have been among them.

---

[205] Wolbert G.C. Smidt, "A Chinese in the Nubian and Abyssinian Kingdoms (8th Century)," *Chroniques yéménites* 9 (2001): 17-28. Du Huan refers to Axum (Ethiopia) as "Laobosa", likely a Sinicization of Al-Habasha (Abyssinia).

[206] Martin Hall and Rebecca Stefoff, *Great Zimbabwe* (Oxford: Oxford University Press, 2006), 26.

[207] Innocent Pikirayi, "The Demise of Great Zimbabwe, AD 1420-1550: An Environmental Re-Appraisal," in *Cities in the World, 1500-2000*, ed. Adrian Green and Roger Leech, 31-48 (New York, NY: Routledge, 2017), 37.

[208] Jeffrey Fleisher, Paul Lane, Adria LaViolette, Mark Horton, Edward Pollard, Eréndira Quintana Morales, Thomas Vernet, Annalisa Christie, and Stephanie Wynne-Jones, "When Did the Swahili Become Maritime?" in *American Anthropologist* 117.1, 100-115 (2015): 103.

This brief survey of Axumite and Solomonic-era sources demonstrates that the earliest urbanized civilizations in the Southern portion of the African continent developed largely through an international trade that connected them to various nations, including African Nazrawi regions such as Kemet and Ag'azi. That is to say, Africans in the South and Southeastern portions of the continent had their first interaction with the Urpeh through the African Urpeh of the North and Northeastern portions of the continent. The implications of these facts are difficult to overestimate. The common narrative for Southern and Southeastern African history and its connection to the Urpeh is that Christianity was introduced through European missionaries and colonists. European colonialism or missionary intervention were unnecessary for the proclamation of the Bisrat on the African continent; Tilli was already spreading the Bisrat through Africans long before colonialism. Indeed, the marginalization of ancient African Nazrawis by European Christendom limited the ability of African Nazrawis to spread the Bisrat across the continent. It is an unfortunate reality that the European Christian contacts that began in the fifteenth century are the only remnants of a religion resembling Christianity whose material evidence and heritage communities survive in the present. There is no extant evidence for the Southeastern African contacts with the Northeastern African Urpeh to have resulted in a sustained Nazrawi community in Southeastern Africa during the Axumite or Solomonic periods. However, what is clear and beyond question is that Southeastern Africans made regular contact with Northeastern African Nazrawis. This means that the first time that the residents of Southeastern Africa heard the name of Yeshua, it was from His African followers in places like Kemet, Ag'azi, and Socotra.[209] The Bisrat was the dominant haymanot across

---

[209] It is also probable that civilizations along the Swahili coast would have come into contact with Nazrawis from the Arabian Peninsula, Mesopotamia, Europe, and the Indian Sub-Continent. This is an area that merits further research.

Northern and Eastern Africa. The Urpeh was also established and present in Central and Western Africa long before European colonialism. The earliest urbanized civilizations in Southeastern Africa also connected with the Urpeh long before the arrival of Europeans, and this contact was through African Nazrawis.

Biblical/Social Justice as a Foundation of the Kingdom of God

Kenneth J. Reid

Introduction

Evangelicals and the wider Christian community have been debating the relationship between social justice and the Gospel over the last twenty years. The debate grows due to the deaths of unarmed African American citizens, a rise in nationalism over the past twenty years that culminated in the election of Donald J. Trump, and the reappearance of blatant racism. These events have brought about the need for a fresh discussion about theology and justice.[210] Yet, some evangelicals have contended that social justice is not consistent with the Gospel.[211]

---

[210] The deaths of unarmed African Americans include Philando Castile, Tamir Rice, and Eric Garner. Ahmaud Arbery, Breonna Taylor, and George Floyd were killed in 2020.

[211] See The Statement on Social Justice and the Gospel," assessed October 21, 2021, https://statementonsocialjustice.com/. Voddie Baucham presents a difference between biblical justice and social justice. He summarizes the Critical Social Justice view, stating that it "assumes that the world is divided between the oppressors and the oppressed." The biblical justice view, summarized on pages 237-38, is not a "definitional" component of the gospel. See Voddie T. Baucham, Jr., *Fault Lines: The Social Justice Movement and Evangelicalism's Looming Catastrophe* (Washington, DC: Salem Books, 2021), 6, 237-39; See also Owen Strachan, *Christianity and Wokeness: How the Social Justice Movement is Hijacking the Gospel – and the Way to Stop It* (Washington, D.C: Salem Books, 2021).

Is social justice incompatible with the Gospel? This is a critical question in our conversation that deals with biblical authority, sexism, racism, and other injustices. Does the Bible support social justice? The implications of this question are enormous. If the Gospel is not related in any way to social justice, then many preachers and theologians are making a critical mistake and departing from Christ's command to share the Gospel. However, if the Gospel is related to social justice, then many evangelicals have neglected a part of Jesus's mission for the church.

The answer to the above question requires a clear definition of both "Gospel" and "social justice."[212] The Gospel that we preach is grounded in 1 Corinthians 15:1-4:

> Now, brothers and sisters, I want to remind you of the gospel I preached to you, which you received and on which you have taken your stand. ² By this Gospel you are saved, if you hold firmly to the word I preached to you. Otherwise, you have believed in vain. ³ For what I received I passed on to you as of first importance: that Christ died for our sins according to the Scriptures, ⁴ that he was buried, that he was raised on the third day according to the Scriptures.

While the Gospel is not less than this, is there more? When Jesus talks about the good news of the kingdom, is he only referring to the evangelistic message that is based on 1 Corinthians 15:1-4? What is the relationship between the Gospel and the two greatest commandments? Because of the intensity of the debate, a definition of social justice is critical. After examining the biblical evidence, Kevin DeYoung and Greg Gilbert summarize that doing justice is about fairness. Kevin DeYoung presents a helpful definition of social justice

---

[212] Many theologians distinguish between biblical justice and social justice. For the purposes of this paper, I will use the term social justice. See my definition of social justice below.

that is grounded in Scripture: "treating people equitably, working for systems and structures that are fair, and looking out for the weak and the vulnerable."[213] If the Gospel is not limited to the evangelistic message, how broad is the Gospel? I submit that the kingdom and Gospel are vitally important theological themes and that our view of the kingdom will inform our theology of social justice.

This paper will explore the relationship between the Gospel and the kingdom of God. I contend that justice is a key characteristic of the kingdom of God, and the African American preaching tradition uses the reality of God's kingdom to encourage African Americans and to provide hope in the face of oppression. This paper will present a preliminary definition of the kingdom of God, and will summarize the classical Protestant liberal, liberation theological, and evangelical views of the kingdom. Finally, the paper will discuss implications for social justice and the kingdom in light of these definitions.

Definition and Views of the Kingdom of God

John the Baptist and Jesus repeat the saying, "Repent for the Kingdom of heaven has come near" (Matt 3:2; 4:17). Jesus performs miracles as a sign of the kingdom. He teaches parables that point to aspects of the kingdom, and he teaches ethics of the kingdom. But what is the kingdom? What is the nature of the kingdom? George Eldon Ladd defined the kingdom as the reign or rule of God.[214] This reign is intimately connected with Jesus Christ as king and his advent.

The Classical Protestant liberal tradition places an important emphasis on the kingdom of God. In the tradition of Albrecht Ritschl

---

[213] Kevin DeYoung, "Is Social Justice a Gospel Issue?," The Gospel Coalition, accessed November 12, 2018, https://www.thegospelcoalition.org/blogs/kevin-deyoung/social-justice-gospel-issue/. My summary of the definition is that people would be treated equitably, working for systems and structures that are fair, and caring for the weak, vulnerable, and the marginalized in the church and society.

[214] George Eldon Ladd, *The Presence of the Future: The Eschatology of Biblical Realism* (Grand Rapids, MI: Eerdmans, 1974), 148.

and Adolf Von Harnack, the kingdom is understood as "the fatherhood of God and the brotherhood of man with the kingdom expressed as the rule of the holy God in the hearts of individuals."[215] Albert Schweitzer contends that the kingdom definition proposed by the Ritschlian School is flawed. Instead, he argues that the kingdom is apocalyptic, would come suddenly. However, he also argues that Jesus was disappointed because the kingdom did not come.[216] Thus, one view correctly envisions the kingdom as an apocalyptic event but denies that it will occur in the future. The other view defines the kingdom solely in ethical terms.

Liberation Theology envisions the kingdom primarily in terms of liberation. The kingdom of God comes as the oppressed are liberated. Gustavo Gutierrez presents a helpful summary of the kingdom as liberation and justice. He states:

> If we believe that the Kingdom of God is a gift which is received in history, and if we believe, as the eschatological promises—so charged with human and historical content—indicate to us, that the Kingdom of God necessarily implies the reestablishment of justice in this world, then we must believe that Christ says that the poor are blessed because the Kingdom

---

[215] Michael Bird, *Evangelical Theology, Second Edition*, 312. Bird cites Adolf Von Harnack, *What Is Christianity?* (New York: Harper & Row, 1957). Abrecht Ritschl states, "The good in the Christian sense is the Kingdom of God, in other words the uninterrupted reciprocation of action springing from the motive of love–a Kingdom in which all are knit together in union with every one who can show the marks of a neighbor; further, it is that union of men in which all goods are appropriated in their proper subordination to the highest good," (Albrecht Ritschl, *The Christian Doctrine of Justification and Reconciliation* [Edinburgh: T & T Clark, 1902]. 334-35).

[216] "Schweitzer's interpretation involved three elements which must not be confused: (a) Apocalyptic is an essential element in Jesus' message of the Kingdom. (b) Jesus' message is exclusively eschatological. In no sense of the word could the Kingdom be interpreted as a present spiritual reality. It is the apocalyptic age to come. (c) Jesus thought that the Kingdom would come at once in his lifetime. These three points must be kept in mind as we continue our survey of criticism, for one may agree with Schweitzer in part if not altogether." (Ladd, *The Presence of the Future*, 5.)

of God has begun: 'The time has come; the Kingdom of God is upon you (Mark 1:15).' In other words, the elimination of the exploitation and poverty that prevent the poor from being fully human has begun; a Kingdom of justice which goes even beyond what they could have hoped for has begun. They are blessed because the coming of the Kingdom will put an end to their poverty by creating a world of fellowship. They are blessed because the Messiah will open the eyes of the blind and will give bread to the hungry. Situated in a prophetic perspective, the text in Luke uses the term poor in the tradition of the first major line of thought we have studied: poverty is an evil and therefore incompatible with the Kingdom of God, which has come in its fullness into history and embraces the totality of human existence.[217]

Gutierrez, while addressing the problem of systemic poverty in his context, envisions the kingdom of God as the elimination of poverty and the presence of social justice in this present age. He argues that the kingdom comes in the experience of material needs being met because poverty is antithetical to the kingdom of God. The emphasis on justice in the present as a predominant characteristic of the kingdom is also present in James Cone's theology. Cone defines the kingdom as the liberating work of the Black Jesus. In response to systemic racism, Cone envisions the kingdom as God's work of liberation today for the Black community.[218] J. Deotis Roberts describes the present and the future aspects of the kingdom, with an emphasis on God's will in action. He comments, "The kingdom is present wherever the will of God is being done, individually and socially in ethics and faith." He continues,

---

[217] Gustavo Gutierrez, *A Theology of Liberation: History, Politics, and Salvation*, trans. Caridad Inda and John Eagleson, Revised edition (Maryknoll, NY: Orbis Books, 1988), 170–71.
[218] James H. Cone, *A Black Theology of Liberation: The C. Eric Lincoln Series in Black Religion* (Philadelphia, PA: J.B. Lippincott Company, 1970), 222.

> My theology considers the kingdom of God (in all times and places) as well as heaven-future. Black theology interprets what happens now and it is based upon the entire Bible: social justice, the ministry of Jesus, the witness of the people of God, and not the Book of Revelation only.[219]

For Cone and Roberts, Black theology's view of the kingdom highlights God's work of deliverance from oppression and the reality of political and social justice in the present age. All three (with Gutierrez) argue that a common feature of Latin American and Black liberation theology from its foundations is its emphasis on the present work of liberation and justice as a primary characteristic of God's kingdom in the present.

Evangelical theologies of the kingdom have been expressed in the Reformed/Covenant and Dispensational traditions. These conversations typically focus on the millennial kingdom as the determining aspect of the definition of the kingdom. In the millennium debate, Reformed/Covenant theologians emphasize the spiritual nature of the kingdom—the kingdom is present entirely in the church age, generally referred to as amillennialism.[220] In contrast, dispensational theologians, especially the classical and revised dispensational approaches, tend to restrict their definition of the kingdom of God to the pre-tribulation millennial kingdom.[221] Both classical and revised Dispensationalism hold to a pre-tribulation rapture, a seven-year tribulation period, followed by Jesus's reign for one thousand

---

[219] J. Deotis Roberts, "Dignity and Destiny: Black Reflections on Eschatology," in *The Cambridge Companion to Black Theology*, eds. Dwight N. Hopkins and Edward P. Antonio (Cambridge, UK: Cambridge University Press, 2012), 219.

[220] Louis Berkhof, *Systematic Theology* (Grand Rapids, MI: Eerdmans, 1996), 2:708-19. Anthony A. Hoekema, *The Bible and the Future*, 0 edition (Eerdmans, 1994), 223–38.

[221] For a helpful summary, see Craig Alan Blaising and Darrell L. Bock, *Progressive Dispensationalism* (Grand Rapids, MI: Baker Publishing Group, 1993), 30–31, 39–48.

years on the Davidic throne from a reconstituted Israel in the Promised Land.

Theological approaches from within evangelicalism have been under some revisions over the last thirty years. Both theologies have evolved, so that new covenant theology and progressive dispensationalism are much closer in their theology of the kingdom. While progressive dispensationalism and new covenant theologies have nuances, a common feature is inaugurated eschatology.[222] Some features of the kingdom are present today because Jesus was present; the presence of Jesus as king means that the kingdom is present with him and, as the risen and exalted king, he has given his Spirit to his church. However, there is an aspect of the kingdom that has not yet occurred. Jesus Christ is not yet ruling and all creation has not been restored. All the promises of the kingdom of God have not been fulfilled. This "not yet" aspect of the kingdom awaits fulfillment in the future new created order.

Note two common features in these definitions. The focus of liberation theology articulates the kingdom in terms of liberation from oppression, though not exclusively. Protestant liberalism in its classical form tends to either emphasize the kingdom as fully present or the kingdom as absent. In addition, classical Protestant liberalism does not envision a supernatural fulfillment of Scripture that God brings to fruition in Jesus Christ. Contemporary approaches within evangelicalism are coalescing into an already-not-yet paradigm. Yet while many evangelical approaches emphasize renewal, many do not explain the already aspect of the kingdom in terms of justice. The next section contributes to that discourse.

---

[222] Russell Moore, *The Kingdom of Christ: The New Evangelical Perspective* (Wheaton, IL: Crossway, 2004), 52–80.

African American Preachers Talk Social Justice and the Kingdom of God

This section of the paper will introduce themes from some speakers and preachers of historic African American churches. This brief review of speeches and sermons from Sojourner Truth, Gardner Taylor, Joseph Harrison Jackson, and Dr. Martin Luther King, Jr. will present important perspectives about the kingdom of God.

Sojourner Truth

Sojourner Truth (1797-1883) was a preacher and an advocate for freedom and women's rights in the nineteenth century. She spoke about the kingdom of God in terms of eschatological judgment. In her speech to a white audience at Framingham, MA in 1854, she contrasted the destinies of white people and Black people. Since Black people suffered persecution in slavery, justice would come to them because the promises of Scripture are for Black people. Thus, they will enjoy the peace and joy in God's kingdom, where the slaveholders and bloodhounds (as instruments that enforced slavery) would not enter into his kingdom. Since her white audience did not suffer from these tribulations, this promise does not apply to them.[223] Sojourner Truth emphasized that God would bring his justice in heaven to the enslaved who suffered. Her messages proclaimed that the kingdom of God will bring about the restoration of Black people. She also spoke later the same year in Battle Creek, Michigan at the Proceedings of the Friends of Human Progress. In her response to acts of dehumanization of African Americans and upon being called an animal, she stated the following as she affirmed her humanity, as well as that of other African Americans: "But I believes in de [the] next world. When we gets up yonder we shall have all of dem [them]

---

[223] Suzanne P. Fitch and Roseann Mandziuk, *Sojourner Truth as Orator: Wit, Story, and Song* (Westport, CT: Greenwood, 1997), 64.

rights 'stored [restored] to us again–all dat [that] love what I'se [I have] lost–all goin to be 'stored [restored] to me 'gain [again]. Oh! How good God is. [*sic.*]"[224]

Sojourner Truth also spoke at the State Sabbath School in Battle Creek, Michigan on June 3, 1863. It was recorded by the National Anti-Slavery Standard on July 11, 1863, page 4.

> Children," she said, "who made your skin white? Was it not God? Who made mine black? Was it not the same God? Am I to blame, therefore, because my skin is black? Does it not cast a reproach on our Maker to despise a part of his children because he has been pleased to give them black skin? Indeed, children, it does; and your teachers ought to tell you so, and root up, if possible, the great sin of prejudice against color from your minds. While Sabbath-school teachers know of this great sin, and not only do not teach their pupils that it is a sin, but too often indulge in it themselves, can they expect God to bless them or the children? Does not God love colored children as well as white children? And did not the same Savior die to save the one as well as the other? If so, white children must know that if they go to heaven, they must go there without their prejudice against color, for in heaven black and white are one in the love of Jesus. Now, children, remember what Sojourner Truth has told you, and thus get rid of your prejudice and learn to love colored children, that you may be all the children of your Father who is in Heaven.[225]

The person who recorded the speech remarked that this was one of the most impactful anti-slavery messages that was delivered in Battle Creek; there was such conviction in the audience that many eyes were

---
[224] Ibid., 117.
[225] Ibid., 119.

filled with tears. The audience's heart or attitude determined if they were near or far from the kingdom.[226] Sojourner Truth grounds the dignity and equality of people on God's creation and his love. If God loves all people, then they too must love all people without prejudice if they are to get into heaven. Her consistent approach is that those who act justly in the present age will enter heaven and live in God's kingdom.

Gardner Taylor

Gardner Taylor (1918-2015) pastored at Concord Baptist Church of Christ in Brooklyn, New York for forty-two years. Many of his manuscripts are stored in the Woodruff Library at the Atlanta University Center. One sermon that he preached in December 1958 is called "The Kingdom Tarries Yet." His main text is Revelation 11:15; he demonstrated that the kingdom had not come due to certain signs.[227] He said,

> But it [the kingdom] has not happened. Sin still stalks angrily through the land. Death's sting still freezes our mortal frames. Man's inhumanity to man seems to grow more deadly as our technical skills of destruction advance. We seem bent on universal suicide with all our gleaming nuclear instruments of destruction.

He also referred to the tragedy of eighty-seven children who died in a fire in Chicago. The absence of the kingdom is demonstrated by tragedies and the reign of death and sin in the world. However, he explained that our preparation for the kingdom depends on our readiness, expressed in how we live. He stated that "we ought to get ourselves ready for the coming of God's Kingdom in our midst by

---

[226] Ibid., 120.
[227] The sermon manuscript is archived at Atlanta University Center Archives, Gardner Taylor collection, Box 21 Folder 22.

living on the things of the Spirit. The New Testament says, 'The Kingdom of God is not meat and drink, but peace and righteousness.'" Taylor emphasized the human dimension, that our role is to get ready by living ethically and with justice today, but he also stressed the eschatological dimension in this sermon. God's kingdom will come when he is ready. He commented,

> For be sure the rule of God is coming to pass. This promise of a kingdom of righteousness which shall appear in our midst is not Fable. This hope of a Kingdom of Truth whose reign shall be without boundary and without border is no figment of the imagination. God has spoken. We can prepare for the King's coming, but we cannot force God's hand.

Joseph Harrison Jackson

Joseph Harrison Jackson (1900-1990) was pastor of Olivet Baptist Church and became the president of the National Baptist Convention in 1953. He led the convention for almost thirty years. He was president when the members of the National Baptist Convention began the Progressive National Baptist Convention in 1961. The split of the convention reflected different views of the strategies in the civil rights movement. Simmons and Thomas note Jackson favored appealing to the courts as an instrument of change over nonviolent civil disobedience. He believed that this strategy was not consistent with the Gospel.[228]

Rev. Jackson delivered the sermon called "Great God Our King" on May 12, 1950, before the closing meeting of the Southern Baptist Convention at Chicago stadium. Rev. Jackson considered the consequences that should occur if God is truly king. In his introduction, he

---

[228] Martha Simmons and Frank A. Thomas, eds., *Preaching with Sacred Fire: An Anthology of African American Sermons, 1750 to the Present* (New York: W. W. Norton & Company, 2010), 546.

describes the New Jerusalem in the New Earth as a place that is characterized by the removal of pride and lust and as a place that would flourish with peace and love.[229] In the first movement of the sermon, he titles it – Since God is our King, We Must Hold a Most Exalted View of the World in which We Live and Have a Most Sacred Regard for All of God's Human Creatures. He advocates for the dignity of all people, which must result in freedom and equality for all.[230]

The second part is titled – God Is Our King, Therefore the Government of the World Is in His Hands. God holds earthly powers accountable for their actions, though they may rule for a while. He states,

> By His patience, long suffering and boundless mercy, God may permit the wrong to reign on thrones of power for a season, and will bless the undeserving, give the light of the sun to the wretched and the weak, and cause the rain to fall on the just and the unjust, but do not mistake patience for poverty of strength and wisdom. God still holds the government of the world in His hand. Dictators may endure for decades, the masters of conflict may reign for years, and the lords of war may wear their well plumed crowns of victory, but only for a while. For at His appointed time, God will send judgment against the unjust and wreak Divine vengeance on the wicked oppressors of truth and righteousness.

> Divine judgment, then, becomes a serious and dangerous fact. Justice cannot and will not be eternally destroyed, if God is our King. The biased decision of a brined judge is not the last word. The verdict of unjust juries will not always stand, for there is a Supreme Court of Eternal Righteousness to which every weary soul may take its appeal. For it is written that

---

[229] Ibid., 552.
[230] Ibid., 555.

"The Judge of all the earth will be right." Look abroad on the wide field of human history and you will see signs of the judgment of truth, of Righteousness and of God.[231]

Thus, God as king requires dignity, freedom, and equality. God as king will judge governments for the wickedness and injustice that they perpetrate.

The third movement in the sermon is titled–If God Is Our King, Those Who Struggle for Righteousness and Truth, Struggle on the Side of the Victorious Forces of the Universe. Rev. Jackson gave the message of hope that God's kingdom will prevail. And that victory will be expressed in tangible ways: the ending of wars, the presence of justice, and peace (shalom) on earth. Victory comes because of the resurrection. Slaves in previous generations were comforted by the promises of God's victory.

Rev. Jackson describes the effect of God's kingdom. In God's kingdom, all people have dignity and can live in the freedom that will allow for human flourishing. God's kingdom brings true justice despite the unjust practices of earthly government, and it brings about victory and shalom. The aspects of the kingdom for this age point to the reality of dignity and equality for all people. His kingdom will come in the future when God judges wickedness and ushers in the new age of justice and peace.

Dr. Martin Luther King, Jr.

Dr. Martin Luther King, Jr. (1929-1968) was perhaps the preacher par excellence who preaches for justice, dealing with ethics while appealing to the prophetic biblical tradition. A few of his messages follow in which his view of the kingdom of God has an impact on his ministry and the social realities of his day.

---

[231] Ibid., 557.

In one sermon, he connected the plight of Black Americans with the hope of God's kingdom. He remarked in his Nobel Prize Acceptance Speech (1964):

> I have the audacity to believe that peoples everywhere can have three meals a day for their bodies, education and culture for their minds, and dignity, equality and freedom for their spirits. I believe that what self-centered men have torn down men other-centered can build up. I still believe that one day mankind will bow before the altars of God and be crowned triumphant over war and bloodshed, and nonviolent redemptive goodwill will proclaim the rule of the land. "And the lion and the lamb shall lie down together and every man shall sit under his own vine and fig tree and none shall be afraid." I still believe that we shall overcome.[232]

Dr. King quoted Isaiah 65, which is a common text depicting the messianic kingdom. Here, he explained that the kingdom promises led to specific acts of justice.

Dr. King preached "Our God is Marching On!" after the march from Selma to Montgomery in 1965. The end of the speech illustrates the glory of the coming Lord in his kingdom, which results in the coming of justice. Dr. King argued that the lie of segregation and prejudice cannot live in light of God's movement. Quoting the Battle Hymn of the Republic, he portrayed God's judgment in the final portions of his speech. This sermon states that God's coming in his kingdom will bring forth truth and justice.[233] Though many have suffered, justice will reign in the end.

Dr. King explicitly tied justice to the kingdom in his sermon called the "Acceptable Year of the Lord" (also named "Guidelines for a

---

[232] Martin Luther King, Jr., *A Testament of Hope: The Essential Writings and Speeches*, ed. James M. Washington, Reprint edition. (San Francisco: HarperOne, 2003), 226.
[233] Ibid., 230.

Constructive Church") in 1966.[234] The text for this sermon is in Isaiah 61. Jesus quotes this passage and proclaims that his ministry fulfills this passage. Dr. King's message applied the text to his audience's experience of disenfranchisement.[235] He commented, "You know the acceptable year of the Lord is the year that is acceptable to God because it fulfills the demands of his kingdom. Some people reading this passage feel that it's talking about some period beyond history, but I say to you this morning that the acceptable year of God can be this year."[236] Dr. King continues to juxtapose the contemporary situation with the prophetic vision of Scripture. Some key phrases demonstrate this prophetic vision and justice:

> The acceptable year of the Lord is any year when men decide to do right.... The acceptable year of the Lord is that year when people in Alabama will stop killing civil rights workers and people who are simply engaged in the process of seeking their constitutional rights....The acceptable year of the Lord is that year when men will keep their theology abreast with their technology.... The acceptable year of the Lord is that year when all of the leaders of the world will sit down at the conference table and realize that unless mankind puts an end to war, war will put an end to mankind.... The acceptable year of the Lord is that year when men will allow justice to roll down like waters, and righteousness like a mighty stream. The acceptable year of the Lord is that year when we will send to Congress and to the state houses of our nation men who will do justly, who will love mercy and who will walk humbly with their God.... The acceptable year of the Lord is that year when men will do unto others as they will have others do unto

---

[234] Much of this section is from Richard Lischer, *The Preacher King: Martin Luther King, Jr. and the Word That Moved America* (New York: Oxford University Press, 1995), 234–36.
[235] Ibid., 235. The following manuscript adds "And the church is called to preach it."
[236] Ibid.

themselves.... The acceptable year of the Lord is that year when men discover that out of one blood God made all men to dwell upon the face of the earth.... These are our guidelines, and if we will only follow the guidelines, we will be ready for God's kingdom, and we will be doing what God's church is called to do. We won't be a little social club. We won't be a little entertainment center. But we'll be about the serious business of bringing God's kingdom to this earth.[237]

Dr. King integrated personal ethics and acts of social/community justice with the promises in Scripture and the coming kingdom. He proclaimed that the church has kingdom work to do. In this way, Dr. King presented his theology of an already-not-yet vision of the kingdom, one that comes on earth by doing justice, yet looks forward to the future reign of our Lord Jesus.

Synthesis and Implications for Justice and the Kingdom

The Protestant liberal tradition describes the kingdom in solely ethical terms in the current age. Liberation theologians primarily emphasize that the kingdom comes in the current age as the oppressed are liberated. Both evangelical theologies and the historic Black preaching tradition will focus on the present and future aspects of the kingdom.

Sojourner Truth, Gardner Taylor, Joseph Jackson, and Dr. Martin Luther King, Jr. collectively focus on the present and future aspects of God's kingdom. Sojourner Truth describes the future aspect of God's kingdom in heaven while preaching that the present acts of justice and love today will make one worthy of entering into the future kingdom in heaven. Similarly, Gardner Taylor preached about the

---

[237] Martin Luther King Jr., *A Knock at Midnight: Inspiration from the Great Sermons of Reverend Martin Luther King, Jr.*, ed. Peter Holloran and Clayborne Carson (New York, NY: Warner Books, 1998), 112–14.

eschatological dimension of the kingdom as our hope while stating that we demonstrate our readiness for the kingdom through our acts of peace and righteousness. He argues that the kingdom is not present because of people's cruelty to each other. Joseph Jackson emphasizes that God's kingdom is present when there is respect for human dignity and the reality of freedom and justice for all people. His hope for the future is God's victory through the resurrection that will bring about justice and shalom. All of the above agree that the kingdom has future orientation but acts of justice in the present point to one's destiny in the kingdom.

Dr. King's messages display that the kingdom's presence should be expected today, and the kingdom of God is evident when war ceases, the killing of those who are fighting for their constitutional rights will stop, and that justice will prevail in this country. In light of Jesus's commands, the character of God, and the reality that all humanity is made in God's image, these Black preachers contribute to the theology of the kingdom by naming acts of justice as a part of that kingdom. Dr. King preached both the hope for the future and the need for kingdom expression in the church. Dr. King emphasized that the kingdom is not primarily future-oriented, but it is expressed in this present age by addressing the contemporary issues of injustice.

A common feature of these preachers is that kingdom is present when there is conformity with Jesus' ethical standards, the prophetic call for justice, and that acts of justice demonstrate one's readiness to enter the future kingdom. Whether one emphasizes a focus on the present or future kingdom, or some combination, all envision justice as intimately connected with kingdom. By recognizing God as king and looking to the already-not-yet aspect of God's kingdom, these preachers highlight the importance of justice and kingdom. They preached eschatologically that the kingdom will bring about shalom because of Christ's victory in the resurrection, the expectation of heavenly reward, and the coming of the New Jerusalem. Yet in the present age, believers should treat one another justly as a sign of the "already" aspect of the kingdom.

Conclusion

This paper has surveyed the different views of social justice in relation to the kingdom of God. It has presented past Black preacher exemplars to demonstrate how they discussed the kingdom of God in light of their battle against injustice.

Creativity, Collaboration, and Improvisation in Christian Systematic Theology

Preston Boone

"Oftentimes, when we come into environments like this to play creative improvised music, you know, someone uses the word 'jazz' and then everyone in the room becomes a f@*%ing Fulbright scholar. And that's cool, you know, but that has nothing to do with where this music's power rests."

—*Chief Xian aTunde Adjuah*[238]

"Jesus spoke of knowledge in terms of intercourse."[239]

—*Carl F. Ellis, Jr.*

---

[238] Christian Scott aTunde Adjuah, "X. Adjuah [I Own the Night]," recorded March 2020, with Elena Pinderhughes, Lawrence Fields, Kris Funn, Weedie Braimah, and Corey Fonville, track 1 on *Axiom*, Stretch Music/Ropeadope, Mp3.

[239] Carl F. Ellis Jr. and Amisho Baraka, *Free at Last? The Gospel in the African American Experience* (Downers Grove, IL: IVP, 2020), 177.

Introduction

In this paper, I will attempt to populate select categories of systematic theology with a hermeneutic shaped by creative improvised music. I will demonstrate ways in which aspects, elements, and customs of the music commonly known as jazz can help articulate classic and timeless truths in fresh new ways. In this way, I hope to sketch the broad contours of what could be called a creative improvised theology. In other words, how can musical concepts illustrate or help illuminate distinctly Christian theological truths? In particular, how can creative improvised music[240] help us in a systematic exploration of the Bisrat—God entering human history to work salvation for humans ahead of history's end?

Three characteristics of creative improvised music will frame my discussion. This music, birthed by African Americans,[241] is creative, collaborative, and improvisational. I will attempt to show how these characteristics can express the creative, collaborative, and improvisational facets of God's self-revelation in Christ, in Scripture, and in creation. My primary theological tools will be analogy and biblical exegesis.

Notes on Discipline and Terminology

I confess here at the outset that I am not a musician. I study theology and this is a theological paper. This creates a real tension, as my research findings reveal an emphasis on praxis over theory. So, I invite musicians as well as theologians to engage honestly with the ideas herein, towards an edifying interdisciplinary conversation.

---

[240] The musical genre historically and traditionally known as 'jazz' will here be designated as 'creative improvised music.' More on this below.

[241] "Most jazz scholars readily concede that jazz, and bebop by extension, originated with African Americans. It was not, however, to remain a domain dominated solely by blacks." Bradley K. Broadhead, *Jazz and Christian Freedom: Improvising against the Grain of the West* (Eugene, OR: Pickwick Publications, 2018), 120

Also, a note about terminology is in order. In 2011, noted multi-instrumentalist, vocalist, composer, producer, arranger, essayist, and social activist Nicholas Payton became the center of a heated discussion about the propriety of the term "jazz." For Payton and others, "jazz" is a racialized label imposed by whites to market music birthed and developed by Black Americans. Thus, "[the term 'jazz' is] not a communal language, it's a capitalist one."[242] He begins his essay, "Black American Music and the Jazz Tradition" by writing,

> There is no such thing as jazz, and any idea of what that might be is false. It's impossible to build a tradition upon something that was never designed to be a true expression of a community. The very existence of jazz is predicated upon a lie, just like racism.

As a corrective, Payton reframes "jazz" as "Black American Music," to denote a tradition that transcends genres and is based in cultural lineage.[243] While the conversation does not end with Payton, I have chosen to avoid the term "jazz" in this paper outside of quotations and citations of original sources. Instead, the musical genre historically and traditionally known as "jazz" will be designated as "creative improvised music," or CIM for short. Three characteristics of CIM will frame my discussion. This music, birthed by African Americans,[244] is creative, collaborative, and improvisational. I will attempt to show how these characteristics can express the creative, collaborative, and improvisational facets of God's self-revelation in

---

[242] Nicholas Payton, "Black American Music and the Jazz Tradition," https://nicholaspayton.com/black-american-music-and-the-jazz-tradition/ (accessed October 16, 2021).
[243] Payton, "Black American Music and the Jazz Tradition."
[244] "Most jazz scholars readily concede that jazz, and bebop by extension, originated with African Americans. It was not, however, to remain a domain dominated solely by blacks." Bradley K. Broadhead, *Jazz and Christian Freedom: Improvising against the Grain of the West* (Eugene, OR: Pickwick Publications, 2018), 120

Christ, in Scripture, and in creation. My primary theological tools will be analogy and biblical exegesis.

Many able scholars have written on this subject, and I enter the conversation with fear and trembling. Thus, I begin with a brief survey of important and/or recent works by Carl Ellis, Jr., Jeremy Begbie, and Bradley K. Broadhead on the topic of theology and improvised music.

Carl Ellis, Jr.: "Jazz Theology"

To date, the greatest synthesis of African American culture and history, creative improvised music, and Christian theology is found in Carl Ellis, Jr.'s *Free at Last? The Gospel in the African American Experience.* In that text, beginning in Chapter 12, Ellis distinguishes "two approaches to music, the formal [associated with 'classical'] and the dynamic [i.e., 'jazz']."[245] He then analogizes from music to theology, which can also "be approached as formal or dynamic."[246] For Ellis, "jazz theology" fits inside a powerful and distinctly African American "soul dynamic" of theology and culture. Whereas the classical approach to theology is systematic, "jazz theology" is concerned "with the hurts of oppressed people."[247] Whereas classical theology examines the acts of God in salvation history, jazz theology appropriates God's deliverance for the contemporary life of the believer.[248] While classical theology emphasizes God's eternal oneness, jazz theology focuses on "the diversity, freedom and eternal freshness of God."[249] Ellis even claims that, "[w]ithin the dynamic of his eternal will, [*God*] improvises."[250]

Ellis sees Jesus' jazz-theological approach most clearly in the "conceal-to-reveal technique" of His parables.[251] Jesus' parables were

---

[245] Carl F. Ellis Jr. and Amisho Baraka, *Free at Last? The Gospel in the African American Experience* (Downers Grove, IL: IVP, 2020), 174.
[246] Ellis Jr., *Free at Last?*, 174.
[247] Ellis Jr., *Free at Last?*, 174.
[248] Ellis Jr., *Free at Last?*, 174.
[249] Ellis Jr., *Free at Last?*, 175.
[250] Ellis Jr., *Free at Last?*, 175.
[251] Ellis Jr., *Free at Last?*, 175, 184.

effective not only because of their content, but also because of the method and quantity.

Another important parallel in Ellis' "jazz-theology" metaphor is Jesus' Hebrew treatment of knowledge as holistic and practical—not just academic.[252] "The great advantage of the jazz approach to theology is its requirement that people be *involved* with Truth."[253] It's something you do; not just something you learn or know. Knowledge and wisdom in this fuller sense necessarily entail implementation or application.

Finally, it is important to note that Ellis sees the "classical" and "jazz" approaches to theology as being ultimately *compatible*; not mutually exclusive.[254]

Overall, I find Dr. Ellis' treatment of "jazz theology" revelatory and substantive, especially as it relates specifically to the African American culture and context, even so many years after *Free at Last* was first published in 1983. However, in light of the more recent discussions around the "problematics" of the term "jazz," Ellis' word choice may be due for revision. I see this paper as a small contribution to Ellis' "soul dynamic" and "jazz theology" frameworks.

Jeremy Begbie

As the leading contemporary theologian of music, Jeremy Begbie has written extensively on the broad topic of intersections and confluences between music and theology. These works as a whole are highly instructive and, in some cases, seminal. For example, in his *Resounding Truth: Christian Wisdom in the World of Music*, he brings out several illuminating ideas. One of which is that he highlights the relationality that is central to music of any kind.[255] He also strikes a similar note to Ellis by emphasizing the music is not most fundamen-

---

[252] Ellis Jr., *Free at Last?*, 176.
[253] Ellis Jr., *Free at Last?*, 177.
[254] Ellis Jr., *Free at Last?*, 181.
[255] Jeremy S. Begbie, *Resounding Truth: Christian Wisdom in the World of Music*, Engaging Culture (Grand Rapids, MI: Baker Academic, 2007), 47, 54.

tally something people collect, curate, or even hear; rather, music is first and foremost something that people *do*.[256]

Bradley K. Broadhead

Broadhead's *Jazz and Christian Freedom: Improvising Against the Grain of the West* is notable not only for the seriousness with which he treats the analogies between improvised music and Christian theology, but also for his application of his analogy as a solution to what he terms "the problem of freedom." This philosophical problem has two poles. One is a postmodern emphasis on individualism and technique in contemporary Western culture which works against tradition and authority. The other is an authoritarian-fundamentalist impulse that stifles healthy spiritual formation and creativity.[257] "Jazz" resolves the tension between the poles by demonstrating that freedom—in both worship and music—requires *both* fidelity to tradition *and* creativity; both unity and diversity.[258]

THEOLOGY PROPER
Trinity as Collaboration

Creative improvised theology is theology in communion with the triune God. Before God is Creator, God is Relator.[259] The Most High exists eternally as One God in Three Persons. Thus, God is eternally in perfect communion with Himself. Although Christian faith hinges

---

[256] Begbie, *Resounding Truth*, 47.
[257] Broadhead, *Jazz and Christian Freedom*, 17.
[258] Broadhead, *Jazz and Christian Freedom*, 103-105.
[259] This is true both chronologically and ontologically. In terms of God's attributes, Trinity is more essential than creativity or God's status as 'Creator.' God was in trinitarian fellowship with Himself prior to creation, and if He had never created, He would still be in trinitarian relationship with Himself. Economic Trinity (e.g., creation—God's Spirit hovering over the waters; God's Word going forth, etc.) expresses immanent Trinity. What God does is an expression of Who God is. In creation, God is both (immanent) Relator and (economic) Creator, but creation flows out of the relation, not vice versa.

upon the Person and Work of Christ in human history (1 Cor. 15:16-20), its theological foundation is its unique affirmation of God as Trinity.[260]

What is important about Trinity for the purposes of this paper is that the Bisrat is essentially an intimate *collaboration* between the Persons of the Godhead. Jesus Himself is, at every step of his public ministry, in correspondence and obedience to the Father (Jn. 5:19-23, 30; 8:28-29; 15:15b). In Jn. 5:19, Jesus uses present active subjunctive language of 'seeing' the Father;[261] the picture is of Jesus performing His ministry while His eyes are on God the Father, who performs the same ministry.[262] Jesus even communicates with the Father, in psalmic language, during His passion.[263] Jesus follows His Father's lead.

Further, Jesus expresses solidarity with the Spirit (Mt. 12:31-32) and arranges for the Father to send the Spirit to believers. (Jn. 14:15-17; 15:26). Jesus is not a solo artist; neither is the Bisrat a solo performance.

The Creativity of God: Creation as Rhythmic Artifact

That God is the creator of the entire universe is clearly posited by Scripture. The point is made explicitly not only at the outset of Genesis, but throughout the biblical canon (Ps. 8; Is. 44:24; Eph. 3:9; Col. 1:15-17; Rev. 4:10-11). The heavens and the earth, then, are artifacts of God's design and manufacture. These artifacts are characterized by order and inherent goodness (Gen. 1:31). Of particular interest as we consider music is God's ordering of time. "Indeed, the

---

[260] "The triune Creator is the foundation for a Christian worldview." J. Lanier Burns et al., "Part One: 'From Dust to Dust': Creation, Humanity, and the Fall," in *Exploring Christian Theology: Creation, Fall, and Salvation*, eds. Nathan D. Holsteen and Michael J. Svigel, vol. II (Minneapolis, MN: Bethany House Publishers, 2015), 68.

[261] The Greek for "sees" in Jn 5:19a is $βλέπῃ$.

[262] The Greek verb denoting the Father's actions ("doing") in Jn. 5:19a is the present active participle $ποιοῦντα$.

[263] Mt. 26:36 (from Ps. 22); Lk. 23:46 (from Ps. 31:5).

[Bible] begins with time: 'God called the light Day, and the darkness he called Night. And there was evening and there was morning, the first day'." (Gen. 1:5)[264]

The Creation narrative of Gen. 1-2 is famously divided into "days."[265] Much ink has been spilled with regard to how to interpret the "days" of creation, but it is clear that the passage communicates the Creator's desire and unhindered ability to impose *order* upon the universe. "He produces an orderly, predictable, and dependable world."[266] Specifically, in terms of time, "God sets the *rhythm* and course of nature, maintaining its *tempo*."[267]

I want to suggest that musical rhythm, and specifically the polyrhythm found in African-diasporic music, including creative improvised music, is an extension of the rhythms God programmed into creation itself. As moderns, we can identify regular (though complex) rhythms of planets rotating around the sun, solar and lunar eclipses, the Earth's spin around its axis, the moon around the Earth, lunar cycles, tides interacting rhythmically with the moon, regular annual seasons, consistent migration schedules of various animals (e.g., the appearance of cicadas in my native Cincinnati every seventeen years), and on and on. Eminent scholar of theology and music Jeremy Begbie has well documented and explained "the Great Tradition" stretching back to classical antiquity, which posited "musical harmony as a metaphor of cosmic order."[268] The Great Tradition predates Christianity but was taken up in some form by prominent

---

[264] Rebecca Skaggs, "Time," ed. Douglas Mangum et al., *Lexham Theological Wordbook*, Lexham Bible Reference Series (Bellingham, WA: Lexham Press, 2014).

[265] Hebrew sg. יוֹם (*yôm*); pl. יָמִים (*yamim*)

[266] K. A. Mathews, *Genesis 1-11:26, vol. 1A, The New American Commentary* (Nashville, TN: Broadman & Holman Publishers, 1996), 121.

[267] Mathews, *Genesis*, 121. Italics mine.

[268] Jeremy S. Begbie, *Resounding Truth: Christian Wisdom in the World of Music*, Engaging Culture (Grand Rapids, MI: Baker Academic, 2007), 78.

Christian thinkers such as Boethius and Augustine,[269] not to mention Martin Luther.[270]

Further, the interlocking rhythms of creation are not only around humans; they are *in us*, as well—think of heartbeats, breathing, digestion, and circadian and menstrual cycles.[271] Thus, the beauty of rhythmic and polyrhythmic music can be seen not merely as an arbitrary aesthetic expression, but as an organic expression of the very creatureliness of the musicians. God, using a "daily" rhythm, produced a rhythmic universal creation, the crown of which is the image-bearing, rhythmically embodied human who expresses I rhythmically.

CHRISTOLOGY
Christ Event as Forecasting Cell

"A Forecasting Cell is a harmonic convention that illuminates the end result of a harmonic sentence preceding its resolution."[272] This musical innovation is the brainchild of Chief Xian aTunde Adjuah, a leading voice in creative improvised music.[273] Adjuah created the forecasting cell as "a means of questioning the improviser, thus forcing him to clarify his/her statements."[274] One journalist describes it as "a new formulation of the typical jazz call-and-response statement, a technique which acts harmonically as a 'musical question' that interrogates the

---

[269] Begbie, *Resounding Truth*, 82, 87-89

[270] Begbie, *Resounding Truth*, 98-101

[271] Jeremy S. Begbie, *Theology, Music and Time, Cambridge Studies in Christian Doctrine, 4* (Cambridge: Cambridge University Press, 2000), 36.

[272] http://www.chiefadjuah.com/stretchmusicbio/ (accessed May 8, 2021). The forecasting cell was first employed on his 2010 album, *Yesterday You Said Tomorrow*.

[273] Adjuah has publicly expressed his preference for this term over "jazz," positing that the latter is "belittling and pejorative." Christian Scott aTunde Adjuah, "X. Adjuah [I Own the Night]," recorded March 2020, with Elena Pinderhughes, Lawrence Fields, Kris Funn, Weedie Braimah, and Corey Fonville, track 1 on *Axiom*, Stretch Music/Ropeadope, Mp3.

[274] http://www.Chiefadjuah.com/stretchmusicbio/ (accessed May 8, 2021).

other improvisers on stage in an attempt to elicit more thoughtful and profound answers."[275]

My intention in this section is to show how the forecasting cell can serve as a conceptual point of reference to the creative, collaborative, and improvisational character of the very Bisrat of Yeshua HaMashiach—the Person and Work of Jesus Christ in His first advent.[276] It is important to note that I do not discern any Christian, theological, or even spiritual intent on the part of Adjuah in his conception or use of the forecasting cell. I am, frankly, appropriating it for my own explicitly Christian-theological purposes.

Divine Creativity

Both the Person and Work of Christ, and the forecasting cell are contextualized artifacts.[277] The context of the forecasting cell seems to include both a musical composition and the performances and recordings of that composition. The distinction between performance and composition is important here, as the forecasting cell functions specifically to influence the course of a solo improvisation. Thus, the forecasting cell does its work in the music as it is performed. Even as the original composition is an artifact in itself, each subsequent

---

[275] Imad Pasha, "Christian Scott aTunde Adjuah Stretches Jazz, Develops New Musical Discourse,"https://www.dailycal.org/2017/06/08/christian-scott-atunde-adjuah-stretch-music, *The Daily Californian* (accessed August 29, 2021).

[276] For the purposes of this section, the Person and Work of Christ *in his first advent* will be considered as one unit. The Person of Christ will not be distinguished from His salvific Work.

[277] While I treat the Person and Work of Christ as a unit here, I want to address the tension that may arise from the idea of Christ as an artifact. God the Son is uncreated and pre-existent within the Holy Trinity. Jesus Christ the God-Man is a hypostatic union of uncreated God and creaturely humanity. God the Son took on flesh and thus ushered in a new dispensation of salvation history. This incarnation, though perhaps foreknown within the Trinity from eternity past (1Pet. 1:19-20, cf. Rev. 13:8), was nonetheless a new development in salvation history. When I refer to Christ's incarnation, sinless life, atoning death, and justifying resurrection as an artifact, I both presume Christ's deity and refer to his distinct, unique hypostatic union with creaturely humanity. In other words, the Christ event was a kind of performance, and a performance is an embodied artifact.

performance of that composition is also a distinct artifact. And the improvisational solos are artifacts completely contextualized by the performances from which they arise.

In the same way, the Person and Work of Christ together stand as a (salvation-) historical artifact within human history, which itself begins with creation as God's creative act and unfolds as a highly complex interplay of divine and human decisions. To be sure, what Christ accomplished in his first advent is complete and sufficient, once for all time. It will not be performed again (Rom. 6:9-10).

The creation project that began in Eden with God breathing life into a novel, unique, dust-wrought race of image-bearers becomes New Creation as God's people are filled with the Holy Spirit (Acts 2:1-4). Jesus, as the Fully Human One, prefigured (Lk. 3:21-22) and prophesied (Acts 1:8) this new union of the collective Godhead with collective humanity.

Repentance as Godward Improvisation

Though contextual (see above), the forecasting cell is also consequential, or determinative. It is a call from the composer which elicits a response, decision, or change of course on the part of the improviser. Recall that the forecasting cell, in Adjuah's own words, "illuminates the end result of a harmonic sentence preceding its resolution." Its objective is to lead both "improviser and accompanist" into

> a constant reevaluation of the topography of the harmonic/melodic landscape, ultimately resulting in the improviser being forced to question before he renders a verdict. This questioning not only makes the intentions of the improviser clearer but also, through a constant reevaluation of the harmolodic landscape, helps in sharpening the communal dialogue of the unit.[278]

---

[278] http://www.Chiefadjuah.com/stretchmusicbio/ (accessed May 8, 2021).

Similarly, the incarnation of God in human flesh and Jesus' subsequent resurrection brought the end of history into the middle of history. The Christ event is an evaluative event: the way people react to it—i.e., the verdict they render on Christ—determines their trajectory into eternity. Christ, in this way, is the revealer of humans' hearts (cf. Acts 1:24, 15:8). Christ illuminates the end result of history, and of individuals' fates, preceding the eschaton.

N. T. Wright has defined justification as follows:

> God's declaration, from his position as judge of all the world, that someone is in the right, despite universal sin. This declaration will be made on the last day on the basis of an entire life (Romans 2:1-16), but is brought forward into the present on the basis of Jesus' achievement, because sin has been dealt with through his cross (Romans 3:21-4:25); the means of this present justification is simply faith. This means, particularly, that Jews and Gentiles alike are full members of the family promised by God to Abraham.
>
> (Galatians 3; Romans 4)[279]

In the same way, the forecasting cell brings the resolution of the soloist's improvisation into the "middle" of the solo itself.[280] Also, the Bisrat is an opportunity for repentance in the same way that the forecasting cell elicits a decision from the improviser. Repentance-and-faith-in-Christ, then, can be seen as *Godward improvisation*—a response to God's forecasting cell, or call, in Christ.

Thus, the forecasting cell is a useful figure for illustrating both the Christ event and its theological and eschatological blessing—namely,

---

[279] N.T. Wright, *Paul for Everyone. Romans: Part Two, Chapters 9-16* (Louisville, KY: Westminster John Knox Press, 2004), 152.

[280] In the Bisrat—specifically, in Christ's second advent—God will eschatologically resolve all human lives, either through vindicating their faith or condemning their lack thereof.

justification. It is a parabolic, prophetic gesture that can be used in Christian theology: The Person and work of Christ become one soteriological and eschatological forecasting cell portending the triune God's ultimate redemption of His people and God's resolution of human history.

Community as Collaboration

The forecasting cell not only brings the resolution of the song into the "middle" of the song, but also disruptively brings the composition to bear upon the improvising soloist. That is to say, it brings the whole into confrontation with the individual—the whole composition and the whole ensemble. It "sharpen[s] the communal dialogue [i.e., the *collaboration*] of the unit."[281]

In the same way, Christ not only brings God's ultimate eschatological victory over sin and death into the "middle" of human history. Christ also (by grace through faith) confronts individual humans with God's cosmic eternal plan, and ushers the believer into "communal dialogue" with neighbors—both inside and outside of God's church. In the next sections, I hope to trace the themes of creativity, collaboration, and improvisation in the context of Christian communal dialogue—both within the church and with the world, respectively.

ECCLESIOLOGY

Biblical Hermeneutics as Collaboration and Improvisation

Creative Improvised Theology is theology practiced in community with God's church. The church, through illumination of God's Spirit, interprets the Bible, God's Word to the World.[282] Theolo-

---

[281] http://www.Chiefadjuah.com/stretchmusicbio/ (accessed May 8, 2021).
[282] Glenn R. Kreider and Michael Svigel, *A Practical Primer on Theological Method: Table Manners for Discussing God, His Works, and His Ways* (Grand Rapids, MI: Zondervan Academic, 2019), 17.

gian Bruce Ellis Benson has written on the role of improvisation in both the inspiration and the interpretation of biblical texts.[283] Benson sees improvisation as a fundamental facet of being (human) in the world, of God's current work in the world, and of the interplay between the two.[284]

Benson models his notion of hermeneutic improvisation on inventio, an idea taken from classical rhetoric: "Inventio is both a repetition and a transformation, for it is the art of taking that which already exists and developing or elaborating upon it."[285] This interpretation is more than pure imitation but stops short of "pure invention."[286] In this way, inventio seems to be closely related to the tension between creativity and tradition noted by Paul Rinzler and drawn upon by Broadhead.[287]

Importantly, Benson sees two basic differences[288] between musical improvisation and Christian biblical interpretation: First, "Christian texts have both human and divine authorship."[289] By this I think he means that divine inspiration sets the biblical canon apart from all other artifacts. In this vein, I concur with his statement that "the Holy Spirit plays a role in both the improvisational writing and the improvisational interpretation of Scripture."[290] Indeed, what he describes here is both improvisation and divine-human collaboration. However, I am not nearly as comfortable with his further point that "there is no reason to think that the Holy Spirit may not be saying new things through the locutions of Scripture." My thinking is along the lines of the her-

---

[283] Bruce Ellis Benson, "Improvising Texts, Improvising Communities: Jazz, Interpretation, Heterophony, and the Ekklesia," *Resonant Witness: Conversations Between Music and Theology*, Jeremy S. Begbie and Steven R. Guthrie, eds. (Grand Rapids, MI: Eerdmans, 2011), 295-319.
[284] Benson, *Resonant Witness*, 295.
[285] Benson, *Resonant Witness*, 300.
[286] Benson, *Resonant Witness*, 300.
[287] Broadhead, *Jazz and Christian Freedom*, 104-107, 109, 113.
[288] "fundamental dissimilarities," Benson, *Resonant Witness*, 303.
[289] Benson, *Resonant Witness*, 303.
[290] Benson, *Resonant Witness*, 303.

meneutical adage which says that "[a] text can never mean what it never meant before / to its original readers or authors."[291]

I do track with Benson when he posits Scripture as "a structure upon which interpreters elaborate."[292] He equates this structure with a "cantus firmus,"[293] which the Concise Oxford English Dictionary defines as "an existing melody used as the basis for a polyphonic composition."[294] Christian tradition—most importantly the Bible and the rule of faith— provides necessary and good constraints within which Christians can creatively navigate contemporary questions and challenges in submission to God and one another.

Divine Creativity and Ecclesial Collaboration in Romans 12

God's transformation of Christians by mental renewal is collaborative in that God accomplishes it in partnership not only with each believer, but also with the church collectively. God accomplishes sanctification, but not by divine fiat. Rather, God is pleased to cultivate Christ-like character through the believer's submissive collaboration—with God's Spirit and with other Christians. This is particularly evident in the twelfth chapter of Paul's letter to Rome.

The major rubric under which all of the Roman Christians' practical application of the mercies of God[295] fit is "to present [their] bodies as a sacrifice." (12:1) Please note here that "bodies" (somata) is plural while "sacrifice" (thusian) is singular. I believe this is intentional. NA28 records no textual variants here. The Roman Christians are to conceive

---

[291] Flame, "Context," track 9 on *Rewind*, Cross Movement Records, 2005, CD. https://genius.com/Flame-context-lyrics?web=1&wdLOR=cEF3519BB-921E-42BB-81CA-D194158986EE

[292] Benson, *Resonant Witness*, 304.

[293] Benson, *Resonant Witness*, 304.

[294] Catherine Soanes and Angus Stevenson, eds., *Concise Oxford English Dictionary* (Oxford: Oxford University Press, 2004).

[295] i.e., the Bisrat as presented in chapters 1-11.

of their multiple bodies, gathered as they are in churches (cf. 16:1 5, 16, 23), as one collective sacrifice. This striking feature of Paul's ecclesiology, implied so subtly in v. 1, becomes more explicit in vv. 4-5: "For just as in one body we have many members, and not all the members serve the same function, so we who are many are one body in Christ, and individually we are members who belong to one another." (cf. 1 Cor. 12:12; Col. 2:19). It is not problematic that Paul speaks of many "bodies" in 12:1 while speaking of one "body" in 12:5 and 1 Cor. 12:12. The careful reader can safely synthesize that the various saints are to present their bodies (their whole selves)[296] as one collective body, which is then offered as a sacrifice. This also resonates with the broader Pauline theme of diversity within unity (cf. 1 Cor. 12:4-7, 13).

Paul then compels his Roman readers with two passive plural imperatives—a negative one, followed by a positive one. "Do not be conformed…be transformed…" (12:2). The implication of the passive voice is that humans are subject to greater forces—one good, others (e.g., "this present world") evil. Just as no individual believer can offer an appropriate sacrifice in and of himself, the Christian life is not a matter of conforming or transforming oneself.[297] Indeed, each individual Christian is warned "not to think more highly of [them]self than [they] ought to think, but to think with sober discernment, as God has distributed to each [believer] a measure[298] of faith" (12:3). We Christians are not only radically dependent on God; we are also dependent upon one another (the other "members"); we are better, stronger, more alive, holier, more pleasing to God *together*.

Not to be missed, though, are the means by which, and the purpose for which, believers are to be transformed. The means is "the renewing of your mind." Interestingly, both the article (tou: literally, 'the,'

---

[296] C. E. B. Cranfield, *A Critical and Exegetical Commentary on the Epistle to the Romans, International Critical Commentary* (London; New York: T&T Clark International, 2004), 598.
[297] Cranfield, *Romans*, 609.
[298] By emphasizing the "measure of faith" given to each *individual*, might Paul be implying that the fullness of faith is only apprehended in Christian *community*?

but rendered by the NET and most translations as 'your') and 'mind' (noos) are singular. Does Paul have in mind here a new collective mind emerging amongst the believing community? I would not want to push this too far, as Christ himself seems to be the head of the body. However, in that vein, Philippians 2:5 does come to mind: "You (plural; lit. 'y'all') should have the same attitude (singular) toward one another that Christ Jesus had."

The telos of the renewing of the mind is "so that you (plural, humas) may test and approve what is the will of God—what is good and well-pleasing and perfect." (12:2) This verse is crucial in that it connects significantly with a couple of previous passages. The koine lemma behind "test and approve" (*dokimazo*; here present active infinitive *dokimazein*) also appears three times in Paul's description of the telos of idolatry in 1:28 ("they did not see fit (*ouk edokimasan*) to acknowledge God" and "God gave them over to a depraved mind..." (*adokimon* noun) and 1:32 ("they... also approve (*suneudokousin*) of those who practice them.").[299] Thus, God's creative work in renewing the mind(s) of believers is the reversal of the natural effects of unbelief. Further, I will posit that, just as idolatry and unbelief naturally lead to the litany of sins itemized in 1:28-32, so also "the renewing of the mind" consists largely in the ongoing practice of Christian virtues in relationship with other Christians. Far from a miraculous supernatural process, this collective sanctification follows the rhythms of creation—sunrise and sunset, week after week, Summer, Spring, Winter, and Fall,[300] year by year. However, time alone does not sanctify us; we must rhythmically practice together the mental habits of life, of holiness, of pleasing God.

Thus, one of the many blessings of Paul's letter to Rome is the role it plays in establishing a distinctly Christian vision of character

---

[299] N.T. Wright, *After You Believe: Why Christian Character Matters* (New York: HarperCollins Publishers, 2010), 153. Kindle.
[300] Or, in other climates, Rainy Season and Dry Season.

development or virtue.[301] This is perhaps most clear in 5:1-5, where Paul lays out a Providential schema by which suffering, the very nadir of human experience, is redeemed and developed into endurance, character, and ultimately hope.

The Greek noun rendered "character" in 5:4 is *dokimein*, from the same root as *dokimazein* in 12:2. The process by which God uses suffering to produce character (and hope) is closely related to, and ultimately inseparable from, the process of transformation by mental renewal. *Both are artifacts of God's creativity.*[302] Further, they make space for faithful human creativity, the fruit of a renewed mind. Wright observes:

> [T]he mind must be transformed so that you can think out for yourself, weigh up and consider, what God's will actually is. Unless the mind is fully involved, not only are you not growing up as a fully (and fully integrated) human being; you are not engaging in virtue at all.[303]

Intertwined with the creativity and collectivity of Christian sanctification is what I am calling collaboration. I draw this from 12:3-8. I've already mentioned Paul's corporate, or 'body' metaphor in v. 5. He uses it to make a point about the respective roles of individual believers with their respective gifts. The gifts are both from God and for others. Also, the idea of the local congregation as a body suggests somewhat subtly that the roles and gifts work together in complementary ways. So, as my first pastor reminded us often, "Christianity is a team sport." If collectivity speaks to the unity of all who love God and are called to be saints, then collaboration speaks to their complementary diversity. Some are prophets; others, teachers; still others, leaders.

---

[301] Wright, *After You Believe*, 18

[302] Wright says Rom. 5:3-5 is "about [among other things] the living God, creating the "new [collective] Temple" through Jesus Christ and then filling it with his own presence." *After You Believe*, 90.

[303] Wright, *After You Believe*, 150

The prophet must be led; the leader must be taught. To conceive of one's gift/role independently or competitively defeats the purpose.

Improvisation as the Fruit of Christian Sanctification

Listening is the key here. Just as the seasoned improvisatory musician must listen to her bandmates in order to know how to play her part, each believer must learn to receive one another in familial love, hearing one another's stories[304] and encouraging one another with the hope of the Gospel.

> ... [P]ut the piano player into a chamber group, or make her instead a viola player in a large orchestra. The good musician is not simply playing the music on the stand in front of her. She is playing, consciously and delightedly as part of a much larger whole, making her own contribution but aware of the music's whole sweep and flow, and of the other contributions which are so different to her own, but so thoroughly complementary.[305]

The sanctifying tension between the individual believer and the church is collaborative in the way that the best of music and sports is collaborative.

> Actually, as with all virtues, once you begin to learn the language, and especially once you begin to speak it in groups where other people are learning it too, it doesn't seem so impossible, but actually begins to acquire its own sense of "second nature," of a second-order spontaneity, as with skilled actors, footballers, or jazz players who have learned the high art of true corporate *improvisation*.[306]

---

[304] Curt Thompson, *Anatomy of the Soul: Surprising Connections between Neuroscience and Spiritual Practices That Can Transform Your Life and Relationships* (Carol Stream, IL: Tyndale, 2010), loc 157. Kindle.
[305] Wright, *After You Believe*, 146.
[306] Wright, *After You Believe*, 211. Emphasis mine.

This is the art of holistic worship to which God calls us, and to which creative improvised theology aspires.

Conclusion

Creative improvised theology is done in communion with the Creator, in community with the church, and in conversation with the world. It joins God's promises with the current of human history. Further, it has deep roots in the African diaspora. African American churches have a long history of creative, collaborative, and improvisational theology and practice, inclusive of our quest for freedom and human dignity.[307] This tradition "overcome[s] evil with good" (Rom. 12:21), and reflects the heart of our creating, collaborating, forecasting, faithful God.

Gospel Haymanot, in full resonance with the soul dynamic, is a space of joining classic biblical doctrine with African and African-diasporic liberation, theology with culture, theory with praxis. I hope this paper supports that worthy project.

As African Americans express and follow a legitimate desire to decolonize their worldviews, it may be wise for Nazrawi activists, apologists, evangelists, teachers, and preachers to mine diverse African and African-diasporic (sub-)cultures for Bisrat analogies. The objective is to express the Bisrat vividly and clearly to our kinsmen according to the flesh.

Moreover, many in today's Western culture experience temptations towards division, fragmentation, and isolation. Conversely, local churches are crucial spaces where the Spirit re-creates image-bearers through collaborative mental renewal and character development. The fruit of this virtue is Godward improvisation. This is where God meets us, and joins us to each other, in profound harmony.

---

[307] Ellis Jr., *Free at Last?*, 48.

Worship, Missiological "Blind Spots," and Reconciliation[308]

Emmett G. Price

Diverse Expressions of Worship in the Bible

From Genesis through the Revelation of the prophet John of Patmos, God both invites and is the sole audience of the worship of God's children. In Genesis 1:1, God is revealed as creator, the one who willed, and it came to be. The eleven "Let there be" statements in Genesis 1 reveals the rich variation of God's expansive palate as God created and populated the entire earth.[309] God's own reflection of the divine and masterful work revealed that "And God saw everything that he had made, and behold, it was very good."[310] By chapter 4, The LORD receives his first offerings, from Cain in v.3 and then Abel in v.4.[311] In Chapter 6:13-16, God invites Noah to build an ark with specific instructions initiating a covenant (v.18) and additional

---

[308] An earlier version of this paper was presented at the 2020 Evangelical Missiological Society's Annual National Meeting, "The Past and Future Evangelical Mission," under the title, "Worship Arts, Evangelical Missions and Conversations about Race in Our Nation Today" (October 9, 2020).

[309] Genesis 1:3; 2:6; 3:9; 4:11; 5:14; 6:14; 7:15; 8:20; 9:24; 10:26; and 11:26.

[310] *The Holy Bible: English Standard Version* (Wheaton, IL: Crossway Bibles, 2002, 2).

[311] *Ibid*, 3.

instructions (v.19-21).[312] Noah was obedient to the LORD's invitation (v.22).[313] From Cain and Abel's offerings to Noah's ark, to the ark of the covenant; from the tabernacle to the temple to the old testament synagogue to the new testament church, sacrifices, prayers, festivals, confession, lament, and the like all took place where God ordained it, where God invited it and on terms that God set and made possible. All throughout the Bible, from Genesis to John's revelation, creativity is a dynamic and crucial aspect of human worship of our Heavenly Father.

Our obedience to God's desire as discerned through the growing intensity of our relationship with God sits at the center of worship. This relationship can best be measured in terms of proximity and intimacy, or distance and depth. The more we spend time with God and the more we avail that time as interactive and engaged time, the more we come to know and receive God's revelation. We are already known by God.

> Worship is relational and transformative, and it is an essential expression of our faith. We are created as worshippers, and worship is the response to the divine invitation for us to engage with our Creator. Worship is where we join our hearts and our minds together as one to petition, hear, praise, heal, and be with God and with one another.[314]

Worship for worship's sake, or transactional, non-transformative worship tends to not express the creative posture that would reflect our proximity and intimacy with our creative God.

Throughout the history of humanity, as reflected in the Bible and beyond, God's children have attempted to respond to the creative nature of our Heavenly Father by responding to God's invitation through our

---

[312] *Ibid*, 5.
[313] *Ibid*, 5.
[314] Emmett G. Price III, *There Is a Balm in Gilead: A Call to Lament Together* (Peabody, MA: Hendrickson Publishers, 2020, vi-vii).

own endowed creative senses. Through music, dance, culinary arts, and even how we practice our various spiritual disciplines, we offer our gifts and talents back to the giver as a sacrifice of praise, an offering of adoration as a response to God's gracious invitation. Our worship is, and should be, as creative, in honor of our creative God, as we can imagine and achieve.

From Pliny's letter to Emperor Trajan (AD 111-113) to the Didache (AD 100) to Justin Martyr's First Apology, we read the creative ways that the early church, even in persecution and in hiding, still creatively responded to God's invitation to engage with God "on the terms that He proposes and in the way that He alone makes possible."[315] The human response to God's initial call to worship has never been as stale as tradition may suggest. Perhaps a better way to make this statement is as a reminder that what may stand as tradition in this season was once the result of innovation, exploration, and contemplation.

Biblical Evangelicalism (Race in our nation)

How we worship has much to do with our ecclesial formation. What we were taught or shown becomes what is desired, expected, and accepted. What we deem as acceptable worship is more about a hermeneutical lens that has been socialized through a systematic theology, than what has been exegeted from the sacred scriptures of the sixty-six books of the Bible. Systematic theologies can sometimes conflict with our own spiritual interaction and engagement with the Almighty God, causing the need for us to reconcile our learned behavior with our spontaneous discerned behavior. This tension can limit the possibilities of our creativity and may lead to a departure from improvised elements of worship.

As believers anchored with both feet in the Bible, we believe, undoubtedly in "being born again" (conversion), the Bible as

---

[315] David Peterson, *Engaging with God: A Biblical Theology of Worship* (Downers Grove, IL: IVP Academic, 1992, 20).

the authoritative, divinely-inspired word of God (biblicism), the importance of the cross as central to Jesus' work on earth (crucicentrism), and in the Great Commission which is often interestingly referred to as activism (to which I will return shortly).[316] As a Black Christian, I tend to stop here, as I find an important distinction between biblical evangelicalism and cultural evangelicalism. Much of the difference between my assertion of the two lies in the tension between our learned behavior and our discerned behavior. For example, being 'pro-life' without affirmation and advocacy of the precious lives of people with differing abilities along with ostracized and disenfranchised ethnic populations, is not a comprehensive theological construct that can pass the test of learned behavior. Similarly, being theologically conservative does not equate to being socially conservative, nor fiscally conservative. Thus, the term 'conservative' needs a contextual qualifier as does the term 'pro-life.' Pro-life, conservative, and other such terms are important to some, yet they tend to be more cultural descriptors than universally understood in practice. These terms are certainly not theological terms. These terms emerge from a hermeneutic that may or may not empower a believer to be a follower (disciple) of Christ.

If our hermeneutic does not allow an interpretation of the sacred Scripture to embody Adam and Eve within our theological imagination as brown-skinned people, then we have embedded blind spots which limit our proximity and intimacy with God. One of the greatest challenges of the Church of Jesus Christ in the United States is our inability to overwhelmingly and comprehensively be empathetically compassionate in our introspective reflection. Many white Christians claim the United States of America as Christian land. Most have no knowledge of the May 4, 1493, papal bull, "Inter Caetera" issued by

---

[316] The Bebbington Quadrilateral is often used as a litmus test for biblical orthodoxy, especially within evangelical settings. It proposes the four tenets of evangelicalism as biblicism, conversionism, crucicentrism, and activism.

Pope Alexander VI that availed the New World, regardless of who the land was already inhabited by, as Christian.[317]

Some white Christians remark that racism is the first American sin[318] without remembering the egregious treatment of the original inhabitants of this land was a conflation of hubris, greed, unjust war, and a host of other sins in addition to discrimination against a people due to their non-European ethnicity. While many of the American evangelical patriarchs, Cotton Mather, Gilbert Tennent, George Whitefield, Jonathan Edwards, and numerous others continue to have a significant influence on the contemporary Church, many choose not to remember these patriarchs as slave holders who did not believe that all of God's creation, in human form, served as image bearers.[319] As missionaries, white Christians believe strongly in the great commission but somehow choose to forget that colonialist actions across the globe have caused more hurt than we will ever realize. This has caused a great stain on the Christian witness for a long time to come. In choosing to not remember, a new biblical narrative is created through a conceived hermeneutic that reveals only white Christians as the extension of the Hebrew Children with everyone else as extensions of the Gentiles, defined loosely as "other than Jews."

Blind spots are not merely what we cannot see. Blind spots are also what we choose not to see or better yet, what we deny is worthy of being seen. The global mantra, "Black Lives Matter," is a cry to the Church, not the world. It is the Church of Jesus Christ that has been commissioned with the ministry of Reconciliation. According

---

[317] See Mark Charles and Soong-Chan Rah, *Unsettling Truths: The Ongoing, Dehumanizing Legacy of the Doctrine of Discovery* (Downers Grove, IL, InterVarsity Press Books, 2019) for more on the Doctrine of Discovery.

[318] See Jim Wallis, *America's Original Sin: Racism, White Privilege, and the Bridge to a New America* (Ada, MI: Brazos Press, 2017) and Carol Anderson *White Rage: The Unspoken Truth of Our Racial Divide* (New York, NY: Bloomsbury Publishing, 2016).

[319] Michael O. Emerson and Christian Smith, *Divided By Faith: Evangelical Religion and the Problem of Race in America* (New York, NY: Oxford University Press, 2000).

to the Center for the Study of Global Christianity, as of 2018, Christians made up one-third of the global population (2.5 billion) with the greatest saturation of Christians on the continent of Africa at 631 million.[320] The next largest concentration was in Latin America with 601 million, followed by Europe with 571 million.[321] Allow this to sink in as a reality check, as of 2018, there were more Christians in Africa than anywhere else on the planet. Second to Africa was Latin America. That most Christians do not know this is clear, and it is an indication that the Church needs to assess and prayerfully eradicate our blind spots.

Towards Healing (with Hope)

Sometimes, our creativity can get in the way. During the Renaissance period, phenomenal artists such as Donato di Niccolo di Betto Bardi aka Donatello (1386-1466), Leonardo da Vinci (1452-1519), Michelangelo di Lodovico Buonarroti Simoni (1475-1564), Raphael Sanzio da Urbino (1483-1520), Hans Holbein the Elder (1460-1524), Hans Holbein the Younger (1497-1543), Jean Fouquet (1420-1481), and numerous other exceptional creatives whitewashed the imagery of Christianity. An example of this in the United States is the 1940 Warner Sallman (1892-1968) painting, "Jesus of Nazareth," that single handedly affirmed and reaffirmed that Jesus was indeed white to Caucasians and people of color. By the end of the twentieth century, the image was reproduced over a half billion times worldwide.[322] The impact of this image was so huge that even in Black households during the civil rights movement, this was the image set in the dining room

---

[320] https://www.gordonconwell.edu/wp-content/uploads/sites/13/2019/04/GlobalChristianityinfographic.pdfPg1_.pdf.

[321] ibid.

[322] William Grimes, "The Man Who Rendered Jesus For the Age of Duplication," New York Times, October 12, 1994, https://www.nytimes.com/1994/10/12/arts/the-man-who-rendered-jesus-for-the-age-of-duplication.html (accessed April 16, 2022).

wall next to Dr. Martin Luther King, Jr. (1929-1968) and President John Fitzgerald Kennedy (1917-1963).

Rather than our hermeneutic guiding our exegesis to disprove that Jesus was of Nordic or Scandinavian decent, we reinforce the images as proof that indeed white Christians are the extension of the Hebrew children and everyone else are "other." The way we see ourselves impacts how we see others. The way we experience our proximity and intimacy with/to God often dictates possibilities for those who we are evangelizing and prayerfully discipling. Our blind spots tend to become the blind spots of others and eventually become encased within tradition as if blind spots were exegeted biblically and vetted theologically. If we have blind spots in our conversionism—believing it is a white God incarnate or, more importantly, that we need to become culturally white in order to have proximity and intimacy with a white God—we are intentionally or, perhaps unintentionally, adding extra-biblical information to our understanding of biblicism. Believing and then intentionally or unintentionally teaching the Bible as if all of God's children are white is an unfortunate and in many ways unjust understanding of crucicentrism. Jesus went to the cross for the sins of the world and not just the assumed Caucasians of the bible. And if our conversionism, biblicism, and crucicentricism is impacted by our blind spots, then indeed our activism is inherently out of alignment and out of balance to the proximity and intimacy of God through Christ Jesus.

I am often asked why there are not more American Blacks serving as missionaries. A second most often asked question is: why are Black Americans not interested in missiology or intercultural studies? I often remark that Black Christians have been missionaries for hundreds of years and even longer, depending on how you see the first and second century Church in Carthage or Alexandria. How we image the powerful Christian witness of Perpetua and Felicitas is a reflection of how we miss the presence of ethnicity in the Bible. Similarly, how we image the second- and third-century influence of Origen and Tertullian or perhaps the third-century ministry of Cyprian or the fourth- and fifth-century ministry of Augustine offers much about how we empower or disempower ethnic equity as narrated by God. Each of the aforementioned were of African descent, deeply influenced by diverse representations of culture on the African continent or spent much of their time in ministry on the continent itself. In many ways, we also have to wrestle with the historical question of what happened to Christian Africa. Especially as we seek continued understanding of how the emergence of Islam led many African Christians to leave Christianity. Choosing not to deal with these questions and choosing not to remember the influence and impact of Christianity on the continent of Africa causes us to begin our African missiological history during the fifteenth century circa 1470s rather than centuries before. Missionaries during the fifteenth to nineteenth centuries came along with colonialism particularly as we trace the influence and impact of Christianity in association with the Middle Passage, the Maafa, the African holocaust. Many Christians (of all ethnicities) choose to embed blind spots rather than the realities and repercussions of said histories. This is partially why we don't see numerous Black missionaries within plain sight. Black Christians are still doing activism in the local sphere both to prospective believers and acknowledged believers who have blind spots that rob sisters and brothers of color of our dignity, agency, and literally our seats within the evangelical church. We have been Bible-believing, trinitarian, Christ followers who affirm and actively engage Jesus' great commission for a long time. In fact, we have been Biblicists with very conservative theological formulations, yet we have been excluded, uninvited, and removed from white Christian spaces for generations. We have been disenfranchised in white evangelical seminaries, ostracized from evangelical denominations, and explicitly seen as the enemy within evangelical cultural circles. Without seats at the table, we are separated and fragmented in the great work that we can and should do together. These reinforced blind spots should not exist, but they have been reaffirmed and overwhelmingly articulated in the public, political, and in certain ecclesial settings which again taints our Christian witness and traditionalizes blind spots.

Here, the importance of invitation is in full frame. As God invites us into his kingdom through the invitation of Christ, our proximity and intimacy with one another is divinely blessed through invitation. The Christian witness to the nations of the world is deeply challenged when white Christians disenfranchise, ostracize, and "otherize" non-white humans who are immigrants, refugees, and asylum seekers. These acts create an overwhelming tension to the possibility and intensity of relationship with them and by extension their relationship with God. Throughout the Caribbean and Latin America, the slave Bible was used by missionaries to proselytize (and I use this term purposefully) into a partial view of the good news of the Gospel. The slave Bible was purposefully published with all of the liberative passages of both the Old Testament and the New Testament removed amounting to about 90 percent of the Old Testament and roughly 50 percent of the New Testament.[323] In essence, of the 1,189 chapters of the protestant Bible, only 232 were included in the slave Bible.[324] Intentional disdain for liberation theology in many evangelical circles remains evident. When we are invited into people's lives generally, their neighborhoods, communities, and courageous spaces, do we add to the safety, or do we cause reason for alarm? Is our intention merely to expand the kingdom of God or to embrace, love, cherish, value, and appreciate our new siblings in Christ? I am fond of the love language Paul uses to his beloved even as he wrote from prison. Do we have that kind of affection for one another as we 'go ye therefore'?

As we study the approaches of worship of our beloved spiritual siblings, are we able to expand our awareness of the brilliant beauty

---

[323] https://www.npr.org/2018/12/09/674995075/slave-bible-from-the-1800s-omitted-key-passages-that-could-incite-rebellion.

[324] https://www.museumofthebible.org/exhibits/slave-bible.

of God's scattering of His beloved, and the Pentecostal affirmation that English or perhaps Greek are not necessarily the heart language of God? Language is for humans, not God. Can we find it satisfactory not to know, but to feel and experience until we know, or is the power dynamic of knowing so important to us it disrupts proximity and intimacy? Do we allow them to solely rely on language?

It is my prayer that, in addition to ethnographic fieldwork with a posture of participant-observer sensitivity, our academic study would be met with our call as believers to uplift the dignity, agency, personhood, and difference of our beloved, not as "other" but as "one another." Jesus' words in Matthew 28:19-20 speak loudly as we "Go," "Baptize," and "Teach," while remembering Jesus is with us. The verb "to teach" is important, as it is not only a directional instruction but also a hermeneutical reminder, teach as I have taught you. Teach from your proximity and intimacy with Christ. Teach based on your proximity and intimacy with Christ. Be proximate and intimate with Christ and then teach creatively as God so inspires.

A Critique of the Nonviolent Ethic's Supremacy in the Black Church's Discourse and Teaching in Light of White Evangelical Theology of Violence

Tyran T. Laws

Introduction

Going back as far as the Doctrine of Discovery, an integral part of the church of England's "redemptive violence" strategy against native Americans,[325] to the most recent act of the January 6 insurrection, white supremacy has made white Evangelical Christians in America susceptible to a theology of violence (which I will define momentarily), albeit with varying degrees of intensity, and typically reserved

---

[325] Mark Charles and Soong-Chan Rah. *Unsettling Truths: The Ongoing, Dehumanizing Legacy of the Doctrine of Discovery* (Downers Grove, IL: IVP, 2019), 13–23. See also R. S. Sugirtharajah's treatment of "Dissident Readings" of Biblical interpretation by colonialist theologians *(Postcolonial Criticism and Biblical Interpretation,* [Oxford: Oxford University Press, 2002]), 43–52.

for "violent-worthy" moments.³²⁶ In contrast to white Christians, Black Christians in America, historically, as evidenced by streams of thought in the Civil Rights movement, have been spoon-fed the ethic of nonviolence. This paper critiques, on biblical ground, the nonviolent ethic's ascendancy in the Black church's discourse and teaching in light of white Evangelical theology of violence and advocates for the Black church's need for more robust theology of resistance (i.e., resistance theology) to combat white Christian America's susceptibility to a theology of violence.

Hermeneutical Concerns

My theology of resistance for African American Christians mostly draws from two streams of thought as reflected in (1) R. S. Sugirtharajah's treatment on postcolonial readings and Oscar Romero whose ideas I will expound on later.³²⁷ Postcolonialism, according to Sugirtharajah, has as its starting point with the assumption that Western hegemonic interpretations have dominated the landscape of Biblical studies. Therefore, postcolonial hermeneutics seek to dismantle *interpretations* that "legitimize, consolidate, and promote the dominant values and ideological interests of the ruling class."³²⁸ In some ways, this paper raises similar concerns. It is questionable to what extent the

---

[326] For an extensive treatise on this, see e.g., Robert P. Jones, *White Too Long: The Legacy of White Supremacy in American Christianity* (New York: Simon and Schuster, 2021), cf. Kristen Kobes Du Mez, *Jesus and the John Wayne: How White Evangelicals Corrupted a Faith and Fractured a Nation* (New York: NY, Liveright Publishing, 2020), 32, 200–1; Raymond J. Haberski, *God and War: American Civil Religion Since 1945* (New Jersey: Rutgers University Press, 2012), 52–53. Haberski's work primarily demonstrates the ways rhetoric of American civil religion has moralized America's war efforts—a theology of violence.

[327] For Sugirtharajah's work, see, e.g., R. S. Sugirtharajah, *Postcolonial Criticism and Biblical Interpretation* [Oxford: Oxford University Press, 2002] 52–55; idem., *The Bible and the Third World: Precolonial, Colonial, and Postcolonial Encounters* (Cambridge: Cambridge University Press, 2001), 75–90. For Oscar Romero's work, see, e.g., St. Oscar Romero, *Voice of the Voiceless: The Four Pastoral Letters and Other Statements* (Maryknoll, NY: Orbis Books, 2020), 125–76.

[328] Sugirtharajah, *Postcolonial Criticism*, 79.

Black Church's ethic of nonviolence actually critiques white Christian America's theology of violence. Rather than critiquing it, one could say the nonviolence ethic absorbs it by intentionally becoming the object of it. In fact, King implicitly states this in a Christmas sermon on Peace at Ebenezer Baptist Church in 1967, "Somehow we must be able to stand up before our most bitter opponents and say, 'We shall match your capacity to inflict suffering by our capacity to endure suffering.'"[329] Thus, I found the post-colonial hermeneutic to be efficacious in critiquing the ascendancy of nonviolence's ethic in the Black church as the ethic relates to white Christian's America's theology of violence. Within the white Christian American's theology of violence, nonviolence, viz., pacifism, as we will see, only promotes the dominant caste's values and interests. However, unlike postcolonialism's hermeneutic, which critiques the biblical texts also, my critique is limited to interpretations of the text and not the texts themselves. In this way, I have adopted the conceptual framework from the postcolonial conceptual framework for our treatment of Scripture, however with evangelical commitments to Scripture.

A Theology of Violence

By white Christian's theology of violence, we mean that white Evangelical Christianity has a pattern of theological justification for its injurious physical force, actions, or treatment of people and property. This theology of violence does not entail that white Christians are themselves carrying out these socially reprehensible offenses. However, a theology of violence will inevitably make allowances, concessions, and mitigations for these offenses.

Sometimes this theological legitimization of violence is subtle, like justifying the unmerited killing of black bodies under the guise of law and order. On the surface, conversations about *law and order*

---

[329] James M. Washington, *A Testament of Hope: The Essential Writings and Speeches of Martin Luther King, Jr.*" (San Francisco: HarperSanFrancisco, 1986), 256.

(e.g., if Black people would just obey the law, they would not be killed) seem to be irrelevant to a discussion about a *theology* of violence. Assuming this would definitely fit well within a stream of Christian thought that, in theory, separates religion and politics. However, that assumption cannot be sustained given that conversations about law and order routinely evoke scriptures like Rom. 13:1–3 or Hebrews 13:17 as a scriptural legitimization of state sanction killings of Black bodies.[330] Concomitantly, this proves that the bifurcation of religion and politics is often a distinction sustained more in theory than in practice. From the Missouri Compromise[331] to turning a blind eye to the repressive mechanism of lynching, white Christians' history continues to demonstrate its propensity to mitigate white violence (even Christian violence) against Black bodies if they so deem it a "violent worthy" moment.[332]

Other times, a white Evangelical Christian's theology of violence has been blatant as in the theological justification for slavery. Generally, however, it is so intrinsically built in the fabric of American history that it comes cloaked in the subterfuge of patriotism and preservation of the "greater good." Thus, when white Christian terrorists (and a handful of Black sympathizers) stormed the nation's capital on January 6, 2021, it resonated with a subculture of white Evangelical

---

[330] White Evangelical proclivity towards a theology of violence as imbued through the conflation of religion and politics is also intimated in the work Anthea Butler, *White Evangelical Racism: The Politics of Morality in America* (Chapel Hill, NC: University of North Carolina Press, 2021), 23–26, 29, 131, 133, 137–38. See especially page 133 where she cites a Facebook post from Franklin Graham who asserts the relevance of Hebrews 13:17 to solving the issue of police violence: "If a police officer tells you to lay down face first with your hands behind your back. Even if you think the police is wrong—you obey."

[331] For a historical treatise on how this shaped American national decision making, see e.g., Robert Pierce Forbes, *The Missouri Compromise and Its Aftermath: Slavery and the Meaning of America* (Chapel Hill, NC: University of North Carolina Press, 2009).

[332] See Robert P. Jones who cites surveys about White Evangelical Protestants: "one in three believe that 'because things have gotten so far off track, true American patriots may have to resort to violence in order to save our country'" ("The Unmaking of the White Christian Worldview," *TIME, Ideas and Religion*, September 29, 2021).

Christianity that ascribes to "violent worthy" moments. The evidence of the religious and violent character is substantiated in the terrorists audible playing of Christian worship songs, and creation of "Jesus Saves" signs, in the context of urinating in the halls, defecating on the floors, leaving behind two pipe bombs,[333] and allegedly killing a police officer.[334] Perhaps, it could be said, however, that it remains to be proven that those who left behind the two pipe bombs were Christians. While that is true, still, the data demonstrates that it is not outside the scope of probability that they were, in fact, Christians, particularly because white American nationalism has sometimes found it feasible to coopt Christian concepts for its national interests.

A case in point is Dylann Roof, the terrorist who murdered nine Black worshippers at historic Black church in South Carolina. As Robert P. Jones argues, the data shows that "Christianity was central to his worldview."[335] To start, he was a member in good standing of the Evangelical Lutheran Church in America.[336] Additionally, in his journal, which ultimately became exhibit 500 in his trial, we find enough cumulative evidence to substantiate the claim that Dylann Roof self-identified as a Christian. Various pages are imbued with crosses. Page six of the journal has a very intricate drawing of White Jesus in the similitude of ancient Christian iconography. The picture depicts the apotheosis of the risen Christ, signified by the halo around Jesus's head and the epithet "Jesus" written above it. Additionally, the drawing has the abbreviations of IC and XC, which are popular Eastern Orthodox abbreviations of the Greek word for Christ. The drawing suggests an

---

[333] W. J. Hennigan, "Who Planted Pipe Bombs in D.C.? Feds Hope New Video Leads to Tips," *TIME*, Politics-Extremism, March 9, 2021.

[334] Paul A. Djupe and Ryan P. Burge, "Trump the Anointed?" Religion in Public: Exploring the Mix of the Sacred and Secular (Blog), retrieved on June 9, 2022, from https://religionin-public.blog/2020/05/11/trump-the-anointed/.

[335] Jones, *White Too Long*, 138–40.

[336] Melissa Ramirez Cooper, "ELCA presiding bishop to attend funeral in Charleston, S.C.," retrieved June 12, 2022, https://elca.org/News-and-Events/7757 .

intimate knowledge with Christian art history. The journal also contains his personal insignia, constructed of a variant of the cross created by the Russian Orthodox Church, with four different white supremacy symbols. Finally, on page 31–32 of his journal, Dylann critiques a certain mode of Christianity as expressed by "modern preachers," who advocated a "Leave it to God; there is nothing you can do about it" form of Christianity. Dylann rejected this type of Christianity for a more "warrior" oriented Christianity.[337] In sum, Dylann Roof possessed a theology of violence, albeit in its extreme form, which was, nevertheless, thoroughly intertwined with his Christian worldview. For all intents and purposes, Dylann is a Christian.

A Resistance Theology

The egregious nature of this type of theologizing from our white brothers and sisters in Christ, particularly in their position as the dominant power brokers of American Christian society, necessitates, then, the Black Christian's need to disturb our white brothers and sisters in Christ' hermeneutical gaze.[338] White Christians in America are susceptible to an *unexamined* theology of violence. It is unexamined because they may not be fully aware of it, and to my knowledge, Black folks have yet to explicitly name it as such. Still, if white Christian's theology of violence has been weaponized against us, African American Christians need a resistance theology, by which they can "fight back" and could include but is not limited to a literal physical self-defense.

At this point, it is fitting to disclose the second paradigm on which I build my proposal for a theology of resistance for the African

---

[337] Dylann Roof, "Personal Journal," cited as government "Exhibit 500" in trial. Posted online at Scribd, retrieved on June 9, 2022, https://www.scribd.com/document/335820753/Dylann-Roof-s-jailhouse-journal#fullscreen&from_embed.

[338] In some ways, this is what Esau McCaulley is attempting to accomplish in his book, *Reading While Black:* particularly in chapter two: "Freedom Is No Fear: The New Testament and a Theology of Policing" (*Reading While Black: African American Biblical Interpretation as an Exercise in Hope* [Downers Grove, IL: IVP Academic, 2020], 25–46).

American church. Bishop Oscar Romero is a bishop in Latin America asking similar questions in his context that I am raising in this paper, and offers the following conditions of what he refers to legitimate violence, i.e., self-defense. I find them to be helpful for delineating my view of a resistance theology that could include literal self-defense, even if other paradigms such as no self-defense is feasible at times: (1) It (self-defense) should not be greater than the unjust aggression (e.g., if it is enough to defend oneself with one's fists, then it is not allowed to shoot an aggressor. (2) It must be in proportion to the need, only after every other peaceable means have been tried. (3) That the violence used in defense does not bring, in retaliation, an even greater evil than that being resisted.[339]

By suggesting this type of theo-political imagination, I am, in some ways, recapturing a more robust political theology that current popular church discourse has seemingly disallowed. However, it is important to highlight that "my recapturing" of this theology signifies a retrieval of a political theology that has historically existed within the Black church's tradition before and during the Civil Rights movement.[340]

For example, we can speak of Black Christians examples of the antebellum period, in which armed resistance was a viable option for activism. As Charles Lattimore Howard has noted, "The movement for liberation from the institution of slavery was fought on many fronts and in many different ways. Some fought for freedom through armed revolt—revolts led by people like Denmar Vesey and Nat Turner."[341] What often goes underemphasized, though, is the fact that both Denmark Vesey and Nat Turner were preachers who *first* shaped the

---

[339] Romero, *Voice of the Voiceless*, 159.
[340] See, e.g., Akinyele O. Umoja, "The Ballot and the Bullet: A Comparative Analysis of Armed Resistance in the Civil Rights Movement," *Journal of Black Studies*, 29.4 (1999): 558–78.
[341] Charles Lattimore Howard, *Black Theology as Mass Movement* (New York: Palgrave McMillan, 2014), 26.

thinking of their followers with a "Black Liberation Theology" before their *actual* "Exodus" from slavery could take place.[342] Thus, as long as Black folks have had even a basic understanding of the scriptures, they immediately began to appropriate a form of theological activism, not limited to pacifism, to resist the violence done to them.

Additionally, in 1966, Martin Luther King, Jr. conceded to proposals of the Student Nonviolent Coordinating Committee (SNCC) and the Congress of Racial Equality (CORE) led by Stokely Carmichael and Floyd McKissick, respectively, to contract the Deacons of Defense, a Black Christian paramilitary group, for security.[343] This was the end result of debates going back to 1964, which ultimately resulted in SNCC and CORE deciding that armed self-defense was a viable tactic and tool in the struggle to achieve human rights.[344] However, despite King's minor concession, which he did out of fear of fragmenting the movement, it was unambiguously clear where he stood with nonviolence resistance, teaching his model in Black churches across the South, even unto his death.[345] Still, what this shows, then, is that, while King's legacy contains a form of activism that prioritized nonviolent resistance, the civil rights movement itself, particularly as it reflects what was seen as a viable tool for Black Christians, was more variegated than what his legacy emphasizes. King, himself, recognizes this in his 1958 essay, "An Experiment in Love." In it he explains why nonviolence philosophy became palatable for Black folks: "It is

---

[342] Justin Fornal, "Nat Turner's Slave Uprising Left Complex Legacy," *National Geographic*, October 5, 2016, https://www.nationalgeographic.com/culture/article/nat-turner-slave-rebellion-legacy; Douglas R. Egerton, "Why They Did Not Preach up This Thing: Denmark Vesey and Revolutionary Theology," *The South Carolina Historical Magazine* 100.4 (1999): 298–318.

[343] Umoja, "The Ballot and the Bullet," 558.

[344] James Forman, *The Making of Black Revolutionaries* (New York: Macmillan, 1972), 374–75."

[345] See also "Southern Christian Leadership Conference," *King Encyclopedia* (Stanford University). Retrieved at https://kinginstitute.stanford.edu/encyclopedia/southern-christian-leadership-conference-sclc.

probably true that most of them did not believe in nonviolence as a philosophy of life, but because of their confidence in their leaders and because of nonviolence was presented to them as a simple expression of Christianity in action, they were willing to use it as a technique."[346] This shows in King's own words the presence of another paradigm for Black Christians. Still, despite the presence of an alternative model of activism, it is not difficult to see how King's assassination and consequent martyrdom status would begin to solidify his form of activism as the *sine qua non* of Black Christian response to white violence, even white Christian violence.

A Critique of Nonviolence's Ethic in MLK's Discourse

King's nonviolent resistance was an amalgamation of Christian political theologizing (e.g., Thomas Aquinas, Howard Thurman), naturalist philosophy (e.g., Henry David Thoreau's civil disobedience), pragmatic inspiration (Gandhi's movement in India), and Scripture. [347] Still, King was a preacher. And, because of the centrality of Black preachers in the Christian community, he would help cement a nonviolent ethic (including no self-defense) as the default Christian response for Black Christians' race relations for generations to come.

Turning, then, our attention particularly to two of King's principles of nonviolence, I offer a few critiques: first, by evaluating the logical flaws in King's own rhetoric and then, secondly on

---

[346] Washington, *A Testament of Hope*, 17.

[347] See e.g., Lawrence Dunbar Reddick, *A Crusader Without Violence: The First Biography of Martin Luther King, Jr., 60th Anniversary edition*, Intr. Derryn Moten (Montgomery, AL: NewSouth Books, 2018) [Kindle version], 18–25. Interestingly, King does not get his nonviolence ideology from Thoreau, who did not disapprove of revolution (in the literal sense) in case of an unjust government (see e.g., Thoreau's, "On Civil Disobedience;" "A Plea for Captain John Brown;" cf. James J. Donahue, "Hardly the Voice of the Same Man:" 'Civil disobedience' and Thoreau's Response to John Brown. *The Midwest Quarterly* 48.2, 247–65 [2007]; James Goodwin, "Thoreau and John Brown: Transcendental Politics," *ESQ: A Journal of the American Renaissance*, 25.3, 156–68 [1979]).

biblical grounds. The two principles of King's nonviolence philosophy subjected to our scrutiny are: (1) "Non-violence seeks to win friendships and understanding" from those who do injustice against you.[348] (2) "It [Non-violence] not only avoids external violence but the internal violence of the spirit."[349] My critique of these two principles will proceed in three progressions: (1) First, I will seek to show that these two principles taken together demonstrate that King erroneously conflates self-defense with hatred. (2) Secondly, I will seek to show that by arguing for love and friendship as the means of deconstructing the cycle of racial animus, King erroneously grounds white racism against Black people as a motif primarily built on hatred and not racial superiority. Consequently, his theology of nonviolence fails to adequately address how in the context of white American racism, the presence of "friendship or love" does not necessarily entail a deconstruction of self-perceptions of white hegemony and concomitantly white violence against Black people. (3) Thirdly, I will seek to counteract some of King's "Christianizing" of his nonviolence principles through his scriptural allusions, by providing an exegetical treatment of some of the passages in Scripture that seemingly coincide with King's principles.

A Summary of Nonviolence's Goal to Win Friendships and Understanding

King expounds on the goal of nonviolence as that which "seeks to win friendships and understanding." He states, "Nonviolence does not seek to defeat or humiliate the opponents, but to win his friendship

---

[348] Martin Luther King, Jr., "Non-Aggression Procedures to Interracial Harmony," Address Delivered at the American Baptist Assembly and American Home Mission Agencies Conference, (July 23, 1956), retrieved at https://kinginstitute.stanford.edu/king-papers/documents/non-aggression-procedures.

[349] James M. Washington, *A Testament of Hope: The Essential Writings and Speeches of Martin Luther King, Jr.* (San Francisco: HarperCollins, 1986), 8.

and understanding."³⁵⁰ In his explanation of this point, King would further express, "The nonviolent resister must often express his protest through noncooperation or boycotts." But these are not an end unto themselves. According to King, nonviolence is "a means to awaken a sense of moral shame in the opponent. The aftermath of nonviolence is the creation of the beloved community."³⁵¹ According to James Washington, a premier MLK scholar, "The year 1966 brought with it the first public challenge to the philosophy and strategy of nonviolence from within the ranks of the civil rights movement."³⁵² This is when resolutions of self-defense begin to sound forth. King responded that, "It was extremely dangerous to organize a movement around self-defense. The line between violence and aggressive or retaliatory violence is a fine line indeed. When violence is tolerated even as a means of self-defense, there is a grave danger that in the fervor of emotions, the main fight will be lost over the question of self-defense."³⁵³ King's own words show that when he speaks of nonviolence, he is also negating the viability of self-defense. In light of nonviolence's goal to win friendships, Black folks' human rights can only be achieved, in King's philosophy, through pacifism.

If we synthesize King's second principle of nonviolence: *winning friendships and understanding* with his objection against self-defense, which he himself relates to nonviolence's goal to win friendships, then we are able to infer a process that looks something like this. (1) Racial opponents of Black people oppress them through legal, social, and economic means, even in violent ways. (2) Black people protest these things through sit-ins and boycotts, which King anticipated would inevitably perpetuate more violence against Black people. Nevertheless, (3) the violence against Black people during nonviolent protests

---

[350] Ibid., 7.
[351] Ibid., 8.
[352] Ibid., 54.
[353] Ibid., 57.

should not in any way result in Black people defending themselves. They should remain nonviolent (i.e., no self-defense) in order to win the friendship of their opponents. This friendship occurs under the assumption that nonviolence (i.e., no self-defense) is perceivably the best way to awaken the moral conscience of the nonviolent protesters' opponents. This would also perceivably lead (4) to the deconstruction of the legal, social, and economic oppression of Black people because whites now see Black people as their friends, resulting in what King calls the "Beloved community."

A Summary of Nonviolence's Goal to Avoid Internal Violence of the Spirit

The second principle under our scrutiny is King's fourth principle of nonviolence: "It (nonviolence) avoids not only external physical violence but also internal violence of the spirit."[354] King expounds on this and says, "At the center of the nonviolence stands the principle of love. In struggling for human dignity, the oppressed people of the world must not allow themselves to become bitter or indulge in hate campaigns. To retaliate with hate and bitterness would do nothing but intensify the hate in the world."[355] Here, King conflates love with nonviolence. Additionally, and perhaps inadvertently, he also conflates self-defense with hate. We know these two assertions are partially true because we have already seen from his treatment of the principle that *nonviolence seeks friendships* that nonviolence includes self-defense.

Further investigation shows that whether intentional or not, King conflates hate with self-defense. This no more evident than when he gave his commentary on his house being bombed. On the night of January 30, 1956, a white terrorist stuck a stick of dynamite on

---

[354] Ibid., 8.
[355] Ibid., 8.

King's porch, bombing his Montgomery home. King says, "Many men wanted to retaliate, to place an armed guard on my home. But the issue there was not my life, but whether Negroes would achieve first-class treatment...Had we become distracted by the question of my safety, we would have lost the moral offensive and sunk to the level of our oppressors."[356] The context of Kings words is that he and his editorial team had to give a defense of nonviolence as the only road to freedom for Black folks against a new wave of strident militancy within the civil rights movement. In the defense of nonviolence, he starts his treatise by saying, "The line between defensive violence and aggressive or retaliatory violence is a fine line indeed." He then uses the bombing of his own house as an example of his commitment against self-defense. It is noteworthy, however, how King skillfully mislabels the concern for the men to guard his house as "retaliation." In the quote above, one notices that King distinguishes between "defensive violence" (self-defense) and "aggressive or retaliatory violence."[357] Yet, when he speaks of the men's concern for guarding his house, he does not speak to it as self-defense but associates it with aggressive or retaliatory violence. Technically, the men were not speaking of *retaliation*; they were not advocating finding the men who bombed King's house and reciprocating a bomb on the white men's houses. Instead, they were only speaking of "guarding his house" (self-defense) if someone tried to bomb it again. So, by labeling their concern as retaliatory in the context of his aforementioned dichotomy, King is stacking the proverbial deck by creating a strawman out of their argument. King goes on with his commentary: "I must continue by faith, or it is too great a burden to bear, and violence, even in self-defense, creates more problems than it solves. Only a refusal to *hate* or kill can put an end to the chain of

---

[356] Washington, *A Testament of Hope*, 57.
[357] Ibid., 57.

violence in the world and lead us toward a community where men can live together without fear."

In sum, a close look at King's use of love and love-oriented words (e.g., friendship, forgiveness, reconciliation) are almost inextricably linked to pacifism.[358] Contrastingly, self-defense is inextricably linked to hatred. This virtually leaves no room for a third choice, in which one can love a person (i.e., show acts of benevolence towards them) and still defend oneself against their assaults.

Problematic Assumptions: The Inadequacy of Solely Addressing Hatred-Oriented Racism

Additionally, it is also clear that racial hatred is key issue that King is trying to rectify. Racism is not just an ideology of racial hatred, though; it is primarily an ideology of racial superiority from which racial hatred flows. This fact has led Isabel Wilkerson to speak of the inevitable narcissism of America's racial caste system.[359] "No matter how degraded their lives, white people are still allowed to believe that they have the superiority. They never become black."[360] What this means for our current discussions is that those in racial castes do not always have to hate their opponents in order to be racist, nor to justify their theology of violence. They could in theory not hate Black people and still think that they are intrinsically superior. Thus, when King grounds his nonviolence theology in addressing the issue of hatred, he is only addressing the symptomatic ideology allowing for the root issue of white superiority to remain.

Historically, in the system of American racism hierarchy, racists could actually perceive themselves to love those at the bottom

---

[358] Ibid., 57.
[359] Isabel Wilkerson, *Caste: The Origins of our Discontents* (New York: Random House, 2020), 268–78.
[360] Wilkerson, *Caste*, 269.

of the racial caste (i.e., reserve affections and no animus towards) other races, viz., Black folks; just as long, "they, the black folks, stay in their place" of subservience. In fact, slave narratives reveal that in a context of American racism, Black children were allowed to be "friends" of white children of the slave master. They grew up together, played together, cried together—shared childhood memories together. These relationships sometimes continued all the way to the adulthood, in which the enslaved Blacks remained in a subservient relationship of slaves to their white "friend"-masters who inherited the authority over the plantations.[361] It is that same logic of thinking that exposes the disjunction between whites who think they are not racist because they have Black "friends" whereas those same Black friends undoubtedly believe that their white "friends" are in fact racist. The perception underlying well-meaning whites is that "if racism is fundamentally an expression of racial hatred, I cannot be a racist since I do not hate Black people." For them, the opposite is true because "I have Black friends." These types of ambiguities created by the ideological racism of white hegemony reveal (1) the need for King to define "friendships" and more importantly (2) that Black people winning the "friendship" of their white opponents in a context where white hegemony has not been first deconstructed, does not automatically entail the eradication of the racial oppression of Black people. To "seek to win friendships and understanding from those who do injustice against you" is a tremendous goal. If we can make friends out of our enemies, by all means, we need to do so (cf. Matt. 5:25). However, King's thinking that Black Christians' (and Black people in general) opting for no self-defense against those who would do violence against them, would somehow awaken, in some lasting manner, the moral conscience of Black people's racial opponent is overly optimistic. It is

---

[361] See e.g., David K. Wiggins, "The Play of Slave Children in the Plantation Communities of the Old South, 1820–1860," *Journal of Sport History*, 7.2 (1980): 21–39, specifically 31–34.

akin to thinking that a high school bully will eventually get a moral conscience about their victimization of one of their peers the more the peer does not fight back. It is possible. However, to the extent that the bully perceives themselves to be the superior and the other child the inferior, the assumption that the other child's lack of self-defense would result in the bully's moral conscience rest on untenable premise. The bully, by the very nature of bullying does not feel diminished in their bullying; they feel empowered. This is because, in the process of bullying and consequent victimization, the bully's self-perceived notion of superiority is reinforced. Similarly, King's second principle: making friends out of our enemies, without first deconstructing the power differentials intrinsic to America's *ideological* racism, viz., the concept of racial superiority only causes Black Christians to absorb the pernicious effects of white violence and does nothing to challenge white Christians' theology of violence. In fact, it erroneously presents an undefined notion of friendship as the catalyst for that deconstruction.

Nonviolence's Ethic in Matthew 5?

Moreover, since King was essentially leading an African American Christian movement, it would be his ability to find resonances with Christian scriptures, especially Jesus's Sermon on the Mount, which served as the primary moral underpinning of his nonviolence theology. After all, it was Jesus who said, "When someone strikes you on (your) right cheek, turn the other one to him as well. (Matt. 5:39 NAB)." I believe due to King's Christianizing of his nonviolent philosophy, the Black church has been guilty of erroneously appropriating MLK's nonviolence ethic in ways that supersede the restrictions Scripture itself puts on the believer.[362]

---

[362] James Washington makes a similar critique, arguing that King relied heavily on the systematic analysis of the Christian concept of 'love' (*agape*) in the works of Anders Nygren, a noted Swedish theologian. Paul Tillich critiques the view of Nygren, and King, even as a

In fact, the more I read Matthew 5, the more I conclude that it was likely not intended to be a paradigm for responding to all acts of violence. First, if we examine Matthew 5 from the literary context of the book of Matthew, we find that, in the book of Matthew, Jesus circumvents being the object of violence when possible. Matthew repeatedly describes Jesus's actions with the word anachōreō, "to withdraw." Almost every time Jesus is the subject of this verb in Matthew, it describes Jesus's action in dangerous situations. When Herod tried to kill baby Jesus, Joseph "withdrew," anachōreō, to Egypt (2:13). When Jesus heard that John the Baptist was taken into custody to be killed, Jesus "withdrew," anachōreō, to Galilee (4:12). When Jesus found out that the Pharisees wanted to destroy him, he "withdrew," anachōreō, from there (12:15). These passages suggest that we are not necessarily called to endure suffering in contexts where God has supplied a way out. It would, then, stand to reason that we do not have to be subjugated to violence in a context where we are legally provided an opportunity to protect ourselves, particularly if it has nothing to do with suffering for the faith.

Secondly, the Beatitudes establishes an important context often neglected in discussing Jesus's sermon on the Mount. In Matt. 5:1011, arguably the climax of the Beatitudes, Jesus pictures a new-covenant community that he says is "persecuted for righteous sake... and on account of Me." Thus, Jesus's conversation about responding to violence, viz., turning the other cheek is not contextualized in light of any and all violence; it is specifically cast in the light of Christian persecution. The context suggests that the people envisioned in Jesus's sermon are those subjected to violence *because* of their faith in Christ as their Lord. After all, to say that Jesus was Lord was to say that Caesar was not. In that vein, their suffering of violence was redemptive (i.e., integral to their Christian witness). But that does not

---

Tillich scholar, overlooks Tillich's critique and still erroneously appropriates the misinterpretation of agape in scripture (*A Testament of Hope,* 16).

mean that all violent suffering is redemptive, neither does it mean that all suffering is for the sake of Christ's name. To be persecuted for Christ is different from being persecuted for one's race. To be clear, King's house was not bombed, and Black people were not being lynched or even being discriminated against because they were Christians; it was because they were Black. Failure to make this distinction, I believe, has led to a type of pernicious racial internalization of a collective expectation of the Black Christian community to mitigate the atrocities done towards it by white Americans under the guise of Christian moral superiority. Thus, when Dylann Roof took the lives of nine Black Christians, three days later, on June 20, 2015, ABC News was broadcasting headlines about victims of the family offering forgiveness. Again, to be clear, forgiveness is not the problem; that's what Christians do. Still, the act of parading Black people using love-oriented language (i.e., forgiveness) of a white terrorist definitely reinforces a familiar trope of the civil rights movement, evoking love-oriented terminology in a context of white violence perpetrated against them. It's the same reason why Brandt Jean, a devout Christian, felt the need to tell Amber Guyger, a white police officer who unlawfully murdered his brother, "I want the best for you, and I don't even want you to go to jail."[363] Brandt seemingly has theological convictions that pressure him to absorb the violence done against him and his family out of Christian commitment, even to the point of mitigating consequences for a white perpetrator of violence, and even when the circumstance had nothing to do with Christian persecution. If Matthew 5 is, as we have argued, to be contextualized specifically in light of Christian persecution, then, there is no reason to use Matthew 5 as a call to let people do any and all sorts of

---

[363] Bill Hutchinson, "Extraordinary Acts of Mercy: Brother of Botham Jean Hugs and Forgives Amber Guyger After 10-Year Sentence Imposed." *ABC NEWS*, October 2, 2019, retrieved at https://abcnews.go.com/US/jury-deciding-sentence-police-officer-amber-guyger-wrong/story?id=66002182 on September 14, 2021.

violence towards us when they deem it necessary under some notion of "Christian responsibility."

In that vein, would we tell a male being raped in prison to resist nonviolently? What redemptive purposes will that have? Understanding the contextual factors of Matthew 5 prevents the Christian community from telling a Christian wife who is suffering violence from an abusive husband to "turn the other cheek," viz., telling her that her Christian duty is to submit and endure physical suffering?[364] The solution, we suggest, would not necessarily entail that the battered wife physically fight back either.[365] We, are, however, suggesting that theologizing Matthew 5 to apply to all sorts of violence outside of being persecuted for The Faith is inappropriate.

Of course, the examples that I just gave about men being raped and wives being abused are not necessarily examples of Christian suffering and, therefore, could undermine my point. However, it actually proves my point. If the aforementioned examples are inadequate applications of Matthew 5 then so is King's application. The racial violence perpetrated against Black folks was not the result of Christian persecution; it was merely because they were Black. Yet, King still advocated that Black people turn the other cheek.

For some, even if they allow for my interpretation of Matthew 5 and my critique of King's misinterpretation of Matthew 5, there remains Luke 22:36–38, which purportedly complicates my thesis. At

---

[364] For how this scripture is weaponized against women in the Christian context, see e.g., D.S., Jayasundara, R.C., Nedegaard, K. Flanagan, et. al., "Leveraging Faith to Help End Domestic Violence: Perspectives from Five Traditions," *Social Work and Christianity*, 44.4, 39–66 (2017), 54.

[365] Some of the challenges of women defending themselves can be seen in the story told by the correspondent, Meredith Vieira, "The Framingham Eight," Airdate: July 20, 1994, https://library.uwosh.edu/streaming/streams/fod100054310. Eight battered women who fought back from domestic abuse and ended up in prison, claiming their actions were in self-defense. The scenarios show the various factors of consequence-oriented ethics but also inherent disparities in our judicial system that necessitate resistance theology consider certain contextual factors.

one time, I would have agreed with this objection. However, upon further investigation, I am no longer sure that Luke 22:36–38 unequivocally complicates my thesis.

Nonviolence's Ethic in Luke 22:36–38?

In this vein, we turn to Luke 22:36–38. The text reads as follows:

> And He said to them, 'But now, let him who has a purse take it along, likewise also a bag, and let him who has no sword sell his robe and buy one. For I tell you, that this which is written must be fulfilled in Me, 'And He was numbered with transgressors; for that which refers to Me has *its* fulfillment." And they said, 'Lord, look, here are two swords.' And He said to them, 'It is enough.

The plain sense of the passage seems to be apparent. Jesus is supplying an opportunity for his disciples to physically defend themselves. However, this plain sense of meaning is often questioned and rejected within most of modern Christendom. To be sure, reasons for doing so are logical, but I suggest it is not the only logical way to interpret this passage.

One of the challenges that Luke 22:36–38 presents is that it appears to contradict what Jesus said in Matthew 5, which we have already argued is not a statement against all and every violence. Secondly, it appears to be in tension with Luke 22:50–51, where Jesus prevents his disciples from using those same swords, which he "prescribed" earlier, to protect him from arrest. The implication appears that he does not intend for his believers to participate in any armed resistance. In this vein, Luke 22:50–51 is used as the interpretive grid for understanding Luke 22:36–38. The result, then, is a need to reconcile what seems to be the plain sense of Luke 22:36–38 with the apparent implications of Luke 22:50–51.

Thus, the following types of interpretation have been presented of Luke 22:36–38: [366] 1) the majority view: Jesus's words are figurative.[367] 2) The minority view: Jesus's words are literal (a view that I will take).[368] According to one argument of the figurative view, buying a sword is to fulfill Scripture.[369] The "for," in conjunction with the "fulfillment formula" in 37, could suggest this. Sharon Ringe's commentary seems to echo this interpretation. Thus, she says, "Their bearing of a sword—even two of them—places Jesus 'among the lawless' who disturb the peace and represent a threat to the authorities,"[370] which could serve as justification for the type of interpretation that occurred directly above. Ringe's assessment shows that she interprets the sword motif in light of Isa. 53:12, which speaks of being "numbered among the transgressors." Nothing, however, in Isaiah's passage speaks of buying a sword or any other item on the list that Jesus mentioned. Thus, it is difficult to see how Jesus's suggestion to buy the sword fulfills Scripture. More likely, Jesus's allusion to Isa. 53:12 and the fulfillment formula in Luke 22:37 is not to speak of their actions fulfilling Scripture but to point to the mere fact that "the changing times," reflected in his

---

[366] Others have three options, but one possibility is just a sub option of one of the two (see e.g., Christopher Roy Hutson, "Enough for What? Playacting Isaiah 53 in Luke 22:35–38," *Restoration Quarterly* 55, 35–51 (2013), 36).

[367] E.g., Douglas Moo, *The Old Testament in the Gospel Passion Narratives* (Sheffield: Almond Press, 1983), 134–35; James Edwards, *The Gospel According to Luke*, Pillar New Testament Commentary (Grand Rapids: Eerdmans, 2015), 640; I. Howard Marshall, *The Gospel of Luke: A Commentary on the Greek Text*, New International Greek Testament Commentary (Exeter: Paternoster Press, 1978), 825; Robert H. Stein, *Luke*, vol. 24, The New American Commentary (Nashville: Broadman & Holman Publishers, 1992), 555; Joseph Fitzmyer, *Luke*, Anchor Bible Commentary, vol. 28a, (New York: Doubleday, 1985), 1432.

[368] See, e.g., S. G. F. Brandon, *Jesus and the Zealots: A Study of the Political Factor in Primitive Christianity* (Manchester: Manchester University Press, 1967), 205.

[369] E.g., Craig A. Evans, *Luke*, New International Biblical Commentary (Peabody, MA: Hendrickson, 1990), 320.

[370] Sharon Ringe, *Luke*, Westminster Biblical Companion (Louisville, KY: Westminster, 1995), 265.

sacrificial death, fulfills Scripture. His death is the fulfillment of Scripture, not the disciples' purchase of anything.

Still, the overwhelming majority of scholars are content to say Jesus's suggestion to buy a sword is figurative or symbolic. For example, I. Howard Marshall asserts the sword "refers to an attitude of mind rather than outward equipment."[371] Darryl Bock communicates a middle ground: the words to buy are literal, but the swords are not to be literally used. Thus, he argues, "They are being drawn into a great cosmic struggle, and they must fight with spiritual swords and resources. The purchase of swords serves only to picture this coming battle."[372] Similarly, Robert Stein says, "The "sword" is best understood in some metaphorical sense as indicating being spiritually armed and prepared for battle against the spiritual foes."[373] Joseph Fitzmyer appears to reckon the "spiritual" interpretation to be too far of a figurative interpretation and seeks to temper it with his own assessment: "Jesus' words about equipping oneself with purse, knapsack, and sword have to be taken in a symbolic sense, even if one may not read into it the sense of spiritual armor of Eph. 6:11–17."[374] (*Luke,* vol 28a, 1432). Upon deeper analysis, all of these interpretations have at least one thing in common: they conclude that the figurative interpretation is the only solution to the tension between Luke 22:36–38 and Luke 22:50–51.

Now to be sure, a figurative interpretation theologically is very possible. My problem, however, is two-fold: first, the figurative interpretation is not the only way to reconcile the tension between Luke 22:36–38 and Luke 22:50–51, for which I will offer another possibility momentarily. Secondly, the inconsistency in American Christian

---

[371] I. Howard Marshal, *Luke*, New International Greek Text Commentary, (Grand Rapids: Eerdmans, 1978), 825.
[372] Darrell Bock, *Luke*, IVP New Testament Commentary (Downers Grove: IVP, 1994), 355.
[373] Robert H. Stein, *Luke*, New American Commentary, vol. 24 (Nashville, TN: Broadman, 1992), 555.
[374] Fitzmyer, *Luke*, 1432.

application of this principle is problematic, to say the least. If Luke 22:50–51 is the interpretive grid through which we should interpret Luke 22:36–38, with the implications that we respond to violence with spiritual weapons and physically arming ourselves is inimical to our identity as kingdom citizens, then let us all—white, Black, Latino, Asian—Christians of all ethnicities collectively embrace this passage, and all become pacifists and hold each other accountable to it. It would be a great collective witness to our unity, appropriating a counter-cultural ethic, showing genuine fellowship, and suffering together across ethnic and social lines. In this way, we would join our Mennonite and Quaker brothers and sisters, who have long since appropriated a "no-sword" approach as a lifestyle.

Suppose this is somehow reasoned to be too impractical. In that case, we need to recognize the factors that are at play for that conclusion. More importantly, we realize in the context of our current conversation that the inconsistency privileges certain Christian groups over others. It reinforces the status quo by policing one population yet feeling no sense of urgency to police another sector of the population with the same theology.

Thus, contrastingly, and against an overwhelming current of consensus, I contend that Luke 22:36–38 is literal. It is interesting to notice the list in which the sword is present. In Luke 22, it is listed among a traveler's bag (small suitcase), a wallet (i.e., money bag), and sandals. All these things are essential for traveling, suggesting that we view the sword as a typical traveling accessory. In fact, it is interesting that they already had two swords, and Jesus never tells them to get rid of them, even after they formally "disclosed" how many they had (Luke 22:38). This would have been a good time for Jesus to say, get rid of all swords; they are unbecoming of my disciples. Rather, he says, "it is enough," not for a war against Rome (that would be absurd), but for simple protection traveling on the road (cf. Luke 22:38).

Even more interesting is the context in which this verse is present. Jesus tells his disciples, "Before I told you not to take" certain things with you on the journey. As missionaries, they were to be at the mercy and the hospitality of their hosts. But now, with Jesus getting closer to his mission of dying on the cross, things are going to change drastically. The type of friendliness and hospitality they received because of Jesus's name will no longer be the default culture. Thus, not only can they no longer depend on the hospitality of the common stranger, it appears that they may need to defend themselves against the common stranger also. In this way, Jesus tells them to buy a sword.

If, however, Jesus's suggestion to take a sword is figurative, as seems to be the overwhelming consensus, then might we expect Jesus's suggestion to take a wallet and a "suitcase" to be figurative too? To be sure, some scholars do interpret these items this way. Still, they fail to demonstrate what this means in application. Are the disciples to literally take all these items (including a sword) but never use any of them because the items only have "symbolic" value? If so, what would be the purpose of carrying around a traveler's bag, wallet, and sword as some sort of spiritual memento? Or is it that Jesus's whole speech is only to be evaluated theologically? If this is the case, what genre of speech shall we compare Luke 22:36–38 to help us objectively make that decision?

Additionally, if they are not literally to take anything for their journey, then why does Jesus compare this situation to a previous situation where the suggestion was literal? It is clear that Jesus literally wanted them not to take anything with them the first time. This suggests, by comparison (i.e., but now), he literally wants them to take sword with them for their journey this time. These observations suggest that while the figurative interpretation seeks to solve one problem, viz., the tension between Luke 22:36–38 and Luke 22:50–51, it appears to create a plethora of other problems, for which it offers no solution.

Luke 22:36–38 speaks of protecting themselves from general danger due to the times changing.[375] However, that doesn't mean that Jesus wants them to physically fight to prevent his going to the cross; that would be counter-productive to his entire reason for coming. This, I believe, is why Matthew 26:52 speaks in proverbial terms of the danger of the sword without forthrightly condemning it.[376] Similarly, the danger of violence even in self-defense has been well documented.[377] We conclude then that Luke 22:36–38 offers a viable scriptural justification for self-defense as integral part of a resistance theology: it's a tool but not the sole tool.

Conclusion and Synthesis

In this paper, I have suggested that the Black church needs a more robust resistance theology to counteract the white Christian American's unexamined theology of violence. The nonviolence resistance theology found in the Civil Rights Movement was pacifism, and, therefore, by its very nature, extreme. Perhaps, it reflected the extremities of its day. However, the ethic in and of itself cannot bear the full weight of resistance of white Christian America's theology of violence. In fact, I have suggested further that in a context where racism is primarily a matter of racial superiority that principles such as using the lack of self-defense as a tool for constructing friendships with our enemies only reinforces the dominant caste interests. The Black Christian's talk of self-defense, then, should not be seen as a departure from our Christian roots nor as slippery slope to a violent revolution, particularly if the white Christian American's theology of violence remains. This speaks to a safety issue for African Americans.

---

[375] See also John Nolland, *Luke 18:35–24:53*, Word Biblical Commentary 35 (Dallas: Word, Inc., 1993), 1076.
[376] Contra our position on Matt. 26:52, see Jon Sobrino, *Jesus the Liberator: A Historical-Theological Reading of Jesus of Nazareth* (Maryknoll, NY: Orbis Books, 1993), 214.
[377] Most notably by Romero, *Voice of the Voiceless*, 125–76, especially 157–59.

The Black church then has a responsibility to stand in the gap by challenging the ideological assumptions of white Christian America's theology of violence.

Consequently, I have offered a small contribution to this end by challenging the ascendancy of nonviolence, viz.., pacifism's ethic in discourse. I have also challenged some of the Biblical interpretations designed to legitimize that ethic and offered my own interpretations as an integral part of my resistance theology, drawing some from Bishop Oscar Romero. Admittedly, however, this essay falls short in that more needs to be said about how my paradigm challenges the idea of racial superiority, something on which I critiqued the nonviolence resistance of the Civil Rights. In that vein, one can see my contribution as deconstructing the assumption that Civil Rights' ethic of nonviolence is the *sine qua non* of Black activism. This will hopefully open the door for more robust constructive theology.

Call, Chant, Cry, Shout: The Rhythms of African-Inspired Diaspora Preaching

Jaclyn P. Williams

Introduction

The sounds and rhythms of African-inspired diaspora preaching testify to the lives of those from whom the word is preached and to whom the word is proclaimed. In the holistically engaged body of the preacher, the call, chant, cry, and shout are witnesses and reflection points. Eyes have seen and ears have heard.[378]

There is a revelation in the heart of the call, in the grounding of the chant, and in the unfiltered emotion of the cry. These crescendos and decrescendos create space, hold, nurture, and motivate towards renewing spaces for the mind, body, and spirit to flourish. Due to repressive realities within the temporal world, there is an imperative need for the space and the renewal. Vocal rhythms are catalyst and creation, as they are inherently connected to formation and transformation through God's Spirit; preaching that proclaims Jesus Christ as Lord, Savior, and Friend, preaching that seeks to discern and disciple. Preachers who accept the call to facilitate spiritual formation by

---

[378] 1 Cor. 2: 9-10 unless otherwise noted, all biblical citations are from the New Revised Standard Version (NRSV).

attuning to the vocal rhythms must consider and incorporate ways to intentionally nurture the formation through God's love and provision.

Preaching is about seeing and hearing the culture and responding with a word that ministers to the moment. Moreover, this informed preaching accompanies the formational movement that is always a part of God's love. Can preachers instinctually move in this flow of revelation and transformation and intentionally work with the flow? Introduction to "amen," harnessing the opportunity of being informed and formed by the very vocal rhythms emanating from pulpit and pew? If so, what might this mean for our communal worship and our collective formation?

This study will address these questions:

- Are the vocal rhythms—call, chant, cry, and shout—within African-formed diaspora preaching moments indicators of spiritual and cultural lived experience within the Church and society?
- If so, does it matter if preachers attune to these vocal rhythms?

As a prophet, priest, pastor, the preacher is the vessel of the word. He or she calls out to God, God provides, and the congregation responds, "Yes, He will. Because He has throughout all of history. Our lives are the witness and the testimony." The Word will allow the community to rise from those pews, travel it home, dare to survive, and be those who manifest a new definition of thriving.

Black Preaching Is...Call and Response

Do we know what is happening in the formation process when the Word is preached? There is an external manifestation of an inward celebration. But what about the inward transformation? Ultimately, much of what is happening, in terms of transformation, is the work of the Holy Spirit. However, does that preclude us from exploring what it might mean for preachers to accept an intentional enhancement of the role of the preacher? Can preachers facilitate edification and invite and usher in transformation using call and response as a homiletical method? Additionally, are the vocal rhythms—call, chant, cry, and shout—within African-formed diaspora preaching moments indicators of spiritual and cultural lived experience within the Church and society?

Bishop Vashti Murphy McKenzie helps us begin to build a framework for defining preaching within the realm of spiritual formation. "Preaching is a mixing bowl in which intellect and emotion are stirred together. Head and heart are blended with divine interaction into a potent feast. It is a tool of social justice and spiritual transformation that empowers its hearers."[379]

Black preaching is connected to Scripture, through relationship, tradition, and doctrine. Furthermore, the preacher is harnessing the emotion and intellect of the people. This emotional and intellectual connection is a manifestation of God opening the spirit and the soul to revelation that meets the needs and desires inherent within the human condition.

Rev. Dr. Teresa Fry Brown shares that "the role of the preacher is to assist the listeners in the identification of spiritual, social, cultural, psychological, and economic issues that have an impact on daily life."[380] This is the delicate and sensitive work of the mind, body, spirit, and soul. This is the work of transformation. The preacher's awareness and willingness to work within God's transformation work is vital. The preacher must surrender to the power of the proclamation and the formation. This requires a manifold submission to the Holy Spirit. This also requires an understanding that the preaching moment is an ongoing moment that can cultivate the fertile soil that God has already tilled and toiled over.

---

[379] Vashti McKenzie in *Those Preaching Women: Volume 4* ed, Ella Pearson Mitchell and Jacqueline B. Glass (Valley Forge, PA: Judson Press, 2004), 9.

[380] Teresa L. Fry Brown, *Delivering the Sermon: Voice, Body, and Animation in Proclamation* (Minneapolis, MN: Fortress Press, 2008), 2.

Rev. Dr. Kenyatta R. Gilbert defines African American preaching as "trivocal"—comprised of the prophet, priest, and sage—and shares that preaching is "is a ministry of Christian proclamation—a theo-rhetorical discourse about God's goodwill toward a community with regard to divine intentionality, communal care, and the active practice of hope—that finds resources internal to Black life in the North American context."[381] These definitions say that preaching identifies the holistic human condition realities that are named and nuanced within the moments of proclamation. Then the truth of the Gospel is offered as the treatment that brings healing. African American preaching is explicitly and functionally illuminating and implicitly formational. It must be if it is to be culturally relevant. Culture necessitates, "I need a word. I need to be changed." If we could only just touch the hem of that garment, we would be healed and transformed.[382]

Fry Brown's preacher as identifier engages with Gilbert's preacher as trivocal illuminator. Both are based on an intentional analysis and understanding of the community of listeners in the pews. The listeners are speaking who they are and what they need and desire in the realm of call and response, and the preacher is seeing and hearing their testimony while responding in kind.

The step further proposed by this study is that the role and work of preaching and the preacher is one of identifier and illuminator, as well of one of facilitator of formation. This is true of those preaching in any pulpit that proclaims the Gospel because the Gospel is transformation. However, there is a particularity found in the preaching of those proclaiming from the purview of the African diaspora that allows for this formational process to be particularly pronounced within homiletical methods and styles. The calls, the chants, the cries, and the shouts are not exclusively practice of the flesh. They are manifestations of inner

---

[381] Kenyatta R. Gilbert, *The Journey and Promise of African American Preaching* (Minneapolis, MN: Fortress Press, 2011), 11.
[382] Mark 5:22-43

needs and desires of the spirit. They acknowledge God's ministry of presence in those needs and desires.

This is to say that, while the preacher is identifying and illuminating, she or he is also explicitly moving with the Holy Spirit's work of formation and flourishing within the people. The preacher cultivates God-given seeds, plants within the God-enriched soil, humbly guarding the nurturing and nourishment, and harvests when the Spirit says, "It's harvest time." From "There is a word from the Lord," to "Amen," the message is a tool of spiritual edification and spiritual formation. Therefore, Black preachers, consecrated and anointed for the preaching call, are also inherently consecrated and anointed for the call of spiritual formation. Within God's template of transformation, one does not come without the other.

Acknowledge and Intentionally Act

The word of God aids preachers in this work of facilitating the call and response initiated by God and manifest in proclamation.

> I thank my God every time I remember you, constantly praying with joy in every one of my prayers for all of you, because of your sharing in the Gospel from the first day until now. I am confident of this, that the one who began a good work among you will bring it to *completion* by the day of Jesus Christ.[383]

The ἔργον [work] of the one who began it and will bring it about is a guide for preachers.[384] Hearing and listening to this guide is a

---

[383] Phil. 1: 3–6

[384] Joseph Henry Thayer, et al., *Thayer's Greek-English Lexicon of the New Testament: Coded with Strong's Concordance Numbers* (Peabody, MA: Hendrickson, 1995), See the definitions for ἔργον: any product whatever, anything accomplished by hand, art, industry, mind and ἐπιτελέσει: to bring to an end, accomplish, perfect, execute, complete for a fuller picture of how Paul is creating this image of formation.

foundational aspect of formation preaching. Paying heed to the vocal rhythms allows the preacher to hear and listen.

Preachers must intentionally acknowledge, accept, and celebrate this aspect of the call to preach. The benefit is found in how preachers process, prepare, and proclaim the word from God. This is a word that seeks not only to inform that Christ has come to "bring good news to the poor, proclaim release to the captives, recovery of sight to the blind, let the oppressed go free, and proclaim the year of the Lord's favor," but also seeks to preach a word that is a vessel, literally, of this transformation work.[385] The word is the wielder's tool, and the wielder is Christ.

Thus, it stands then that a definition of preaching as "theological" and "rhetorical," such as the description offered by homiletician Frank A. Thomas, must add the qualities of "practical" and "formational."[386] Dr. Thomas shares that African American preaching is theological—dealing with God and people—and rhetorical—persuasive and influential building —based upon the characterization offered by Lucy Lind Hogan and Robert Reid.[387] The message speaks to belief as well as renewal. Black preachers, based on tradition—historical and societal trajectory—know that the people in the pews need a way out of no way. Yes, it is inherent, but perhaps we can push what is ingrained into the actualized realm of what is intentional, making the implicit explicit, so that we might believe in transformation and surrender ourselves to being transformed by the word of the Lord and the Word that is Lord. Perhaps we must more intentionally press into the practical and formational aspects as we adhere to the theological and rhetorical import.

---

[385] Luke 4:18–19 NRSV.

[386] Frank A. Thomas, *Introduction to the Practice of African American Preaching* (Nashville, TN: Abingdon Press, 2016), 16.

[387] Lucy Lind Hogan and Robert Stephen Reid, *Connecting with the Congregation: Rhetoric and the Art of Preaching* (Nashville, TN: Abingdon Press, 1999). See the arguments presented in Chapter 1.

The Hum and the Rhythm

The history of African American preaching begins with enslaved peoples expressing religious freedom. By the time enslaved peoples had a Christologically focused religious and spiritual outlook, Black bodies were gathering in brush harbors, barns, gullies, and under trees participating in the invisible institution, so named by historian and scholar Albert J. Raboteau.[388] Here, we see the historical connection to needing holistically safe sacred spaces that allowed God's word to ring unencumbered by distorted and destructive interpretation. A vision of worship "was traditionally African with 'shouts,' 'ring dancing,' hand-clapping, and ecstatic expressions and utterances and led by one of their own."[389] All the while, preaching was the formation, resistance, healing, and a facilitated communion between divinity and humanity.

These first preachers proclaimed from a pulpit positioned in deep oppression and need and sought to illuminate hope and practical survival that transformed oppression into freedom. This work was formed around a framework of call and response due to the roots of this tradition within the people's history. Professor Elochukwu E. Uzukwu connects African initiation rites and Christian ritual practice.

> In African village life, rituals are designed for important stages along throughout one's life; and they connect people with the community's life at the deepest levels both for the society and for the individual. Because they are body language more than

---

[388] Albert J. Raboteau, *Slave Religion: The "Invisible Institution" in the Antebellum South* (New York, NY: Oxford University Press, 2004). See a complete description in Section 2, "The Invisible Institution." This institution birthed the first African American leadership and the first African American preachers.

[389] Frank A. Thomas, *Introduction to the Practice of African American Preaching* (Nashville, TN: Abingdon Press 2016), 21.

intellectual processes, these African rituals of initiation do transmit life and transform behavior.[390]

Uzukwu is critical of traditional Christian initiatory practice because it depends primarily upon cerebral knowledge rather than knowledge gained through action.[391] This work by Professor Uzukwu aids this study by articulating that the bodied and vocalized expression of call and response, chant, cry, and shout can be connected to a psychic memory and a sense of marking the seasons and manifestations of development in the seasons of life. This is not to say that ecstatic worship is only present in African American congregations. It is not to say that there is only one manifestation of the vocal embodied rhythms discussed. The rites are manifest in many indicators, rooted in the entirety of the individual and communal experiences. There are inherited hums and echoing rhythms that are an inherent part of shared life that allow us to respond to the call of God.

Call and Response: Chant, Cry, Shout

When speaking of call, chant, cry, and shout, this study is not speaking of a two-dimensional manifestation that negates the fully realized expression and experience of the fully realized people of the African diaspora. From "Let there be light"[392] to "Come Lord Jesus come,"[393] preaching from the living word of God to the people of God means proclaiming and modeling a life-breathed, life-forming message that encompasses in modality, method, and mission an actual process of renewal. There are sub-rhythms of chant, cry, and shout within the call

---

[390] Elochukwu W. Uzukwu, *Worship as Body Language Introduction to Christian Worship* (Collegeville, MN: The Liturgical Press, 1997). See the specific explanation throughout Chapter 2 "Ritual-Symbolic Action as Creating and Re-Creating Community."

[391] Ibid. Uzukwu expands his argument that it is through active and embodied rituals that people can move to a new level of knowing self, others, and God.

[392] Gen. 1:3

[393] Rev. 22:20

and response. Chant symbolizes resilience and endurance. The cry is a lament. The shout is joy. Thus, the listening community can bring the whole community of experience into the space of worship, opening themselves to the work of being renewed.

These are vocalized rhythms that we are flowing with and in and through. It is the with and in and through of the moment of proclamation. But it is also the with and in and through of formation, holistically. We—those whose breath emanates from the breath of God—are created with the capacity to be a manifestation of "right now" transformation. There is a spiritual, emotional, and physical pulse that arises. This kind of testimony is instinctual, inherent, truth representing and presenting. It's not about the particular movement—quiet head nod or fully-body ecstasy—but about the interchange and movement of the Triune God's work within us.

Spiritually and culturally, we are rooted in call and response. Chant, Cry, Shout. We will frame our discussion of chant, cry, and shout around Barbara A. Holmes' *Joy Unspeakable*, as it speaks to the emotional expression of the internal reality of the Black church.

> Joy Unspeakable
> is not silent,
> it moans, hums, and bends
> to the rhythm of a dancing universe.
> It is a fractal of transcendent hope,
> a hologram of God's heart,
> a black hole of unknowing. For our free African ancestors,
> joy unspeakable is drum talk
> that invites the spirits
> to dance with us,
> and tell tall tales by the fire. For the desert Mothers and Fathers,
> joy unspeakable is respite
> from the maddening crowds,
> and freedom from

> 'church' as usual. For enslaved Africans during the
> Middle Passage,
> joy unspeakable is the surprise
> of living one more day...[394]

God Created by Call and Response

When we preach, we proclaim a creator God of progress—redemptive, restorative, and resurrected—and flow with that progress. If proclamation can be named as a manifestation of God's continual revelation of Self to creation, then proclamation can be named as a part of how God is calling to creation. The moment of proclamation is an outpouring of a cycle of calling instigated by God.

The first call, from God, is creation. The call to be. We, the receivers, respond by living. The second call is to an intentional relationship. We respond by being intentionally present. The call cycle continues, mostly perfectly in the Incarnate Word that is Jesus Christ. When we preach, we are illuminating this continuing call. We are advocating for a response. To God. With our presence. With our surrender. With our service. With our method of proclamation. We are being formed by this cycle of call and response, facilitated by the message and invitation within the message. This is also a way of encouraging a worldview that expects the call, listens for it, hears it, and responds.[395]

---

[394] Barbara A. Holmes, *Joy Unspeakable: Contemplative Practices of Black Church* (Minneapolis, MN: Fortress Press, 2017) 19.

[395] Gen. 1: 1- 5. "In the beginning God created the heavens and the earth. Now the earth was formless and empty, darkness was over the surface of the deep, and the Spirit of God was hovering over the waters. And God said, 'Let there be light,' and there was light. God saw that the light was good, and he separated the light from the darkness. God called the light 'day,' and the darkness he called 'night.' And there was evening, and there was morning—the first day."

Chant: Praise, Protest, and Repeat

...and the freeing embrace of death
chosen and imposed. For Africans in bondage
in the Americas,
joy unspeakable is that moment of
mystical encounter
when God tiptoes into the hush arbor,
testifies about Divine suffering,
and whispers in our ears,
'Don't forget,
I taught you how to fly
on a wing and a prayer,
when you're ready
let's go!' Joy Unspeakable is humming
'how I got over'
after swimming safely
to the other shore of a swollen Ohio river
when you know that you can't swim.
It is the blessed assurance
that Canada is far,
but not that far.[396]

Chant is repeated rhythmic phrasing. It can travel the spectrum from praise to protest. It is the relentless manifestation of hope and faith in God's love and provision. A chant is simple and portable. Yet, the chant reaches the depths of who we are and what our soul is counting on and yearning for holistically. Chants are found in the Psalms[397] and other culturally significant manifestations.[398]

---

[396] Barbara A. Holmes, *Joy Unspeakable: Contemplative Practices of Black Church* (Minneapolis, MN: Fortress Press, 2017) 19-20.

[397] Psa. 117: 1-2 "1 Praise the Lord, all you nations; extol him, all you peoples. 2 For great is his love toward us, and the faithfulness of the Lord endures forever. Praise the Lord."

[398] Chisholm, Hugh, ed. *Encyclopedia Britannica. (11th ed.)* (Cambridge University Press, 1911) *846.*

Cry: Let us Lament

> For Africana members of the
> 'invisible institution,' the
> emerging black church,
> joy unspeakable is
> practicing freedom
> while chains still chafe,
> singing deliverance
> while Jim Crow stalks,
> trusting God's healing
> and home remedies,
> prayers, kerosene,
> and cow patty tea. For the tap dancing, boogie woogie,
> rap/rock/blues griots
> who also hear God,
> joy unspeakable is
> that space/time/joy continuum thing
> that dares us to play and pray
> in the interstices of life,
> it is the belief that the phrase
> 'the art of living'
> means exactly what it says.[399]

Historian Katherine Guerrero defines the cry as an expression coming from deep in the soul. She also challenges society to lean into, rather than away from, the cry. Her definition expands into how a community or culture may attune to the cry and formulate care for the soul. Her words acknowledge the impact and the pathway to transformation

---

[399] Barbara A. Holmes, *Joy Unspeakable: Contemplative Practices of Black Church* (Minneapolis, MN: Fortress Press, 2017) 19-20

offered by listening to the cries of individuals and communities.⁴⁰⁰ There is a core of pain that escapes with the cry. Preachers must prayerfully seek to hear the cry and the message behind the cry. Then, the preacher can intentionally create a space, through the sermon, that accompanies God's transformation and healing.

Shout: Freedom Found

> Joy Unspeakable
> is
> both FIRE AND CLOUD,
> the unlikely merger of
> trance and high tech lives
> ecstatic songs and a jazz repertoire
> Joy unspeakable is
> a symphony of incongruities
> of faces aglow and hearts
> on fire
> and the wonder of surviving together.⁴⁰¹

The shout is freedom found. It breaks through the bounds of finite temporality and engages the limitless spirituality offered through God. Dr. Thomas expresses,

> The nature and purpose of African American preaching is to help people experience the assurance of grace (the good news)

---

⁴⁰⁰ Katherine Guerrero, "The Liturgy of a Scream" in *Liturgy*, 36.2 (2021) 51-53. "The liturgy of their scream shows us how to pay attention to the place of rupture, to the cries of [those] who face violence and oppression around the world, past and present. It is a liturgy that challenges us. What if we were to pay attention to what their screams hold? What if we were to see their cry as one that escapes our ways of understanding yet, in that inexplicability, teaches us something about how to hold grief in our present moment and breathe? What if it were to teach us how to survive a world built from our dismay."

⁴⁰¹ Barbara A. Holmes, *Joy Unspeakable: Contemplative Practices of Black Church* (Minneapolis, MN: Fortress Press, 2017) 20.

that is the Gospel of Jesus Christ. Whenever the assurance of the grace of the Gospel is received and appropriated, the natural response is one of celebration and praise to God.[402]

The shout is a natural and needed expression of the soul, individually and communally. There is a resilience and insistence present in the shout. The urgency of the truth from a shout must be met with a similar sense of urgency from the preacher. This shared urgency is a tangible manifestation of being seen and heard by God and God's ministering presence.

Black Preaching Does...Feed Us and Form Us

As we name and explore manifestations of the call, chant, cry, and shout, we are being formed as we express ourselves freely. We implicitly acknowledge a connection to our cloud of witnesses, our psychic connection to our ancestry, and we engage with God's power to transform us. There is so much more happening than surface expression. There is an excavation process happening, and the vocal rhythms are guideposts.

> All preachers, no matter what their background, would like to move their listeners from praying 'Help 'em Lord!' to 'Amen!' and 'Glory Hallelujah!'...I want to look at those qualities of preaching which encourage an authentic response of 'Glory Hallelujah!' from the human heart, whether that ascription of

---

[402] Frank A. Thomas, *They Like to Never Quit Praisin' God: The Role of Celebration in Preaching* (Cleveland, OH: Pilgrim Press, 2013). Thomas shares, "The best of celebrative design excels at giving attention to emotional context by incorporating these five elements of emotional process: use of dialogical language, appeal to a core belief, concern for emotive movement, unity of form and substance, and creative use of reversals. Celebrative emotional process manages these five elements to generate creative and powerful sermonic forms to help people experience the assurance of grace that is at the heart of the gospel."

praise is spoken aloud or uttered through those sighs that lie too deep for words.[403]

When the preacher and the people exchange vocal rhythms, they dive into the cycle of awareness, reflection, edification, encouragement, healing, and catharsis. In addition, they are responding to the movements of God's hand. This is all happening simultaneously. We are caught up in the sacred cacophony, and it changes us.

At its best, Black preaching affirms the people in the pews and encourages the unfiltered expression of the call and response. Black preaching is disruption and integration. Preaching is disruption as a response to disruption in the world. Therefore, preaching is formational. Spiritually, emotionally, mentally, and physically freeing, an uncompromising space is created for an unashamed utterance of transformation. Preachers must intentionally invite the listeners into the space that God is creating for wholeness. They must hold the space with the help of the Holy Spirit and the empowerment of Christ. This goes beyond the exuberance of the moment and extends into all aspects of renewal and lived theology.

Caught up in the call and response, surrounded by the chant, the cry, and the shout, molded by the moments and movements of proclamation giving, we are changed. Each of these is reflexive, visceral, and holistic. They are Holy Spirit contemplation, exploration, and transformation. They are seeds that are individually relevant and communally catalytic.

---

[403] Evans E. Crawford, *The Hum: Call and Response in African American Preaching* (Nashville, TN: Abingdon Press, 1995), 16. Crawford goes on to say, "Although rooted in the black church, the clarity and wisdom represented by these oral responses illumine a variety of traditions. Even preachers not accustomed to spoken response from the congregation find these phrases helpful in understanding the silent encouragements of their listeners…That transformation of spirit requires far more than learning the tasks of exegesis and the development of a successful outline. As essential as these are, their mastery is not the focus here. Instead, … That movement represents not simply the preacher's desire to deliver a successful sermon, but the deeper yearning that draws preachers to their calling in the first place: to awaken in others a sense of wonder and thanksgiving toward God."

Preachers as Facilitators of Formation

> Does not wisdom call,
> and does not understanding raise her voice?
> On the heights, beside the way,
> at the crossroads she takes her stand;
> beside the gates in front of the town,
> at the entrance of the portals she cries out:
> "To you, O people, I call, and my cry is to all that live."[404]

We have identified the vocal rhythms that are present with the various manifestations of Black preaching. Acknowledged as expressions of the spiritual and emotional inner-life of the congregation, these vocal rhythms are markers and hints for preachers. They point to what is happening and to the need into which God is calling and revealing. Therefore, these rhythms are indicators and resources for processing and healing. How might preachers intentionally utilize the vocal rhythms of call and response, chant, cry, and shout as resources in the ongoing spiritual formation and societal transformation of those deeply engaged in the call and response of God's self-revelation to creation?

Preachers can lean into modes of formational preaching that lift and honor the vocal rhythms reverberating in the community and the congregation. Preachers can encourage the call, cry, chant, and shout in the content of the message, not only in the delivery method. The preacher can name what is happening. This serves as an invitation for the receivers of the word to engage with the Triune God.[405] Addition-

---

[404] Prov. 8:1-4
[405] Adetokunbo F. Knowles-Borishade, "Paradigm for Classical African Orature: Instrument for Scientific Revolution?" in *Journal of Black Studies,* 21:4 (June 1991), 488–500, 497–98. "Responders (audience) are the community who come to participate in the speech event. They are secondary creators in the event, containing among them a vital part of the message. It is they who either sanction or reject the message—the Word—based upon the perceived morality and vision of the Caller (rhetor) and the relevance of the message. This notion of community or group sanctionis the basis of the African call-and-response tradition."

ally, preachers can re-present the call and response model initiated by the Triune God. In Matthew 5–7, the Sermon on the Mount, Jesus preached a practiced paradigm and lived theology. He preached a way of being that moved and formed the people. He spoke and expected creation to respond, even if people did not.[406] So, we re-present this paradigm and the truth of God. We re-present how to live it out practically and spiritually without dualistic compartmentalization that generates false and shadow self-realization. Lastly, preachers can expect restoration. Preachers must hold healing space in all its manifestations and stages because healing is expected through God's faithfulness and love. This is akin to a space where good fruit grows in fertile soil. We may not be fully aware of all God is doing, but we trust and believe it is being done. There is immediate formation, meantime formation, and forthcoming formation. We do not dictate the timing, but we hold the space with expectation.

Conclusion

This study does not suggest that this acclimatized and faithful formation preaching is without barriers. Attuning to the vocal rhythms that speak to the holistic needs of the people is in and of itself a spiritual discipline. However, we are bolstered by the reality that this is the work of God. Preachers are receivers as much as they are proclaimers. We surrender to the sacred cacophony. As articulated by Douglas Jones, we want to labor with,

> This repertoire of ecstatic embodied practices—dancing, shrieking, frenzied gesticulations, rapt transfixion, among other behaviors that collectively, consolidated into a distinctive worship style that not only countered the noetic rhetorical and textual traditions that ecclesiastical authorities upheld as

---

[406] Matt. 5–7

doctrinal necessities in order to reinforce sociopolitical hegemony but also implored persons to experience God personally and without intercession, which is a sacred imperative of evangelicalism.[407]

This is not imitation that merely skims the surface for the sake of delivery, but rather the by-product of a deep and wide excavation process, mining the foundations of a spiritual practice of call and response preaching. Preachers are not standing in God's place as the one who transforms, but instead, we are recognizing and relating to call and response, the chant, the cry, and the shout. Then we explicitly offer our message and ourselves as a messenger to raise our and others' expectations of the transcendent and immanent God's movements.

Whatever the manifestation of the vocal rhythms—quiet storm or expert whooper—this is an authentic and accountable ministry of preaching and formation. We utilize our spiritual, cultural, and homiletical history tools and intentionally preach from formation methodology while riding the Spirit's wind of incarnate word.

---

[407] Douglas A. Jones Jr., "Slave Evangelicalism, Shouting, and the Beginning of African American Writing" in *Early American Literature,* 53.1, 69-95 (2018), 70-1.

Dismantling the Optional Service Mentality: A Dire Call for Christian Preachers and Educators to Abandon Me-Centered Teachings that Steer Believers Away from Serving the Church, and Learn Practically How to Spark a Culture of Volunteerism

Charonda Woods

Introduction

Individualism is alive and well in the United States. Globally, America stands paramount in this regard.[408] And sadly, for American Christians, this individualistic mindset has invaded many local churches, leaving church volunteerism to decline. Frequent

---

[408] *Country Comparisons–Individualism.* https://www.hofstede-insights.com/country-comparison/nigeria,senegal,the-usa,zambia/. https://www.hofstede-insights.com. Web (accessed November 11, 2021). When comparing America's individualism rate to most countries in this world, America excels considerably. Furthermore, since this paper seeks to contribute to predominately African American churches, it's important to view how America's individualism rate far exceeds many African countries (countries from which Africans were stolen, and they lived and served in a collectivist society before U.S. chattel slavery) versus an individualist society in which we see many in the African diaspora participating in highly today.

churchgoers report higher rates of volunteering in low individualism cultures.[409] People have the proclivity to follow the values and norms of their community in choosing to volunteer in these cultures.[410] Yet amongst individualistic cultures, people follow their personal needs and desires for volunteering, rather than volunteering as a community or communal norm. A recent poll of Black American churchgoers identified their top two priorities for choosing a church were a welcoming environment and inspiring sermons.[411] These priorities reflect a me-centered mindset, because they don't speak to what a Christian can do for others, they speak to what a Christian personally gains from attending a church.

As this paper focuses on predominately African American churches, it is important to note that most Black Protestants in America attend predominately Black churches.[412] African Americans hold the highest church membership rate throughout the United States. However, the percentage of Black adults who state that church involvement is "desirable" has declined from 90 percent in 1996 to just 74 percent today.[413] Additionally, only 19.3 percent of Blacks reported that they volunteered at least once over the course of the year.[414] A small percentage of church members serve while a

---

[409] Gil Luria, Ram Cnaan, and Ammon Boehm, "Religious Attendance and Volunteering: Testing National Culture as a Boundary Condition," *Journal for the Scientific Study of Religion*, 56.3. https://onlinelibrary.wiley.com/doi/abs/10.1111/jssr.12360. (2017), 592. (accessed November 11, 2021).

[410] Ibid., 595.

[411] "Faith Among Black Americans," https://www.pewforum.org/2021/02/16/faith-among-black-americans/, https://www.pewforum.org, Web (accessed November 11, 2021).

[412] "2. Religious Affiliations and Congregations," https://www.pewforum.org/2021/02/16/religious-affiliation-and-congregations/, https://www.pewforum.org, Web (accessed October 20, 2021).

[413] "Most Black Adults Say Religion & the Black Experience Go Hand in Hand," Barna, https://www.barna.com/research/sobc-2/, https://www.barna.com, Web (accessed October 1, 2021).

[414] "U.S. Church Membership Falls Below Majority for the First Time," https://news.gallup.com/poll/341963/church-membership-falls-below-majority-first-time.aspx. https://news.gallup.com, Web (accessed September 8, 2021). "Who Volunteers in America?" https://lifewayresearch.com/2018/07/26/data-paints-a-picture-of-volunteerism-across-the-nation/, https://lifewayresearch.com, Web (accessed September 9, 2021).

large percentage of church attendees sit on the sideline spectating or continuously receiving social support and spiritual encouragement. I submit that a substantial percentage that sit on the sidelines are impacted by what they hear in and outside of the church. Church members are inundated with me-centered teachings. Therefore, I assert that teaching about serving, matters. This paper will argue that the quantity of church volunteerism is decreasing due to individualistic church teachings that render serving as *optional*. And I am urging Christian preachers and educators to reverse this emphasis on serving-as-*optional* by perpetually modeling and proclaiming the servitude of Christ Jesus.

Volunteerism Background and a Biblical Call for Service

In my experience church volunteerism can be characterized as a long-term, planned effort to invest one's physical resources and/or spiritual gifts without expectation of financial gain in return. Synonymous phrases for church volunteerism include but are not limited to "outreach and missions work" or "ministry service." The Apostle Paul tells us that Christian service includes presenting our bodies as a sacrifice to God by serving others in love and humility (Rom. 12:1-8). Service includes believers using their gifts to serve one another well (Rom. 12:6-8). Although serving is listed as a gift in Romans 12:7, it is clear from other New Testament passages (Jn. 13:14-15, Gal. 6:10) that believers serving each other is *not* an elective. Paul gives Christians a further evangelistic call to serve not only those who are free in Christ, but also those of other backgrounds, for the cause of the Gospel (1 Cor. 9:19). Serving others and serving them well points to the truth of the Gospel believers proclaim.

Moreover, the second chapter of James' epistle shows us that faith and works go hand in hand. If someone professes Jesus as Lord but does not demonstrate that they genuinely have faith, then their faith profession is questionable.[415] A believer shows their faith by meeting the needs of others. James then says that faith unaccompanied by works is dead; those in Christ must reflect their living Savior's nature. Faith in Jesus produces actions that reveal the character of Christ.[416] James shows us the intimate relationship between Abraham's faith and his works: faith 'worked with' (*synergei*) his works (*ergois*).[417] Abraham's faith not only did something to his works; his works also did something to his faith: they *completed* it. The 'completed/perfected' verb used here is *teleioō*, which means 'to perfect' or 'bring to maturity'.[418] James then adds Rahab as another example of the relationship between faith and works, in that she recognized the truth of God delivering Israel, hence she hid the Israelite spies from her countrymen; she demonstrated a *working* faith.[419] James' argument stands true today. A true believer possesses a faith that works. Teaching and reiterating what James shows us in chapter 2, *matters*.

Unfortunately, the value of this matter has become quite tested. Recruiting and retaining volunteers has become a task for many ministries with this ethic. According to a 2015 Church Volunteer study, over 70 percent of respondents stated that recruiting volunteers is continually challenging or even impossible.[420] I have repeatedly experienced this challenge myself as a church leader. Likewise, I bemoan the stories of struggles to find volunteers that I hear from others who serve in ministry leadership. Several Black church leaders

---

[415] T. D. Lea, *Holman New Testament Commentary: Hebrews, James (Vol. 10)* (Nashville, TN: Broadman & Holman Publishers, 1999); James 2:14.
[416] Ibid., James 2:17.
[417] D. J. Moo, *James: An Introduction and Commentary (Vol. 16)* (Downers Grove, IL: InterVarsity Press, 1985); James 2:22.
[418] Ibid.; James 2:22.
[419] K. A. Richardson, *The New American Commentary: James (Vol. 36)* (Nashville: Broadman & Holman Publishers, 1997); James 2:25.
[420] "Who Volunteers in America?" https://lifewayresearch.com/2018/07/26/data-paints-a-picture-of-volunteerism-across-the-nation/, https://lifewayresearch.com, Web (accessed September 9, 2021).

continuously witness the number of congregants serving in their church plummet. Prior to the Covid-19 pandemic, many Black church leaders struggled with motivating, recruiting, and retaining volunteers. Now amid the Covid-19 pandemic, the state of volunteerism is even bleaker as those with needs to be served in our communities continue to increase.[421]

Church volunteerism is vital because individuals inside and outside of churches are languishing in physical and spiritual darkness, and believers are called to bear the good message of hope, the Gospel (Mk. 16:15). Church volunteerism remains critical for individuals who are estranged from their family or do not live near relatives. These individuals substitute support from church members for family support and they identify church members as their surrogate family.[422]

The dominant *optional* service mindset in many churches has left the sick, broken-hearted, and lost to suffer and grieve alone with no hope. The absence of modeling and teaching on serving one's brothers and sisters has left already neglected populations like the formerly

---

[421] "2020 AHR: Part 1 – PIT Estimates of Homelessness in the U.S." https://www.huduser.gov/portal/datasets/ahar/2020-ahar-part-1-pit-estimates-of-homelessness-in-the-us.html, https://www.huduser.gov/, Web (accessed November 8, 2021). While serving the homeless isn't the only way that the church should serve people in our community, Scripture provides us with examples on how we ought to serve the poor (Prov. 19:17, Gal. 2:10, Lk. 14:12-14). This HUD homelessness report is heartbreaking because between 2019 and 2020, homelessness increased significantly among unsheltered populations and people experiencing chronic homelessness. Additionally, the report found that people of color are significantly over-represented among people experiencing homelessness. African Americans and indigenous people (including Native Americans and Pacific Islanders) remained considerably overrepresented among the homeless population compared to the U.S. population. Almost four of every ten people experiencing homelessness in January 2020 were Black or African American (39 percent or 228,796 people). A higher percentage of people in shelter(s) were Black or African American (47 percent or 167,205 people) than were people experiencing homelessness in unsheltered locations (27 percent or 61,591 people). The church should fill these gaps and meet these needs.

[422] Ann W. Nguyen et al, "Church support networks of African Americans: The impact of gender and religious involvement," *Journal of Community Psychology* 47.5, 1043-1063 (2019), 1044.

incarcerated and the elderly without church support. When looking at overall support in the church, older persons reported receiving less support than their younger counterparts.[423] Respondents who were previously incarcerated received support less frequently than others.[424] I contend that the type of instruction and training (or lack thereof) that congregants are receiving has created this void. Congregants are being submerged in me-centered teachings on topics such as "How to find your boo," "God's got a financial miracle for you!" or giving praise to God in worship services only for temporal things such as a new job or car. While I understand that in preaching and teaching self-indulgent messages are used to pique the interest of your audience, the number of me-centered teachings has engulfed the minds of those we are educating. It has affected the way they regard their neighbor. Or in most cases, they don't even see their neighbor. Teaching about serving, matters.

Teaching About Serving, Matters

Data reveals that the information Black Americans are taught, and subsequently believe, affect their desire for and commitment to volunteerism. Only 44 percent of Black Americans in the past year stated that the Bible should be taken literally (compared to 59 percent in 2014).[425] While 38 percent responded that everything in the Bible should not be taken literally in the past year, and 16 percent reported that the Bible was written by people and it is not the word

---

[423] Ibid., 1051.
[424] Ibid., 1051.
[425] (2021 Study) "3. Religious beliefs among Black Americans," https://www.pewforum.org/2021/02/16/religious-beliefs-among-black-americans, https://www.pewforum.org/, Web (accessed September 12, 2021).
(2014 Study) "U.S. Public Becoming Less Religious," https://www.pewforum.org/2015/11/03/u-s-public-becoming-less-religious/, https://www.pewforum.org, Web (accessed September 12, 2021).

of God in the past year.⁴²⁶ While these findings can't adjudicate a Black American's exact stance on serving within a church, it does show us that the Bible may not be authoritative in the lives of many Black Americans. This has ramifications for volunteerism. Another startling finding from this same study revealed 51 percent of Black Americans maintain that it is a religious leader's duty to convert non-believers.⁴²⁷ "Do these lay Black Americans believe they are not responsible for spreading the Gospel?" If so, then this belief can drive their praxis. Church leaders must lay the foundation of a ministry by teaching their flocks that ministry and mission are the vocations of *every* believer. Again, teaching about serving, matters.

Factors Contributing to the Church Volunteerism Decline

Data reveals multiple contributing factors to the church volunteerism decline. Firstly, church attendance. A 2013 study by Joseph Johnston showed that increased religious beliefs and church attendance are associated with greater religious institution volunteerism.⁴²⁸ Now, concentrated servanthood teaching may be mentioned in weekly church services but only one-third of Black Christian adults reported that they attend weekly church services.⁴²⁹ Weekly attendance has decreased 20

---

[426] (2021 Study) "3. Religious beliefs among Black Americans," https://www.pewforum.org/2021/02/16/religious-beliefs-among-black-americans, https://www.pewforum.org/, Web (accessed September 12, 2021).
(2014 Study) "U.S. Public Becoming Less Religious," https://www.pewforum.org/2015/11/03/u-s-public-becoming-less-religious/, https://www.pewforum.org, Web (accessed September 12, 2021).
[427] "3. Religious beliefs among Black Americans," https://www.pewforum.org/2021/02/16/religious-beliefs-among-black-americans, https://www.pewforum.org/, Web (accessed September 12, 2021).
[428] Joseph B. Johnston, "Religion and Volunteering Over the Adult Life Course," *Journal for the Scientific Study of Religion*, 52.4, 733–52 (2013), 748.
[429] (2021 Study) "4. Religious practices," https://www.pewforum.org/2021/02/16/religious-beliefs-among-black-americans, https://www.pewforum.org/, Web (accessed September 12, 2021).

percent since 2014.[430] Nevertheless, Black Protestants rely on religious organizations for volunteer support more than other groups (i.e., Catholics and mainline Protestants), and religious institution involvement acts as an affluent approach for an individual's movement into volunteering.[431] Church attendance results in a *"meditation"* of certain religious beliefs, highlighting key Christian principles.[432]

Another factor contributing to the church volunteerism's decline is the sharp incline of content consumed from media sources.[433] Although good teaching can be delivered through radio, TV, podcasts, and social media, and these media sources can be a great vehicle to connect people, psychological studies reveal that individuals who maintain high social media usage report isolating more compared to those who utilized social media less.[434]

A third contributing factor to the decline in church volunteerism is the prosperity Gospel. This ideology magnifies personal success at the expense of communality, servitude, and contentment in Jesus Christ. A Pew Forum Study revealed that many Black pastors worry that too many other church leaders that preach personal success have devoted themselves and their church's mission to the "prosperity Gospel," which links strong faith to financial achievement and good health instead of alerting society (and their churches) to the injustices that

---

[430] (2014 Study) "U.S. Public Becoming Less Religious," https://www.pewforum.org/2015/11/03/u-s-public-becoming-less-religious/, https://www.pewforum.org, Web (accessed September 12, 2021).

[431] Joseph B. Johnston, "Religion and Volunteering over the Adult Life Course," *Journal for the Scientific Study of Religion,* 52.4, 733–52 (2013), 748-749.

[432] Ibid., 749.

[433] R.J. Taylor, L.M. Chatters, "Religious Media Use Among African Americans, Black Caribbeans, and Non-Hispanic Whites," *Journal of African American Studies,* 15.4 433–454 (2011), https://doi.org/10.1007/s12111-010-9144-z.

[434] Dar Meshi & Morgan Ellithorpe, "Problematic social media use and social support received in real-life versus on social media: Associations with depression, anxiety and social isolation," *Addictive Behaviors.* 119. 106949. (2021), 119.

anger God.⁴³⁵ Some posit that the rise of megachurches that preach prosperity Gospel is a response to Black Americans' basic needs being unmet.⁴³⁶ While I sympathize with this sentiment, Scripture instructs believers to serve others and fight for justice (Ps. 106:3).

The prosperity Gospel has invaded so many of our churches, through various outlets, that a shift has occurred from a *collective* sense of prosperity to an *individual* focus on prosperity.⁴³⁷ Thus teaching about serving, matters much in this generation as a reclamation of ethic and ethos. How often do we hear sermons on how congregants should use their day-to-day gifts to serve the church? Quite seldom, according to the data.⁴³⁸ An analysis was conducted on 50,000 online sermons including Black Protestant messages from the pulpit.⁴³⁹ The most common words were recorded and although it is good that we see repeated words such as "God," "Jesus," and "love," none of the commonly repeated words in these sermons included outreach or missional words such as "help," "serve," or "justice."⁴⁴⁰ Words in teaching and preaching matter to motivate people in furthering the Lord's Kingdom agenda of servitude.

---

[435] "9. Interviews with Black pastors," https://www.pewforum.org/2021/02/16/interviews-with-black-pastors/, https://www.pewforum.org, Web (accessed September 14, 2021).

[436] "9. Interviews with Black pastors," https://www.pewforum.org/2021/02/16/interviews-with-black-pastors/, https://www.pewforum.org, Web (accessed September 14, 2021).

[437] Alan Greenblatt and Tracie Powell, "Rise of Megachurches: Are they straying too far from their religious mission?" https://edge.sagepub.com/system/files/Chambliss2e_13.1CQR.pdf, https://edge.sagepub.com.,Web (accessed September 19, 2021), 14.

[438] "The Digital Pulpit: A Nationwide Analysis of Online Sermons," https://www.pewforum.org/2019/12/16/the-digital-pulpit-a-nationwide-analysis-of-online-sermons/, https://www.pewforum.org, Web (accessed September 29, 2021).

[439] "The Digital Pulpit: A Nationwide Analysis of Online Sermons," https://www.pewforum.org/2019/12/16/the-digital-pulpit-a-nationwide-analysis-of-online-sermons/, https://www.pewforum.org, Web (accessed September 29, 2021).

[440] "The Digital Pulpit: A Nationwide Analysis of Online Sermons," https://www.pewforum.org/2019/12/16/the-digital-pulpit-a-nationwide-analysis-of-online-sermons/, https://www.pewforum.org, Web (accessed September 29, 2021).

Historical Examples That Inform Us Today

Foundationally, the United States of America stands tall in individualism, and it breeds millions of self-serving Americans today. However, many African Americans did not always live by this me-centered creed. In fact, during the Trans-Atlantic Slave Trade, upon reaching North American soil, African captives sought to look out for one another as they were in a bondage struggle *together*.[441]

Throughout African American history, Black churches have collectively taken on numerous religious, political, economic, and civic roles in Black communities dating back to the antebellum period. The Black church's motivation to serve one another well was their unified endeavor for *freedom*: freedom to read the Bible, to hold their own church services, to marry, to have ordained ministers, and many other civil liberties because of racism. In the nineteenth century, Black churches played a vital role in helping Black communities inside and outside of the church with education, professional development, and wellness initiatives that helped Black society thrive.[442] Some of these initiatives (i.e., job training, athletic wellness) remain, but the number of Black Christians behind them and serving their local churches has changed. Though the activities of freedom may look different now than they did in the antebellum period, the mission of the church and the need for physical and spiritual liberation are the same.

Consider the following examples of historic Black servants and how they inform us today. At the start of the Civil War, Sojourner Truth agitated for the inclusion of Blacks in the Union Army and once they were permitted to join, she volunteered by bringing them food and clothes. Truth also fought for land to resettle freed slaves, and

---

[441] Henry Louis Gates, *The Black Church: This Is Our Story, This is Our Song* (New York: Penguin Press, 2021), 21.

[442] "10. A Brief Overview of Black Religious history in the U.S." https://www.pewforum.org/2021/02/16/a-brief-overview-of-black-religious-history-in-the-u-s/#fn-34217-30, https://www.pewforum.org, Web (accessed September 14, 2021).

she saw the 1879 Exodus to Kansas as part of God's divine plan for Blacks to gain basic rights of freedom.[443] Many Blacks passed through St. Louis en route to Kansas and they wondered how to survive their flight with no resources. In response, we see unity personified with St. Louis clergy and business leaders forming committees to assist the freed Blacks so that they could survive and make their way to Kansas.[444] Food and funds were collected from the local community as well as from supporters from Iowa to Ohio.[445] These Midwesterners' services, plus Truth's model of serving and teaching, was what brought many Blacks to join in the effort to support others to freedom.

Consider Harry Hoosier, who was better known as Black Harry. He was a powerful servant preacher during the eighteenth century. Harry was the traveling partner of Bishop Francis Asbury of the Methodist church. Asbury would preach to white audiences, then Hoosier would preach to Black audiences. Due to the dynamic preaching of Hoosier, white audiences started requesting Hoosier to preach to them.[446] Hoosier not only preached a salvific message, he also lived it. He spoke frequently about freedom and justice, in his most notable sermon, "The Barren Fig Tree."[447] Hoosier called for Christians to bear fruit according to Luke 13:6-7 by attending to the physical needs of their oppressed brothers and sisters.[448] Hoosier attended to the needs of bonded African Americans by outreaching to all races to energize

---

[443] Damani Davis, "Exodus to Kansas: The 1880 Senate Investigation of the Beginnings of the African American Migration from the South," *National Archives Prologue Magazine* 40.2 (2008).

[444] Robert G. Athearn, *In Search of Canaan: Black Migration to Kansas, 1879-80* (University Press of Kansas, 2020), 25–36.

[445] Ibid., 28.

[446] Carter Godwin Woodson, *The History of the Negro Church* (Washington, DC: Associated Publishers, 1921), 56-57.

[447] Stephen H. Webb, "Introducing Black Harry Hoosier: The History Behind Indiana's Namesake," *Indiana Magazine of History* 98.1 (2002), 38.

[448] Stephen H. Webb, "Introducing Black Harry Hoosier: The History Behind Indiana's Namesake," *Indiana Magazine of History* 98.1 (2002), 30–41.

anti-slavery efforts for decades.⁴⁴⁹ Hoosier embodied Christian unity through his service and teaching on servanthood.

Finally consider, Miss S. Mattie Fisher who was one of the first Black social workers in the United States of America. In 1918 in Chicago, she sought to serve Olivet Baptist Church with her education and experience.⁴⁵⁰ Fisher used her professional training as a social worker to develop an all-inclusive survey to assess the needs of Black migrants in her neighborhood and to help her church establish systems and programs to address to their physical and spiritual needs.⁴⁵¹ Fisher served the body of Christ well. Teaching about these historical examples will help to revive the ethic of volunteerism.

Jesus Christ—Our Best Model of Servanthood

Surpassing these historical Black servant leaders, Jesus Christ, our Lord and Savior, is the best example of servanthood. If we claim our identity is rooted in Christ Jesus, a suffering servant, then this is the reason we must serve. Jesus Christ was on a mission when he came in his full divinity and humanity to earth. Our Savior walked in authority and power, and he performed miracles for the downtrodden (Lk. 9:42-43, Mt. 14:26, Jn. 2:11). Jesus spent much of his earthly ministry teaching the disciples; to serve others, to sacrificially give (Jn. 6:1-13, Jn. 13:12-17, Mk. 12:43-44). Likewise, Jesus teaches us in the Gospel of Matthew the importance of outreach to meet others' physical needs (Mt. 25:35-40). Ultimately his example of a bondservant included him laying down his life for all of humanity (Jn. 3:16). Jesus said that all authority in heaven and earth has been given to him. He then

---

[449] William D. Piersen, "Welcome to the Harry Hoosier Project," https://harryhoosierproject.org/highlights, https://harryhoosierproject.org, Web (accessed October 12, 2021).

[450] Milton C. Sernett, *African American Religious History: A Documentary Witness* (Durham and London: Duke University Press, 1999), 368.

[451] Eric Mason, *Urban Apologetics* (Grand Rapids, MI: Zondervan, 2021), 45.

commanded us, as believers, to go and make disciples by teaching and baptizing (Mt. 28:19-20). It's our duty as Christian preachers and educators to continuously speak into our fellow brothers' and sisters' lives, encouraging them to go do Kingdom work (Heb. 10:24-25).

Dismantling the Optional Service Mentality

I will now present specific educational and behavioral exhortations by which ministry leaders can dismantle the *optional* service mentality of this generation.

1. *Model servitude first.* When thirty Black pastors were interviewed from different denominations, most pastors agreed that the Black church's influence has declined since the Civil Rights Movement, and partly because they are seeing fewer Black clergy in social activism.[452] Since 75 percent of Black Christians report that opposing racism is essential to their faith, it's up to religious leaders to model that the Gospel and social justice go hand in hand, and then encourage them to fight for justice as well.[453] In most cases, people watch what you do *first* before they listen to what you say. If you aren't displaying the behavior of a bondservant like Christ shows for us (Jn. 4:27, 19:30), then you will not see this type of behavior in your local church. It starts at the top; Senior pastors, bishops, and Christian educators must live what they teach.

2. *Promote a sense of belonging.* Higher church volunteerism rates are linked to higher church attendance. To increase church attendance, church leaders must show that everyone belongs.

---

[452] "9. Interviews with Black pastors," https://www.pewforum.org/2021/02/16/interviews-with-black-pastors/, https://www.pewforum.org, Web (accessed September 14, 2021).

[453] "6. Race in the religious lives of Black Americans," https://www.pewforum.org/2021/02/16/race-in-the-religious-lives-of-black-americans, https://www.pewforum.org, Web (accessed September 14, 2021).

Letting others *feel* that they belong helps combat individualism and it breeds a sense of communal ownership for members and visitors to serve.[454] Pour out so much irresistible love onto your church members and visitors that they will come running back to your church to eventually serve. Promote a sense of belonging because Jesus lovingly invited everyone to his table (Mt. 9:9-13). Moreover, to create an ethos of belonging, address personal sufferings that Black men, women, and families encounter. Then, show them practically how they can communally help others who suffer from similar issues (i.e., racial discrimination, financial hardship, divorce, or sin struggles). While I encourage sermons and teachings that sympathize with Black American struggles, we can't stop at sympathizing. We must empower congregants and students to serve others that are hurting. In the Fall of 2020, 4,517 distinct Black church sermon messages were analyzed, and it showed that Black Protestant pastors often discussed racism, the Covid-19 pandemic, and the presidential election in their sermons.[455] Although I appreciate the recognition of voter suppression and the effects of the Covid-19 pandemic on Black communities highlighted, I do not see a charge or a repeated exhortation given for congregants to serve, help, reach out, and spread the Gospel.[456] Promote a sense of belonging then motivate your congregants and students to serve.

---

[454] Ian A. Gutierrez and Jacqueline S. Mattis, "Factors Predicting Volunteer Engagement Among Urban-Residing African American Women," *Journal of Black Studies* 45.7 (2014), 599–619, 609.

[455] Dennis Quinn and Aaron Smith, "Pastors Often Discussed Election, Pandemic and Racism in Fall of 2020," https://www.pewforum.org/2021/07/08/pastors-often-discussed-election-pandemic-and-racism-in-fall-of-2020/, https://www.pewforum.org, Web (accessed October 4, 2021).

[456] Dennis Quinn and Aaron Smith, "Pastors Often Discussed Election, Pandemic and Racism in Fall of 2020," https://www.pewforum.org/2021/07/08/pastors-often-discussed-election-pandemic-and-racism-in-fall-of-2020/, https://www.pewforum.org, Web (accessed October 4, 2021).

3. *Teach Bibliology & Bible Study Methods.* Based on the Pew Study that reported some Black Americans' low regard of Scripture, Christian preachers and teachers must provide a robust Bibliology—that is, how and why the Bible should be authoritative in a Christian's life.[457] Teach how the Bible was formed and teach about the sufficiency of Scripture (2 Tim. 3:16-17). Also, educate about African presence in the Bible, show your Black audience about the contributions Africans have made to theology, so they can see *themselves*. Teach Bible study methods so that your students and congregants know how to interpret and apply Biblical passages. For example, they may find Scripture to attest that their high social media usage can be an idol; they will find that serving is a biblical mandate. Your congregants and students need to hear about the reliability of the text and how God expects us to live by His Word.

4. *Draw the link between serving and spiritual fulfillment.* Many Christians are seeking spiritual fulfillment and what they do not realize is that they can experience an immense amount of joy and fulfillment from serving others. Hold frequent testimony services so that you and your Outreach Teams can share how God moved in and through you and the Outreach Teams as they served and shared the Gospel. This propels others to serve. Communicate to your congregants that they become like Jesus when they serve (Mk. 10:45). Furthermore, share the *physical* benefits that others receive from your congregants serving. Regarding African American

---

[457] Nathan D. Holsteen and Michael J. Svigel, eds., *Exploring Christian Theology: Revelation, Scripture, and The Triune God, vol. 1* (Minneapolis, MN: Bethany House, 2014), 256. Bibliology contains the study of the Bible and how God reveals Himself. Bibliology starts with inspiration and it includes the following four corollaries: inerrancy, authority, sufficiency, and canonicity.

mental health outcomes, church support is associated with lower rates of depressive symptoms, serious psychological distress, and anxiety.[458] Prior empirical work has indicated that higher levels of social integration within a church network and social support from church members can protect against a range of mental health problems, such as suicidality and psychological distress.[459] Share with your congregants that when they serve others, they are being used by the Lord to heal, strengthen, and save lives.

5. *Continuously repeat the church's charge.* Remind your congregants and students repeatedly about the Great Commission. Making disciples is a mandate for every Christian. Bring them along as you evangelize others. Turn Sunday morning worship experiences into missional events and go serve the community as a church after a morning worship service. Always remind the church of their privilege to make disciples of Jesus Christ.

6. *Teach about other religions and secular philosophies that don't align with God's Word.* Oftentimes believers sincerely want to serve their neighbors or invite them to church but they shy away from interfacing with them because they may not understand their neighbor's religion or secular beliefs. So, utilize Sunday morning messages and weekly small group Bible studies to prepare your congregants with apologetics as you preach to them to live a missional lifestyle. Teach them about other religions.

---

[458] L.M. Chatters, R.J. Taylor, K.D. Lincoln, A. Nguyen, S. Joe, "Church-based social support and suicidality among African Americans and Black Caribbeans," *Arch Suicide Res.* 15.4 (2011) 337-53.

[459] A.W. Nguyen, R.J. Taylor, L.M. Chatters, M.O. Hope, "Church support networks of African Americans: The impact of gender and religious involvement," *Journal of Community Psychology* 47.5 (2019), 1043-1063.

Additionally, tap into written resources such as Dr. Eric Mason's *Urban Apologetics*, or my own *Exchanging Cultural Lies for God's Truth* small group Bible studies. These types of resources will prepare your congregants and students as they interface with their friends, neighbors, and co-workers on religious and secular philosophies that do not align with God's Word.[460] Train your fellow brothers and sisters to watch out for subtle and loud cultural messages that speak against God's word. Then show them how to missionally defend their faith.

Excursus: apologetics against excuses. Because I am speaking about apologetics, I would like to provide my fellow ministry leaders with apologetics against some of the excuses we receive from our ministry teams on why they cannot serve their church and/or local community:

Excuse #1 "I got too much going on."

Apologetic: Yes, I understand that you have a lot going on; I have five jobs. However, for believers, fulfilling the law of Christ is not optional. Scripture tells us just to do it. Paul says in Galatians 6:2 that we must carry each other's burdens and that, in doing so, we will fulfill the law of Christ. Let's pray now; then look at your calendar to see how you can faithfully make time in your schedule to help your brother right now who is battling with a sin struggle.

---

[460] See the 'Products' page for Small Group Bible Studies to prepare your churches to engage the culture to learn how to best serve them. Charonda Woods—Revolutionary Teacher, Speaker & Writer. https://charondawoods.weebly.com/#/.
Also, when reading *Urban Apologetics* by Dr. Eric Mason, you will be informed on some cults, religious groups, and ideologies that are prevalent in the Black community. This book will prepare your churches to engage with the culture to know how to best serve them. *Urban Apologetics* book by Dr. Eric Mason: https://www.amazon.com/Urban-Apologetics-Restoring-Dignity-Gospel/dp/0310100941.

Excuse #2 "I'm tired."

Apologetic: I hear you! I stay tired. In your toil, the Bible tells us that God will not forget how you have helped his people (Heb. 6:10). Keep going, don't get weary. And let me pray with you now that God would give you strength to carry on in your current struggles and I will pray to see how I can serve you as your ministry leader. Then let's look at your calendar to see how you can continue to do good in serving others. I'm not going to let you give up on serving others. The Bible also says that when you refresh others then you will be refreshed (Prov. 11:25). Pouring into others could be the refreshment you need to ignite your strength.

Excuse #3 (Background: Ministry leader asks a churchgoer to serve in a particular area in the church). Response from churchgoer: "I'm not interested in doing that."

Apologetic: I understand that the Lord has given you specific gifts to serve the church and this may not be one of them, and while I realize that you are looking for a passionate connection to serve in this area, Scripture highlights our mandate to serve our brothers and sisters well. Your sister in Christ needs you right now, and Paul tells us in Romans 12:13 that when God's people are in need, be ready to help them. We should be eager to practice hospitality. Let's look at your schedule this week to see how you can live sacrificially for your sister.

7. *Lecture on spiritual gifts.* Teach your fellow believers that they are endowed with spiritual gifts to use. Assign mature leaders to sit with babes in Christ to help them affirm the gifts with which the Lord has endowed them. Then encourage them to use their gifts to edify the church (Eph. 4:7-16).

8. *Increase your technological outreach footprint.* The Gospel has always been shared through the lens of the culture, and today's culture is entrenched in technology. Hence, technology can be useful to increase church volunteerism. Add a 'Get Involved' button to the home page of your ministry website, front and center, so visitors know that your ministry stands tall in outreach. Blast the importance of serving, plus your outreach activities on your social media pages frequently. Create streamlined processes for people to sign up and get connected to a leader so that they can hit the ground running.

9. *Provide practical ways for members' trades/careers to be bridges to serve others and spread the Gospel.* Jesus caught Peter and Andrew by using their everyday lingo of fishing. The text says that they "...left their nets immediately and followed him" (Mt. 4:20). Spend time with those to whom you are preaching and teaching and learn what they do daily; then ask God to show you how to help them use their day-to-day work and gifts to serve their local community and church. See examples below:

    - Master chefs/cooks—They can cook meals to serve the community, or they can teach healthy cooking classes to assist urban areas in eating a better diet.
    - Entrepreneurs—Grab some burgeoning entrepreneurs, then assign them a task, i.e., to write Gospel-centric business plans for your church, schools, or community programs, that serve the formerly incarcerated, elderly, and various underserved communities.
    - Drivers—Those who drive as a trade, ask them to give rides to members or visitors to church services or events, as well as provide rides to medical appointments for the elderly.

- Artists/entertainers—Observe local artists in your church and community doing their secular-based artistry (such as painting, song, or dance). Next, talk to them about ways they can infuse Jesus into their artistry and serve ministries within your church to build cultural ministry bridges.

Paul was a tentmaker, and this was his bridge to share Christ with Aquila and Priscilla (Acts 18:1-3). Teach your brothers and sisters how to use their *work bridges* to serve others. Educate them on how to live out the Gospel per their trade.

10. *Celebrate/honor church volunteers.* Show your volunteers that eternal life with our Triune God isn't their only reward. Celebrate and honor them for how they are serving (Rom. 12:10). Honor volunteers with your sweet, uplifting words and through celebration brunches, small gifts, trips, and/or dinner parties. People stay where they are appreciated.

Senior pastors can equip their church leaders with these ten behavioral approaches to dismantle the optional service mentality. Those church leaders can then teach these same principles to their ministry teams. Moreover, engage your local community by holding community leadership training courses to teach these principles. Educate your community on how they can apply this model to their everyday routine. Train others to replicate this practical biblical model to spark a culture of volunteerism.

Summary

In recent years, the quantity of church volunteerism has decreased due to the teaching of an individualized ethos which made serving optional. To reverse this optional serving mentality, I argued that teaching about serving, matters. I provided examples from African American church history of servant leaders personifying Christian unity that inform us today. I then presented a praxis to demolish me-centered attitudes with practical theological instructions to teach the authority of Scripture, model evangelism, expand your technological outreach footprint, and show direct ways in which one's day-to-day work helps them serve others while spreading the Gospel. I continuously reminded you that *teaching about serving, matters*. It is my prayer that consistently teaching, and modeling Christ-like servanthood will create an explosion of church volunteers to meet the needs of those suffering in our churches and communities. Let the dismantling begin.

Koinonia as Economic Development in the African Diaspora

Walter S. Augustine, Ph.D.

One hundred years ago, the African American community known as the Greenwood District of Tulsa, Oklahoma, was destroyed in what became known as the Tulsa Race Massacre. Founded in 1906 by Black entrepreneur O.W. Gurley, Greenwood was designed to be a community "for Black people and by Black people."[461] Gurley contributed to his vision by purchasing the forty acres known as Greenwood, and subsequently making business loans to other African American entrepreneurs hoping to start businesses in the community. Another early AfricanAmerican entrepreneur in Greenwood—J.B. Stradford—successfully convinced many of his fellow entrepreneurs that they would be more successful as a community if they pooled their resources together to help one another start their own businesses.[462] Through collaboration with other entrepreneurs such as John and Loula Williams, Mabel Little, A.J. Smitherman, and Simon Barry, Greenwood grew to become one of the greatest self-sustaining enclaves of African

---

[461] Quote from Hannibal Johnson, author of *Black Wall Street: From Riot to Renaissance in Tulsa's Historic Greenwood District*, in Alexis Clark, "Tulsa's 'Black Wall Street' Flourished as a Self-Contained Hub in Early 1900s", originally posted September 4, 2019, updated January 27, 2021, https://www.history.com/news/black-wall-street-tulsa-race-massacre.
[462] Ibid.

American-owned businesses and wealth, which eventually became known, thanks to Booker T. Washington, as Black Wall Street.[463]

This community was destroyed over the two-day period of May 31st to June 1st, 1921, by white Tulsa residents resentful of the wealth of Greenwood. The massacre was incited by the accusation that a Black shoe shiner assaulted a white woman who was an elevator operator, and the subsequent defense of that shoe shiner by members of the Black community. Over that two-day period, it is estimated that approximately 300 Black Greenwood residents were killed, 6,000 were held in internment camps, 10,000 were made homeless, and over 1,200 homes were destroyed. The businesses which had been built over the years were also destroyed in the massacre, resulting in a near-complete devastation of the community.[464]

However, this is not the end of the story. Within a five-year period after the massacre, much of Greenwood was rebuilt through the efforts of many of the remaining residents in collaboration with the NAACP, other Black business owners and Black townships in Oklahoma, and donations from Black churches; and by 1942, Greenwood was once again home to more than 200 Black-owned businesses.[465] So why is Greenwood no longer a community of thriving Black-owned businesses today?

Two major factors contributed to the eventual demise of the Greenwood district. One factor was the federal, state, and local governmental policies of urban renewal, which led to a federal highway being

---

[463] Alexis Clark, "9 Entrepreneurs Who Helped Build Tulsa's 'Black Wall Street,'" originally posted and updated May 14, 2021, https://www.history.com/news/black-wall-street-tulsa-visionaries.

[464] Tom Huddleston, Jr., "'Black Wall Street:' The history of the wealthy Black community and the massacre perpetrated there 100 years ago," originally posted July 4, 2020 and updated May 28, 2021, https://www.cnbc.com/2020/07/04/what-is-black-wall-street-history-of-the-community-and-its-massacre.html.

[465] See Clark, "Tulsa's 'Black Wall Street' Flourished as a Self-Contained Hub in Early 1900s" and Huddleston, Jr., "'Black Wall Street:' The history of the wealthy Black community and the massacre perpetrated there 100 years ago."

constructed right through the heart of the Greenwood community, displacing many families and businesses in the process. Ironically, though, the other factor was integration. As one article put it, "As Tulsa neared the mid-century mark, increasing integration across the country meant that Black residents no longer needed to only spend their money at Black-owned businesses, which sent money outside of the community."[466] In other words, O.W. Gurley's philosophy of "for Black people and by Black people" was no longer valued as highly as the ability of Black residents to purchase goods and services from white-owned businesses, or even to work in white-owned establishments in positions that previously had been unavailable to them, increased.

While both factors were indeed crucial to the dissolution of both an economic base and a sense of community, this paper will focus primarily on the second factor—that of the economic and communal consequences of integration. Specifically, this paper will look to raise three major arguments regarding economics and community within the African American community and, indeed, much of the African diaspora as a whole. The first argument is that economic integration in the United States has led to a widespread values shift within the African American community—one that economically prioritizes the neo-capitalistic values of exchange and consumption and an individualistic worldview over a communal-based worldview. In other words, economic integration has resulted in a shift of values in the African American community away from placing people before profit, towards placing profit before people, and away from valuing community before consumption, towards valuing consumption over community. The second argument is that the New Testament concept of *koinonia* can serve as a Christian alternative approach to economic values and practices which both develop economy and build

---

[466] Huddleston, Jr., "'Black Wall Street:' The history of the wealthy Black community and the massacre perpetrated there 100 years ago."

community. The final argument of this paper is that this concept of *koinonia* is one which has historically been embraced and utilized throughout the African diaspora and should be reclaimed in new ways for our communities today.

Regarding my initial assertion of an economic values shift within the African American community, Greenwood serves as just one example of a people who previously valued community before consumption. The Wilmington, North Carolina race massacre of 1898 and the Atlanta race massacre of 1906 both occurred under the false pretenses of assaults on white women by Black men; but they were in truth due to the resentment of Black community wealth and success by white residents of the cities.[467] One article about Black Atlanta before the massacre notes that "Black businesses were springing up" and "Women took it upon themselves to provide community services to poor Blacks, and to instill in them middle class standards and values. The men's organizations invested their energy into building social and fraternal organizations that worked for community betterment."[468] With the advent of economic integration, however, the sense of community began to erode. This new phenomenon was a concern of Martin Luther King, Jr., whom King scholar Thomas Jackson wrote "criticized middle-class Black individualism and consumerism by insisting that Christian service mattered more than worldly success."[469] These assumptions of neo-capitalism—namely individualism and consumerism—are described further by the Harvard economist Stephen Marglin. In his book titled *The Dismal Science,* he writes:

---

[467] Clay Cane, "Not Just Tulsa: Race Massacres That Devastated Black Communities in Rosewood, Atlanta, and Other American Cities," Updated May 31, 2021, https://www.bet.com/news/national/2019/12/17/not-just-tulsa--five-other-race-massacres-that-devastated-black.html.

[468] "The Rise and Fall of Jim Crow," https://www.thirteen.org/wnet/jimcrow/stories_events_atlanta.html (accessed October 16, 2021).

[469] Thomas F. Jackson, *From Civil Rights to Human Rights: Martin Luther King, Jr., and the Struggle for Economic Justice* (Philadelphia: University of Pennsylvania Press, 2007), 8.

> ...economics relies on value judgments implicit in foundational assumptions about the self-interested individual, about rational calculation, about unlimited wants, and about the nation-state, and it is these assumptions that make community invisible. In arguing for the market, economics legitimizes the destruction of community and thus helps to construct a world in which community struggles for survival.[470]

It is observations such as these which lead to my initial assertion that the efforts of African Americans towards economic integration within the larger United States society have resulted in the unintended consequences of value shifts towards exchange, consumption, and an individualistic worldview. Furthermore, I would argue that these shifts have played a significant—though not exclusive—part in the destruction, economic and otherwise, of many African American communities. The beginning of solutions to these issues, however, can be found in both the Scriptures and in the African diasporic cultural heritage.

In light of these shifts in values, my research focuses on the New Testament conception of *koinonia* as an alternative way of envisioning and practicing economics within a community. Based on the root word *koinos*, meaning shared or common, *koinonia* is an event word that describes the various tangible and intangible ways that a community both demonstrates and develops its nature and its values. The concept is first encountered in Acts 2:42-47, where it is used to indicate a common sharing of tangible economic resources for

---

[470] Stephen A. Marglin, *The Dismal Science: How Thinking Like an Economist Undermines Community* (Cambridge, Massachusetts and London, England: Harvard University Press, 2008), 2-4. Marglin defines the market as "a self-regulating *system*, a world in which markets collectively allocate resources, set prices, determine the distribution of income—in short, a system in which markets provide for our needs and wants and from which we derive our sustenance. And something more: a system that not only regulates itself but also regulates ourselves, a process that shapes and forms people whose relationships with one another are circumscribed and reduced by the market."

the benefit and betterment of the community. Through actions that redefined the meaning of ownership, Acts 2:44 indicated that they held all of their possessions in common, thus resulting in them selling their possessions and giving the proceeds to others within the community as they had need.[471] In this one passage alone we see the values of people before profit and community before consumption being demonstrated within the early church. New ways of envisioning the distribution and consumption of economic goods were being practiced within the community, and the text indicates that doing so contributed to this new community having favor with those outside of their community, as well as the growth and development of the community.[472] This is not the only time a form of economic *koinonia* is practiced in the New Testament church. Similar actions can be seen in Acts 4:32-37, Romans 15:26-27 and Philippians 1:5 and 4:15. The Acts 4 passage clearly indicates the shift in values, as in the verse 23 claim by the Apostles of the members of the community as their own. This act is mirrored in verse 32 where the members of the community do not count any of their possessions as their own, but hold everything in common. In other words, people and community were more valuable to them than profits and resources; and economic resources were meant to be used for the development of community.

While some might call this giving, economic *koinonia* is actually something different. Borrowing an illustration from Christian Ethicist Oliver O'Donovan, in a giving relationship, what's mine becomes yours. I no longer have any interest in the resource that I have given to you, and you alone possess it. However, with *koinonia* what's mine now becomes ours.[473] Resources are held jointly, or in common,

---

[471] Acts 2:44-45, *New American Standard Bible: Updated Edition* (Anaheim, California: Foundation Publications, Inc, 1998).
[472] Acts 2:46-47, *New American Standard Bible: Updated Edition.*
[473] Oliver O'Donovan, *The Ways of Judgment* (Grand Rapids, MI and Cambridge, U.K.: William B. Eerdmans Publishing Company, 2005), 242-245.

with one another. By design, then, this type of economic engagement necessitates an ongoing relationship between those who are sharing that which they have in common. The way in which God gives— God shares, because since everything belongs to God, God can never completely divest God's Self from God's possessions. God gives—God shares for the purpose of building community, as seen in the lease-giving of the land to the Israelites in Leviticus 25:23 and even in the giving of the Son in John 3:16.

It is also different from the modern economic concept of exchange, in which what's mine becomes yours, and what's yours becomes mine.[474] This exchange does not necessitate an ongoing engagement in mutual community between the parties in the exchange, and as seen earlier, can even contribute to a dissolution of community amongst those involved in the exchange—the engagement can be purely transactional in nature, without care for the wellbeing of the other. Economic *koinonia*, on the other hand, has as its end goal the development of community; and the means for doing so is through sharing of resources together—what's mine becomes ours. This practice of economic *koinonia* did not end with the New Testament church but was actually practiced frequently throughout Christian communities during the first three centuries of the Church's existence. One of the most notable examples of this was the community founded by the North African Bishop of Hippo—Augustine—who practiced this economic lifestyle with a small community of close friends and family that eventually expanded into a monastic community.[475] Their community was concerned mainly with the "common good," or wellbeing of the community as a whole; therefore, their economic practices were

---

[474] Ibid.

[475] Peter Brown, *Through the Eye of a Needle: Wealth, the Fall of Rome, and the Making of Christianity in the West, 350-550 AD* (Princeton and Oxford: Princeton University Press, 2012), 167-169, 174-177.

ordered towards that goal. In summation, I affirm that the New Testament concept of *koinonia* in its economic manifestation can serve as an alternative method of economic development with a goal of developing community. This is because *koinonia* is a practice that involves a mutual sharing of resources for the purpose of participation in and development of community.

As noted earlier, I argue that this solution can be found not only in Scripture, but also in the cultural heritage of those within the African diaspora. I now turn to the late Jamaican theologian Lewin Lascelles Williams, along with Afro-Canadian Christian ethicist Peter J. Paris, to support this claim.

The economic and communal value of "for Black people by Black people" was not something that was peculiar to O.W. Gurley or other historical African American communities. Instead, this economic value which placed community over consumption and people over profit was a value rooted in a predominantly communal worldview, derived from the biblical concept of *koinonia* as implemented by their African ancestors and practiced throughout the members of the African diaspora. Lewin Williams began to make these connections through his work on the development of Caribbean theology in 2005. Williams served as President of the United Theological College of the West Indies in Jamaica. A native of Jamaica, Williams' scholarship focused primarily on the development and systemization of an indigenous Caribbean theology largely free from the influence of colonial missionary theology. He sought to systematize and encourage further development of nascent Caribbean Christian theologies—theology for the Caribbean people, by the Caribbean people.

Initially grounded in liberation theology, Williams noted Caribbean theology's political and economic emphasis as opposed to a completely spiritualized Gospel. He wrote "from the very genesis of its chief thoughts, Caribbean theology was so radically opposed to such an abstract spirituality emphasis that it called for disengagement with the Euro-American tradition."[476] He also notes, though, that over time a pendulum swing began in Caribbean theology and spirituality, moving away from an either/or approach to somewhat of a both/and, truly holistic approach. He wrote, "Functionality means that the Church, the embodiment of the "Spirit," has an understanding of ministry in which the function of its spirituality matches the sociological, political, and economic needs of the context."[477] Thus, for Williams, a theology that addresses not only the spiritual but also how the spiritual impacts and shapes the other aspects of Caribbean life became the basis for the development of Caribbean theology.

For Williams, the development of Caribbean community is a major emphasis in his work; and similar to myself, he lamented the dissolution of community taking place in the Caribbean. Moreover, he noted that the factors for the dissolution of community were both external and internal, by stating:

> The lack of real community within the Caribbean society as a whole, no doubt, has its root in the original polarization strategies of the dominance of colonial and contemporary major power dealings…Yet the responsibility for the trust that will cement the Caribbean into community is the Caribbean's. In other words, territorialism is only a bigger version of the political games played locally for power and recognition.[478]

Another similarity in my ways of thinking aligning with Williams can be found in his emphasis on the role of economics in the development of community. However, while I identify the issue within neo-classical capitalistic values, Williams identifies the

---

[476] Lewin Williams, "Social Conditions and Spiritual Solutions in the Caribbean," in Dwight N. Hopkins and Marjorie Lewis, *Another World Is Possible: Spiritualities and Religions of Global Darker Peoples* (London: Routledge, 2009), 276.
[477] Ibid, 277.
[478] Ibid, 274.

issue within the rise of globalization, which extends those same values to underdeveloped countries worldwide. He gives as evidence of this a pernicious double impact of economic globalization. One impact is that cultural value differences amongst various countries and communities are often ignored by those seeking to extend economic globalization, forcing communities to abandon their values in order to embrace globalization. The second is the undervaluation within the global marketplace of goods produced in underdeveloped countries. This double impact, he notes, contributes to both ongoing poverty and community dissolution within underdeveloped countries.[479]

A final area of discussion is found in the usage of *koinonia* as an economic alternative, similarly noted in both of our works. This is where Williams begins identifying ways in which African diasporic economic and communal thinking and practices adapted the concept of *koinonia* to African diasporic thought. Williams wrote,

> '*Koinonia*' specifies the area of the religious community (referring to the Christian church) that has utilized it. Yet while the term emerged as an egalitarian effort within the early Christian church, the principle it represented, and other like principles, have been universalized throughout the ages. It is not a stranger to some socialist structures and even to indigenous African traditions such as Nyerere's *Ujamaa* in Tanzania. In any case *koinonia*, which here appears as a suggested response to globalization, is a much broader application of the principle observed in the early church.[480]

---

[479] Lewin L. Williams, "A Theological Perspective on the Effects of Globalization on Poverty in Pan-African Contexts," in Peter J. Paris, ed. *Religion and Poverty: Pan-African Perspectives* (Durham and London: Duke University Press, 2009), 88.
[480] Ibid, 89.

For Williams, the concept of *koinonia* is tied into both a communal focus and an emphasis on the Old Testament concept of *tsedaqah*, or treating each other rightly in relationships. He also connects it to the New Testament concept of *oikonomia*, or household management. In addition, for Williams *koinonia* is the true meaning of globalization, because it recognizes the theological and cosmological implications of God being the owner of the entire world, and all humanity therefore living within the household of God.[481] It functions as a means of practicing *tsedaqah*, so that all of God's broad and diverse household can thrive. Williams believed that this principle could be practiced not only on a micro level, but on a macro level as well, changing and impacting how entire nations practiced economy and developed community both internally and externally. He stated,

> It may not be childish naivety to believe that good community, socially ordered, can bear the fruits of economic growth and development. Jamaica should not have to turn to Venezuela for better oil deals when Trinidad has the capability in Jamaica. Guyana should not have to fear that its rice will not be bought on the Caribbean market, and that its citizens will not be treated with respect in Barbados.[482]

While he recognized that trying to implement this alternative economic ethic on a global basis would be a daunting task, he also believed that implementation on a smaller scale might be possible. He desired a worldwide embracing of the concept, values, and economic practices of *koinonia*, and so began its implementation through a "for our people, by our people" approach.

---

[481] Ibid, 100.
[482] Williams, "Social Conditions," 274-275.

Peter J. Paris, the Afro-Canadian Christian ethicist, is also helpful to the discourse here, as he has done extensive work on the virtues of African peoples throughout the African diaspora. He argues that Africans who came to the United States and other countries around the world brought with them, above all, a value for the wellbeing of community. This value of community wellbeing thus becomes the rubric through which economic and all other human activities are measured. Moreover, regarding the difference between African American communal thinking versus white individualistic thinking, Paris asserts,

> the communal traditions of African Americans (deeply rooted in Africa and preserved through slavery in the family, music, and religion) have made it psychologically impossible for the vast majority of them to embrace fully the basic value system of white Americans.[483]

Though this communal value system and its corresponding moral virtues have been communicated and transmitted differently through the ages—largely due to the circumstances of those dispersed to different parts of the world due to slavery—Paris argues that these basic, common values and virtues can still be found throughout the descendants of African people worldwide. Therefore, moral virtue amongst those of the African diaspora is significantly influenced by the teleological goal of community wellbeing.

Paris identifies a number of prominent virtues common to those throughout the African diaspora. Of those virtues, Paris argues that none is more prominent and praiseworthy than the virtue of beneficence. This, Paris notes, is because beneficence serves the ultimate goal of communal wellbeing through prioritizing the wellbeing of others over the individual's own wellbeing. The virtue of beneficence

---

[483] Peter J. Paris, *The Spirituality of African Peoples: The Search for a Common Moral Discourse* (Minneapolis, MN: Fortress Press, 1995), 126.

can be interpreted through various synonyms, but Paris' synonyms which are most economically relevant are generosity, liberality, and magnanimity.[484] These synonyms represent how the virtue of beneficence manifests itself with regards to the distribution and consumption of economic resources. For example, when beneficence is manifested economically, the private acquisition of property is for the usage and enjoyment of the community, and not just the individual. In addition, economic decisions are not made primarily based on efficiency, but on the ultimate benefit to the community.[485]

Finally, Paris notes that this virtue manifests itself in various ways in both South Africa and the United States, and is exemplified through leaders such as Nelson Mandela and Martin Luther King, Jr.[486] It is in this virtue of beneficence, which is rooted in an African Diasporic value of community, that sharp contrasts can be seen between the traditional economic values and approaches of those of African heritage and the values and approaches of our current neo-classical capitalist philosophy today. He writes,

> Commensurate with their African roots, African Americans have borne no small disdain for the philosophy of individualism and the cultural spirit it has fostered. They have had similar contempt for the logical extension of such a philosophy in the moral development of self-centered persons who pursue their own autonomous purposes with little or no regard for the well-being of others. Such persons, morally shaped in accordance with the principle of individual autonomy, differ sharply from those who are formed in consonance with a historical principle of communal belonging. The thought of the former sacrificing either their own lives or even a substantial

---

[484] Ibid, 25.
[485] Ibid, 25-26.
[486] Ibid, 26-30.

part of their property for the good of others is totally repulsive to them. Consequently, the predominant moral and religious values of the two groups differ sharply, a difference clearly manifested in their respective thought about person, family, community, and religion, as well as their understandings of music, property, and politics.[487]

It is this historically sharp contrast that I am arguing has progressively begun to blur, especially within the United States. Many African Americans have begun to adopt those same individualistic values noted by Paris above. Yet it is the communal value and corresponding moral virtue of beneficence that has historically existed amongst members of the African diaspora. I assert such value legacy supports the argument of Lewin Williams that the concept of *koinonia* has historically been embraced and utilized throughout the African diaspora. Therefore, the concept of *koinonia* must be reclaimed for African diasporic communities to successfully develop economically stable and vibrant communities.

While I concur with Williams in his embracing of *koinonia* as an alternative economic approach for people of the African diaspora, I would quibble just a bit with his framing of *koinonia* as egalitarianism. From my point of view, egalitarianism implies sameness, which I would argue is a somewhat different picture than what we find in both the Old and New Testaments with regard to economic resources. Instead, I would argue for a framing of *koinonia* as partnership, where each party contributes according to their ability and each party receives according to their need.[488] New Testament *koinonia* is often framed in a manner where some share tangible resources

---

[487] Paris, *The Spirituality of African Peoples*, 126.
[488] While I inherently recognize the difficulty in defining what is need, and who determines that definition, I would humbly submit that need can be defined as the resources necessary for a person to fully contribute to and thrive within a community for the betterment of that individual and the community.

and others share intangible resources within and amongst communities (knowledge, teaching, etc.—see Romans 15:26-27). While each party shares something different, all are able to contribute, and the common goal is always kept in sight—the development of the community. And the community operates best when each member is free to contribute to the development of the community in their own unique ways.[489]

In addition, while the concept of *koinonia* is useful, the theological term itself is somewhat unwieldy in our times; and the corresponding term used by Paris—beneficence—can be just as difficult to explain. I believe that a more common alternative term that can be used to explain the concept of *koinonia* is investment. The term is used today in both an abstract and a concrete way to indicate the devotion of one's resources (e.g., time, effort, energy, money, etc.) to "a particular undertaking with the expectation of a worthwhile result."[490] This, I would argue, conveys well the concept of *koinonia*, where people share their resources with one another with the expectation of the development of community. It also describes the practices that were taking place within the Greenwood community, where loans were being made to budding entrepreneurs and community members were pooling their resources in order to start businesses that would help develop the community. It is with keeping practices such as those that took place in Greenwood in mind that I turn to my concluding thoughts.

One key question is how might communities within the African diaspora recapture the concept and practices of *koinonia* today? I would like to suggest a few initial practical steps that can be taken. First, churches can paint the vision for this type of community

---

[489] Again, I recognize that this concept can get sticky when considering how to place value on the contributions of each member of a community, but that is a concept for another paper.
[490] "Invest," Lexico, Powered by Dictionary.com https://www.dictionary.com/browse/invest (accessed October 17, 2021).

through preaching and teaching on the concept of *koinonia* as economic development, or investment, within the church. Passages such as those on the Lost (or Prodigal) Son in Luke 15:11-32 or the Parable of the Unjust Steward in Luke 16:1-13 convey the economic value shift that is expected within the kingdom of God. In addition, sermons on Acts 2:32-37 and Acts 4:32-37 can give concrete examples of how the early church implemented these concepts and values in their everyday lives. A second step that churches can take is to recognize and support entrepreneurs who are members of their churches. As long as the member is conducting a business that is helping to build the community, they can be recognized by the church and members of the church can be encouraged to support their endeavors. But the support doesn't have to stop at the four walls of the church. There is a powerful impact when churches show their concern for the wellbeing of their surrounding communities. Thus, if churches look to identify and celebrate *koinonia*-minded entrepreneurs within their communities, it can go a long way towards building up partnerships and relationships with others in the community, possibly paving the way for larger collaborative efforts down the line. And finally, once those relationships with other entities, organizations, and businesses within the community have been established, even larger common economic and community development goals can be reached. These are just a few ideas of ways to begin the process. No doubt other ideas for implementation can be identified based upon specific contexts. In addition, questions can rightly be raised regarding the limitations of this approach to economics and community development. As King noted,

> However much we pool our resources and 'buy black,' this cannot create the multiplicity of new jobs and provide the number of low-cost houses that will lift the Negro out of the economic depression caused by centuries of deprivation...In short, the Negroes' problem cannot be solved unless the whole

of American society takes a new turn toward greater economic justice.[491]

Nevertheless, I would contend that a reclaiming of the biblical, cultural economic value, and virtue of *koinonia* will help to prepare communities within the African diaspora for economic growth while also reifying their value of community. To put it in the words of James Weldon Johnson, it would allow our communities to remain "True to our God, True to our native land."[492]

---

[491] Martin Luther King, Jr., *Where Do We Go From Here: Chaos or Community?* (Boston: Beacon Press, 1967), 50.

[492] "Lift Every Voice and Sing," Black Culture Connection: PBS, https://www.pbs.org/articles/lift-every-voice-and-sing (accessed October 17, 2021).

Book Reviews

What Makes a Church Sacred? Legal and Ritual Perspectives from Late Antiquity, Mary K. Farag, University of California Press (ISBN: 978-0520382008), 344 pp., $34.95 (paper)

Mary Farag has composed a magnificent work that examines the legal and ecclesial function of church buildings in the late antique Roman Empire. Farag's work primarily focuses on the testimonies of emperors and bishops in how church spaces were defined as *res sacrae* ("sacred space") during the fourth, fifth, and sixth centuries (p. 2). The book explores the nature of sacred building space in legal and ecclesial contexts during the late antique Roman Empire and how the concept of sacrality was received by Christians and modified from its previous traditional Roman ("pagan") uses (p. 6). Farag also provides examples of the Christian construction of sacred space in collaboration with and in contention with the Roman Empire.

Part One deals with the legal definitions of *res sacrae* and how early Christians applied and contested this concept to church structures in ritual contexts (p. 11). Chapter 1 details the nature of *res sacrae* and its uses by late antique Christians of the Roman Empire. Emperor Justinian was significant in building upon and expanding extant concepts of sacred space as that space which has been so ordained by patriarchs (p. 17). Patriarchs were instrumental in resolving conflicts wherein bishops maintained conflicting claims on land upon which both may have consecrated sacred space, such as the case of Synesius of Cyrene (p. 29). The conflict between

Augustine and the bishop Crispinus demonstrated the degree to which the "right" and "wrong" kinds of bishops vied for imperial recognition of their sacred space (p. 37). While the explicitly Christian dominance by which sacred space would be defined came into practice under Justinian in the sixth century, Farag demonstrates that Christian space already began to be recognized as *res sacrae* in the traditional Roman category following the time of Constantine (p. 40). Chapter 2 analyzes the laws and canons used by jurists in the maintenance of sacred space (p. 42). As *res sacrae*, churches were inalienable, that is, unable to be privately transferred between multiple parties (p. 45). However, Emperor Justinian attempted to impose allowances for emperors to have prerogative over alienation status, a prerogative that was challenged in some sectors of the empire (p. 52). Justinian also established various rules on how property could be loaned—or hypothecation. Two common scenarios included ecclesial property being loaned for temporary use (usufruct) or the leasing of church property (emphyteusis), both of which retained various restrictions (p. 63). Laws were instituted against committing any act of violence in *res sacrae*, punishable by death in some cases (p. 65). Bishops often attempted to exert their personal will against civil regulations on *res sacrae*, prompting the Council of Chalcedon in 451 CE to promote greater cooperation between church and state (p. 69). Chapter 3 elucidates various manners in which churches, as protected places, also provided protection. The manumission of slaves was one of the most common cases in which churches could serve as protecting places. A variety of laws and canons developed that outlined who had the authority to manumit slaves and the church's responsibility following manumission (p. 73). Refugees seeking asylum were another category that sought protection in church space. The Christian councils of Gaul, outside of the Roman Empire, provide some of the most detailed canons dealing with accepting those seeking asylum awaiting trial, having recently obtained a verdict, or those engaged in theological debates (p. 76). Roman emperors also issued decrees outlining the roles churches were to play in the ransoming and rehabilitation of captives (p. 84). This section outlines a particular incident in which John Chrysostom was accused of denying asylum to a particular *comes* ("Count"), thus committing sacrilege against the church as a place of protection. John denied these charges and claimed to use church space for the poorest and most oppressed (p. 92). Thus, the execution of church space as a place of protection was often contested.

Part Two focuses on the ritual performances in ecclesial sources that engaged and challenged the framing of *res sacrae* in juristic circles. Farag draws here on anthropologist Igor Kopytoff's concept of "singularization": Christian clerics "singularized" Christian space in order to stave off their re-commodification (p. 97). While the juristic prescriptions emphasized the "protected" aspect of Christian space, the ritual constructions of Christian space emphasized the "protecting" nature of *res sacrae* (p. 101). Chapter 4 focuses on donations and dedications in Christian space. Farag likens the process by which *res sacrae* were "singularized" to a marriage gift exchange, wherein the exchange of goods signals the initiation of an eternal bond (p. 107). The reciprocity of the marriage gift continues as a metaphor to demonstrate that church spaces were simultaneously gifts given and favors received (p. 120). Farag juxtaposes examples from traditional Roman ("pagan") religion with Christian donor mosaics to illustrate the similarities between religious leaders and celestial beings reciprocally entrusting religious space. A complication arose for the ritual "singularization" of *res sacrae*: how could bishops honor the expensive adornment of churches and leverage Christian real estate for the empowerment of the poor? Bishops often found themselves caught between donors who expected an eternal return on their investment, legal statutes alienating Christian property, and biblical mandates to serve the poor (p. 127). Chapter 5 analyzes examples of church consecrations, which helped to form "circles of sanctity" in which God, Christians, and the church building visibly depicted the invisible transformation of the soul (p. 130). Farag advocates the term "regifting" rather than "recommodification" when conceiving of the "circle of sanctity" by which the builder of the church "regifts" the church building to the God who gave it through the name of the saint after whom the church is named (p. 138). Homilies accompanying church dedications provided Christians with directions on how to use church space as a model for inward transformation (p. 140). Homlists such as John Chrysostom, Shenoute of Atripe, Ambrose of Milan, and Rabbula of Edessa defended the adornment of churches but exhorted Christians to remember that this outward adornment was only for the purpose of inward sanctification (p. 153). The monastic leader Pachomius even intentionally defaced a chapel that he himself built because it evoked pride in his heart (p. 154). Therefore, the "circle of sanctity" had a variety of approaches to the value of church space. Chapter 6 highlights Christian constructions of holy space in Non-Chalcedonian communities that resisted the dominant Chalcedonian Christology of the imperially-sanctioned Church following the Council of Chalcedon in 451 CE (p. 157). Farag focuses on pseudonymous works attributed to well-known Church fathers as a means of legitimating *res sacrae* apart from imperially recognized space (p. 161). Non-Chalcedonians did not appeal to juristic definitions of *res sacrae* like their Chalcedonian counterparts, as the empire and its legal processes were held suspect. Emperor Justinian responded to the discord by placing "orthodox" (i.e., Chalcedonian) churches in Jerusalem as a symbol of hegemonic Chalcedonianism to the Non-Chalcedonians in the region (p. 174). Such tensions underscore the overall theme of Farag's exceptional work: religious and civil leaders had a variety of approaches to establishing the sacredness of

Christian space (p. 180). This book offers scholars of early Christianity an invaluable resource that highlights an ancient question that the modern world still grapples with: the nature and purpose of religious—specifically Christian—property in a pluralistic society.

Vince L. Bantu
Meachum School of Haymanot
Fuller Theological Seminary

Redemptive Kingdom Diversity: A Biblical Theology of the People of God, Jarvis J. Williams, Baker Academic. (ISBN 978-1-5409-6462-5), 207 pp., $24.99 (paperback)

In this text, Jarvis Williams offers an analysis of the Biblical and Theological theme of the People of God. It is redolent with crisp exposition as Williams aims to provide examples of how God formed and related to the people who were in covenant with him. It is apparent throughout that the scope of the text was not to be exhaustive in its treatment of this theme but to be circumspect with regard to the manner that the people of God are discussed throughout. At the outset of the text, Williams lays a foundation that portends his *raison d'etre* to ensure that the reader is aware of his aims: to uphold a multi-ethnic, diverse people created to relate and serve God. This is a project which has not been addressed in this manner despite the historic challenges that evangelicalism has faced within recent history. This perspective of an Evangelical African American scholar is a welcome addition to many texts that focus on Biblical Studies.

Chapter 1 presents Williams' ambitious analysis of the Pentateuch and this catena of texts. Herein the infrastructure of Redemptive Kingdom Diversity is established. Williams notes that obedience to the law and God's preservation of Abraham's posterity would be maintained through God's maintenance of his promise to the Patriarch. Through observance of Torah and covenant keeping, the people of God would be granted access to relationship with God. This relationship, though tenuous at times, demonstrates God's determinism to ensure that his vision of ethnic diversity is upheld.

Chapter 2 ambitiously covers the Historical, Wisdom, Poetic, and Prophetic books. Williams makes clear that God remains committed to his people and would fulfill his promises to them if the covenantal stipulations were kept. Williams maintains a clear expositional focus upon these texts by paying attention to how the people of God are depicted throughout each while establishing how God preserved his people in the wake of an ever-growing and expanding matrix of difficulties. As he moves toward the Wisdom genre, Williams reads the plight of the people of God through the lens of suffering, righteousness, salvation, and redemption. Each of the books throughout this section is summarized as presenting the people of God as "those who fear the Lord, remain faithful to him," (p.61) through the varied experiences and emphases that the wisdom books feature. Within the Prophetic material, Williams aims to "highlight selected themes in the prophetic literature that give insight into Israel's identity as the people of God, including faith in the God of the Jews, even in the face of suffering and exile, faithful obedience to Torah (p.74).

In chapter 3, Williams analyzes the New Testament by beginning with the Gospels and Acts. The People of God are presented through their ethnic lens with key indicators of the unique settings of each Gospel writer. He notes, "each Gospel has its own distinct message about Jesus and the formation of his people, but each Gospel likewise demonstrates that Jesus, an ethnic Jew, entered into this world as a Jew with a heritage that included gentiles" (p.103). Williams provides the reader with the same crisp exposition of key themes that discuss the People of God, while doing so in how each relates to the Messiah, Jesus Christ. Herein lies the added emphasis that the Gospel writers demonstrate. Jesus, as a Middle Eastern Jew, particularizes the manner that individuals interact with him. Since Jesus' Jewish identity is redolent within the Gospel writer's apostolic memoirs, it comes as no surprise that the book of Acts displays a type of celebration of the diverse crowds of both Jew and Gentile who adhere in obedience to the message of Jesus.

Chapter 4 witnesses Williams' expositional within the Pauline Corpus. Williams notes that "the primary concepts…are the Gospel's saving power for both Jews and gentiles" (p.132). Under the canopy of this reality are a bevy of issues that all relate to Jewish and Gentile perseverance within the household of faith. Reading through this chapter, one notices Williams' content expertise as it is by far the most incisive argumentation thus far. Centrifugal to this idea is his manner of reading through Galatians as a tractate on God's "multiethnic kingdom, with a brown-skinned Jewish Messiah reigning as king" (p. 117).

Chapter 5 demonstrates the manner that the people of God are addressed throughout the General Epistles and Revelation. As the salient themes of each book are addressed, Williams missed an opportunity to express how false teachers infiltrated the people of God throughout the books of 2 Peter, Jude, 1, 2, 3 John, and the resultant issues that these situational texts addressed. Given the rather opaque treatment of ethnicity and identity within these letters, Williams adequately addressed what the future of ethnic diversity and the people of God will resemble in the eschaton. It will be a "new multiethnic community filled with many diverse ethnic communities from all over the world" (p. 147).

By far the shortest chapter, Williams synthesizes his treatment of The People of God in the Old and New Testaments in chapter 6. He opines, "the biblical witness suggests that this new chosen multiethnic community in Christ should obey the Gospel, be opposed to racism, and be in pursuit of Spirit-empowered love for one another as we seek to incorporate others…" (p. 151). As his evaluation of the Biblical texts concludes, Williams now turns his attention to the practical outworks of what the presentation of the people of God can instruct for those living in today's fractured and hostile world in relation to racism and division.

The final chapter 7 is focused on the pressing issues *de jour*. In other words, Williams lays the groundwork to address the current moments in our world that are fraught with racism, the fracturing due to a global pandemic, racial supremacy, and the concomitant features that are attached to these issues. These chapters reflect Williams' deep commitment toward sharing anti-racist practices and outcomes from the reading of the biblical texts. His conclusions extend to the people of God and their diverse spectrum of political affiliations.

Given the tenuous political and social climate in the west, Williams writes an at times acerbic and powerful statement lobbying for the realization of a multi-ethnic and diverse people of God who contend for this reality. To the average reader, one might assume that the tone at times takes a bellicose turn. This would be unsubstantiated, for even in the most direct positions that the author holds, he writes with an urgency and generosity not found in many texts that choose to discuss racism and bigotry. The non-white readers of this text will notice that Williams has written with their interests in mind; a text that will likely help church practitioners and teachers of scripture attend to the challenging battle for the realization of a multi-ethnic Kingdom of God to be inaugurated in our time.

Ernest Gray
Meachum School of Haymanot

Divine Revelation and Human Liberation, Harry Singleton III, Lexington Books (ISBN: 978-1978702998), 147pp., $36.54 (paper)

This is a genre-defying book in that Singleton is not engaging in a descriptive project defining the mechanisms of revelation; nor is he developing a constructive project for a new understanding of revelation: he simply focuses on divine human liberation. Instead of asking *what is* or the *how is* of revelation, Singleton develops a heuristic for evaluating any theological presentation of revelation for its coherence with the biblical narrative of the God who liberates full humanity. In a sense, Singleton has gifted us with an apologetic for a theology of liberation that is based on God as revealed in the Scriptures. Singleton develops a simple but instructive heuristic by creating a framework for revelation using a structure/content model, or what he also calls the first and second order of revelation. This duality of revelation is a constant thread throughout the book and serves as a way to analyze, diagnose, and offer a remedy to Western theological deficiency and racialized view of revelation. Singleton has basically organized his book into three sections—preliminary information, historical analysis, and concluding remarks/recommendations (this is my organizational interpretation, not Singleton's). I will briefly review each section.

In the introductory sections, Singleton establishes the basic outline and premise of the book: revelation consists of two parts—structure and content. The Western church has spent an inordinate amount of time concentrating on the structure of revelation, that is, the mechanisms of revelation instead of the content. The two-fold scheme is effective because it necessitates that the content of revelation must include that God has revealed Godself to Israel and in Jesus Christ as the One who liberates from human oppression. Without stating it explicitly, Singleton argues that the Western Christian tradition has created a view of revelation that condoned, and in some cases created, a racialized church of white hegemony. Singleton will spend the majority of the book explicating the disastrous results of a Christian theology that views revelation from the aspect of structure instead of the content of God's liberating action. Elsewhere, Singleton refers to the mechanisms of revelation as first and second order, where the first order is more in line with the epistemological process of revelation and the second order is the actual content. In what I call the second section, Singleton spends the majority of the book explicating a case for revelation as liberation.

Singleton begins this section where theology should begin with the doctrine of God. Singleton's starting premise is that when Western Christianity, especially in America, accepted slavocracy and white supremacy as moral, Christian theology needed to reshape God in the image of white supremacy. Not only does this begin Singleton's premise, but it also establishes the literary pattern for this section: describe the problem, give historical examples, then list historical counter voices. For example, taking on the role of a historian of theology, he uses theologians like Richard Baxter in order to strengthen his original argument that American Christianity developed a theology that required, almost demanded, White Christians to dominate inferior Black flesh in order to fulfill God's plan for the world. This created a Christian God within the context of white supremacy, a God who approved of white hegemony and Black inferiority. On the other hand, counter voices like Fredrick Douglass understood God's message as one of liberation. Singleton uses this scheme of historical problem and then counter voices throughout the remainder of the book, using theological categories such as the doctrine of God, ecclesiology, sacred symbols, and eschatology to adumbrate how revelation became distorted and was/is used to oppress non-whites instead of liberating them. This format allows Singleton to take us on a theological, historical, and philosophical journey towards an analysis of the development of American theology, a theology that stressed a first order revelation over a second order revelation which resulted in a doctrine of white supremacy.

Obviously, I oversimplified the book, but I believe I was faithful to the basic structure and content of Singleton's work. The strength of this work is that it provides an overview of how the church misused the idea of revelation to allow for slavery, and America's ongoing problem of white privilege/supremacy, and the church's complicit participation in America's original societal sin. Singleton uses theological categories in a way that is accessible to laypeople while engaging with the theological *loci* that allow those in the academy to reflect on their own views of revelation. Even though it is not stated in this particular term, the book clearly explains that the Haymanot Gospel is missing from the American theological imagination, which has been dominated by white theologians and institutions. The content and purpose of God's revelation are clear, consistently revealed in Israel and in the revelation found in Jesus Christ: God is the God who identifies *with* and liberates the marginalized and oppressed. The glaring weakness of the book is that his analysis did not go deep enough. I believe this is primarily due to spatial limitations which prevented this from becoming a full-blown work on the history of revelation. Although Singleton did mention a few key figures, he did not engage with scholars like Schleiermacher or Gadamer on hermeneutics, which is expected when discussing a topic like revelation.

Overall, considering that Singleton is writing to a broad audience, I do believe this book is worth the read just to understand how revelation as a theological topic has been discussed from the ivory towers of academia instead of from the margins. Also, Singleton has done the church a service by providing a heuristic tool that critically assesses the topic of revelation as that which impacts our Christian lives instead of it being a Platonic concept grounded out there in the abstract. I believe this work can aid in the continued conversation surrounding revelation and its indispensable relation to human liberation.

Leon Harris
Biola University

Faithful Anti-Racism: Moving Past Talk to Systemic Change, Christina Barland Edmondson and Chad Brennan, InterVarsity Press (ISBN: 978-0-8308-4723-5), 240 pp., $25.00 (hardcover)

Anti-racism is a concept that claims that racism thrives at a systemic level and that it is insufficient to "not be racist" nor to abstain from racist acts. Successful anti-racism demands an internal posture and ongoing praxis to address racism and its effects on society. There have been many significant contributions that further this idea. However, very few, if any, stress the spiritual dynamic of racism and its processes. We must treat systemic racism as a spiritual stronghold. Reliance upon the Holy Spirit and a grounding in the scriptures must inform discipleship and praxis. Dr. Christina Edmonson, an expert in ethics, equity, and Christian leadership development, and Chad Brennan, the leader of a Christian consulting ministry dealing with race and diversity in faith-based organizations, have contributed a volume that addresses these needs. Their data-driven and evidence-based analysis and biblically informed praxis allow readers and organizations to confront systemic racism and engage in measurable change.

The authors' intentions are explicit: "we are not primarily concerned with what we must *say* or *know*—though incredibly important—but what we must *do* and stop *doing* in order to see change" (p. 7). Unlike their predecessors, they show how systemic racism is a spiritual deformity that manifests in systems and actions that oppress and harm those on the underside of a white-controlled social hierarchy. Chapter 1 shows how any meaningful anti-racist effort requires wisdom—a way of life that takes God and His ways seriously and respects how God has ordered his creation. Chapter 2 lays the biblical foundation for a social ethic that incorporates God's desire to restore the proper relationship between God and humanity and the right relationships among humanity. These critical chapters lay the foundation for what follows.

The strength of this work is not only in its theological grounding but also in its interdisciplinary research. The authors draw upon survey and racial climate data from highly regarded research organizations that study racial dynamics on a national scale. They also bring a sociological and historical analysis rooted in biblical presuppositions about human nature and the pursuit of justice as an essential part of the Christian community. They understand that any healing of long-term conflicts, especially identity-based ones like interpersonal and systemic racism, requires an honest assessment of the present and an evidence-based understanding of the past (Chapters 3, 4, and 5). They persuasively link current facts to the historical evidence of systemic racism's origins, reminding readers of its processes and effects on the oppressed and marginalized (Chapter 6). Finally, they reveal the folly of frequently touted but ineffective approaches to dealing with racism (Chapter 7).

In the last four chapters, the authors get practical about how to engage in healthy, *faithful* anti-racism. As said before, anti-racism is a direct outcome of the divine command to love God and neighbor. Thus, Chapter 8 encourages readers to emulate and follow the examples of biblical and historical predecessors who dealt with the racial dynamics of their day. Chapter 9 confronts a prominent blind spot: the idea that one can address evil on an individualistic basis without help from others. Faithful anti-racism happens in community. Here the authors stress the need for mentors who challenge our faulty presuppositions about racial dynamics. It also emphasizes the radical posture of repentance and humility necessary to pass on what one has learned to others.

The final two chapters discuss the external praxis necessary to promote systemic change. Chapter 10, in particular, confronts one of the frustrating tendencies of churches and Christian organizations: the willingness to pass off performative but ineffective actions as evidence of their commitment to racial justice. These actions look meaningful and may make these organizations look good, but they avoid accountability and do not result in measurable change. Edmonson and Brennan provide a vital service to readers (especially decision makers in organizations and churches) by giving examples of assessments and metrics that identify needed change and demonstrate meaningful progress, chiefly through the Racial Justice Unity Center. With Chapter 11, the work comes full circle. Assuming readers have undertaken the sober work of anti-racism, it explains how communities and individuals can exercise their new muscles of wisdom to disrupt racist systemic forces through their economic, political, and religious commitments.

There are very few critical faults to find with this effort. That said, I wish the writers had emphasized cross-cultural collaboration at the organizational level. This might seem obvious, and sure the authors would wholeheartedly agree. However, all too frequently, many churches and Christian organizations (especially predominantly white institutions or churches that claim to be multicultural but still operate with a white cultural ethos). They fail to see the need for accountable partnership with Black- and Brown-led organizations. One cannot be faithfully anti-racist without meaningful cross-cultural relationships to decenter one's experience. The same applies to organizations, all the more so given the demographic shifts within American Christianity.

In conclusion, this is an essential contribution to the work of discipleship for the church and its communities going forward. This is a valuable resource for those who seek to grow in their faith and to be better neighbors, especially across racial and ethnic dividing lines. A further recommendation would be to work through this volume in the community with fellow believers or members of organizations seeking the common good. Edmondson and Brennan's work—including the contributions of experts and research efforts—are essential tools for robust and redemptive Christian witness.

Nicholas Rowe
Independent Scholar

www.ingramcontent.com/pod-product-compliance
Lightning Source LLC
Chambersburg PA
CBHW060352080526
44583CB00012B/273